OUT OF
SIGHT
OUT OF
MIND

OUT OF SIGHT OUT OF MIND

A MADMAN'S JOURNAL

MICHAEL J. HARRISON

Deeds Publishing | *Atlanta*

Copyright © 2018—Michael J. Harrison

ALL RIGHTS RESERVED—No part of this book may be reproduced in any form or by any electronic or mechanical means, including information storage and retrieval systems, without permission in writing from the authors, except by a reviewer who may quote brief passages in a review.

Published by Deeds Publishing in Athens, GA
www.deedspublishing.com

Printed in The United States of America

Cover design and text layout by Mark Babcock

Library of Congress Cataloging-in-Publications data is available upon request.

ISBN 978-1-947309-16-6

Books are available in quantity for promotional or premium use. For information, email info@deedspublishing.com.

First Edition, 2018

10 9 8 7 6 5 4 3 2 1

For my parents, Joe and JoAnne Harrison. Thank you for being the best Mom and Dad a human could ever hope to have. I pray that I can be half the person that your example set me up to be.

For my lovely daughters, Jennifer and Jessica. Thank you for being so supportive through the bad times, as well as the good.

And for my beautiful wife, Diane. Thank you for picking this old, worn out vagabond up by the chin straps and convincing him that he could still make something of himself.

"With the great number of wrongful convictions being overturned with DNA evidence, what are the percentages of wrongful convictions in cases where DNA doesn't apply?"
—Barry Scheck, The Innocence Project

Contents

Preface xiii

PART I: LOSS OF DIRECTION 1

Climbing Everest 3
Against the Wind 9
The Perfect Storm (Fall 2008) 13
Titanic 21
Jailbird 25
Plea Jockies 31
Playing God 39
Debtors Prison 53

PART II: SALT IN MY WOUNDS 59

Rants and Raves 61
The Colbert County Hilton 67
273811 73
Hellmore 79
A.D.O.C. (Alabama Department of Corruptions) 91
"A Made Man" 101
Hurry up and wait! 111
Uncomfortably Numb (Reflections on all the socially redeeming factors at Elmore Correctional Facility) 115
Deaf Ears (S.O.S.) 117
The Pillars of Southern Society 125
"The Criminal" 133

PART III: ROCK BOTTOM 139

ANIMALS (The Goon Squad) 141

Hell's Bells! (Will the real criminals please stand up?)	149
"Soda"	155
The Callous Palace	163
The Dark Side of the Moon	167
M—I—C—K—E—Y—M—O–U—S—E	177
Highway to Hell	187
Riding the Storm Out	193
Someday I'll Be Saturday Night	199
Waiting My Turn To Get On The Plane!	205

PART IV: TREADING WATER — *209*

Going Home	211
Every Silver Lining Has It's Cloud	221
The Song Remains the Same	227
Ramblings	231
First Blood	235
Law School Fodder	243

PART V: BACK FROM THE DEAD — *253*

A Commentary from Monte Cristo	255
I Know You're Out There Somewhere	259
Losing My Religion	267
Hair of the Dog	275
Sweet Home Alabama	279
Baggage	287
Reflections and Resolve	297
Winding Down	309
Turn the Page	321
Postscript	327
Acknowledgments	331
About the Author	333

Preface

*Failing does not make you a failure:
it just means you had the balls to try."*

—fuelrunning.com

Have you ever awakened from a nightmare in which you were naked and exposed in a crowd, falling off a cliff, or being run over by a train? Maybe you were being chased through the streets by zombies or cannibals. Maybe you found yourself in a pit filled with snakes. When you come to, you are sweating profusely, only to realize that the situation was only a dream. But what if you woke to find that the nightmare around you wasn't a dream?

Life is a tangled web of twists and turns. One day you can be on top of the world, the next you can be tumbling down the slopes suffering the agony of defeat. A prince overnight can become a pauper and a hero can become a villain. Life deals hard lessons.

To prepare you for my story, I will need to give you a little background. This is a real story, not some-action packed, super-hero page turner. However, I'll try not to bore you totally, so grab yourself your favorite beverage, settle down, and let's begin. "I'll have Old Forester with a splash of water—Cheers! Here we go."

Remember the old myth turned children's tale about King Midas and his golden touch? He was so wrapped up in wealth that he wished for and was granted the ability to turn everything he touched to gold. Only after he had turned his food, his water, and even his daughter to gold did he realize his mistake. All of a sudden, there were more important things in life. The lure of wealth didn't mean so much anymore. Maybe that time spent with the kids at a t-ball game was worth more than that new bass boat. Maybe appreciating the wonders of the universe was more fulfilling than cruising around in a new Porsche.

At one time in my life, I seemed to have that Midas touch. I was a successful business man and every button I pushed seemed to work. Complacency, however, is a curse. Sometimes we need to slow down and examine what can happen to prevent complacency from coming to pass. Truman Capote once said, "Failure is the condiment that gives success its flavor." The "F" word (failure) had never crossed my mind. I watched as the business I had started from scratch grew and grew until I had to strain just to keep it under control. No problem. I just keep hiring, kept growing, and charged ahead like a bull in a china shop. What could go wrong?

On May 14, 1960, I was born into a blessed life. I was not born into a life of financial wealth, but born to parents who loved me more than one human could ever hope to be loved. Although we were comfortable financially, my parents had come from poor Southern families who had survived the Great Depression and had persevered and climbed into middle class, blue collar America. A baby boomer, my name is Michael Joseph Harrison. My friends call me Harry.

Although both my parents were "Joes," I was named after Michael Landon of "Little Joe Cartwright" fame from the T.V. show *Bonanza*. My parents' friends called me "Little Joe" for many years, until I finally outgrew the "little" part.

How did I come to be called Harry? Well, when you are born into my generation with the name Michael and you are on the golf course with a group of friends around the same age, when someone yells "Mike," several heads are going to turn. Therefore, all of us "Mikes" went by our last names. Eventually a friend shortened Harrison to Harry and it stuck. Soon, even I began to refer to myself as Harry.

I was an only child. People make jokes about only children being spoiled and I am sure some level of being pampered is indeed true. However, there is also a large amount of pressure associated with being the only offspring of a relationship. As an only child, you are the eldest and the baby, the smartest and the most challenged, the golden child and the black sheep. Bottom line though, my parents worshipped me.

My dad was a "Simple Man." I hear the old Lynyrd Skynyrd song by that title and my mind automatically turns to memories of my dad. Named after General Joe "Fighting Joe" Wheeler of the Civil War and Spanish American War fame, my dad was a hard worker and a conscientious employee. His friends, coworkers, and supervisors knew him as "Good Ole Joe." He was a pipefitter and proud union member of the Plumbers and Steamfitters Local out of Muscle Shoals, Alabama, a town famous for its music and its recording studios. For thirty plus years, he worked at a local aluminum plant in "The Shoals."

Dad died in 1999, two years after his retirement, from mesothelioma lung cancer caused by the years of asbestos exposure on the jobsite. To sum my dad up in one short statement: he was the closest thing that I can imagine to what Jesus Christ was like when he walked this earth. I say that not only because he did not drink, smoke, or curse, but also because he had the kindest, warmest, and most caring heart of anyone I have ever known.

Although I pray that God put some of my dad's qualities in me, I am probably more like my mom, JoAnne. This statement is not saying anything negative. My mother is a wonderful person. She was, and is, a moral and loving wife, mother, and a great friend. However, she has a level of mischievousness, stubbornness, and ambitiousness about her. A small spark of spitfire that was somewhat tempered by her marriage to Daddy. I think some of these traits have surfaced in me over the years. The bottom line on Mom, or Jodi as I call her, is that she daily defines and exhibits the term "unconditional love." She is my rock and has stood behind me every step of my life, through the good and the bad, with unflinching resilience and support. When others abandoned me, she was always there to pick up the pieces and to put Humpty Dumpty back together again.

My parents raised me in church, and somewhere beyond the mistakes that I have made in my life, that Christian foundation is still solid. However, unlike some Christian upbringings, I was raised to think for myself, to develop my own relationship with God, to study, and to discern right from wrong. I was taught to determine my own faith, not to just believe something because it was screamed at me from a pulpit.

I was given a good education, first in the Russellville Alabama City School System, then at the University of Alabama, and finally at the University of North Alabama where I received a Bachelor of Science degree in marketing. After school, I went to work in management for a large textile manufacturing company. A few years later, I went to work for a local stone quarrier/fabricator where I got my start in the dimensional stone industry. In 1990, I began ArcStone, Inc., my own business.

During this time, I married my high school sweetheart, DJ. She gave me the two greatest joys in my life, my two daughters, Jennifer and Jessica. For the next nineteen years, I lived the typical highs and lows associated with being a self-employed businessman. I lived and worked off my reputation of being honest and doing good work. I was well known regionally in the granite and marble industry, and as I said before, I always seemed to be able to push the right buttons to succeed.

Sometimes though, things are not always as they seem on the surface. Having always prided myself as a small "hip pocket" operator, I made snap decisions and didn't sweat the small stuff (I didn't mind my Ps & Q<u>s</u>). My mentality worked fine during good economic times, but not when the housing market turned on me. I discovered then that this mentality exposes a soft underbelly that can destroy you and that your shortcomings will rise to the surface. You discover that maybe you weren't such a good businessman after all. Also, you find out that many of your "friends" really weren't such good friends. Whoever came up with the term about kicking a man when he is down had obviously been through this type of ordeal. This book is about my undoing. It is about my failures, as well as the failures of an entity called the Alabama Justice System. Many people from other parts of our country, including Hollywood, still view the Southern political scene to be like it is portrayed in *To Kill a Mockingbird, Cool Hand Luke, Mississippi Burning, A Time to Kill, Crazy in Alabama,* or even *My Cousin Vinnie*. We have, however, made great strides since the days of "segregation now, segregation forever." Public Klan hangings are at an all-time low. Chain gangs are made up of only Yankee carpetbaggers and others deemed unfit to be socially acceptable in our genteel society.

In all honesty, we have come a long way. However, we still have a long way to go. Southern justice is still doled out according to the size of your bank account or by who your friends happen to be. If you think that the Southern good ole boy system has been totally washed away, think again.

WARNING: Some content may be sensitive and disturbing to some readers! An open mind and common sense are required!

If the text of this journal reads like the soundtrack from the movie *Joe Dirt*, I offer no apologies. A cheap transistor radio and a couple of rock-n-roll stations helped me to retain any small amount of sanity that I might still possess. Am I a madman, you ask? I don't know. But I do know that I am a Mad Man. Hopefully the following pages will offer an explanation as to why.

In advance, I do apologize for the language and some of the trains of thought that are in this book, including my own. As Mark Twain once said, "Under certain circumstances, profanity provides a relief denied even to prayer." This being said, I am trying to, in real terms, portray the undoing of my life, as I had known it. This is my story: Some names have been changed to protect the guilty.

PART I:
LOSS OF DIRECTION

Climbing Everest

*"I had the right to remain silent,
but I didn't have the ability."*

—Ron White

Imagine that you are standing at the base of Mt. Everest. Your goal is the peak. There at the peak, hidden in a crevice, is something that you desperately need. Something that you have to obtain to go forward in your life. Something necessary for your survival as you know it. That something is called hope. Hope for your future. Hope to reclaim and salvage your life.

Imagine, however, that you have to reach the summit without the aid of oxygen. Also, you have no climbing gear or skills. You have no funds left to purchase such things or to hire a team of Sherpas to assist you in your ascent.

You are past your prime physically, and despite chronic medical problems with your back and wrist, you must still start your trek. Pain cannot be an issue. You must do whatever is necessary. Your life, reputation, and future depend on it.

Also, finally, imagine that all the easier paths up the mountain have been made off limits to you. You are either prohibited or are rejected by the guardians and overseers of the trails. Every attempt to follow one of these paths ends in rejection. "YOU, cannot come this way," you're told, "YOU, are forbidden to take this path."

Finally, at wits end, you look up at the sheer face of the mountain. Regardless of how difficult it will be, you must attempt to climb it. Neither failure nor suicide is an acceptable option. Even if you die during your attempt, you must push forward.

So up you go, one hand and one foothold at a time. You have to be extremely careful of loose rocks and debris falling from above. Every step has to be sure, or a fall into the abyss awaits you.

Although you have no gear, you are carrying a cargo with you, strapped to your back. It slows you down and hinders your progress, trying to deny you your goal of Hope. It is heavy and keeps you off balance, threatening to make you fall. The cargo is an overbearing weight, a burden, a curse. The cargo is something intended to be strapped to you for the rest of your life. The cargo is labeled in bright letters, for all of those that you approach in your attempt to succeed, to see. The cargo is labeled "CONVICTED FELON."

AUGUST 2011—Here I was, staring at my Everest. Having just been released from a yearlong prison term with the Alabama Department of Corrections (ADOC). It was now time for me to start my trek towards hope.

Having lost my home prior to my conviction, I was moving in with my Mom till I could sort through some things. My divorce papers had been signed just a couple of weeks before my release. I had no job, no car, and no money. I knew the job situation was going to be a big hurdle in my climb to recovery.

In the three months between my conviction and my sentencing, I had sent out approximately 85 resumes in an attempt to find a decent paying job. I needed it! I had hoped that a potential "restitution paying" job would be considered in my sentencing (I owed a lot of restitution). At that time, it had been decades since I had been having to look for a job.

Out of the 85 resumes and other applications that I had filled out then, I was called on approximately 15 interviews. This was encouraging, because the economy was really struggling. I attributed the high response to a strong work history and years of sales and manufacturing experience. Some of the employers that didn't grant me an interview notified me that I was overqualified for the position that was involved. I had applied for anything and everything. At least the notifications made me feel good.

All of the interviews had gone well at first. Most of the personnel people seemed impressed and interested. Then came the dreaded word—Felony! As soon as they came to the line on the employment application designated to mark this, the brakes went on. I was usually then out of their office within minutes. You would have thought that I was carrying leprosy! Apparently, there were too many people hunting jobs for them to even consider a convicted felon. It was an automatic elimination, regardless of what the applications said. Also, many companies have strict policies against hiring someone with a record.

Now, here I was again. A year had passed and I was going to be facing the same thing again. National unemployment had risen to 9 ½%. The State of Alabama's rate was over 10%. Over 1/3 of the citizens of Alabama had applied for food stamps! Could I lean back far enough to see the peak of Everest hidden above in the clouds?

When I wasn't beating the bushes looking for a job, my mind would wander to other aspects of my future. What about my personal life? With the finalization of my divorce pending, would I ever find someone else to share my life with? Would I ever find a woman that I could love and that would love me in return? I could just imagine the kind of ad that I could run in the personals:

SINGLE WHITE MALE SEEKS FEMALE COMPANIONSHIP
AGE: 51 (doesn't look a day over 50)
HEIGHT: 6'2"
WEIGHT: 195# (at least I lost some weight during my time away)
EYES: Green
HAIR: Salt & Pepper (mostly salt)
MARITAL STATUS: Divorced
RELIGION W.A.S.P. (WHITE ANGLO SAXON PROTESTANT)
JOB: None

Intangibles: No home, no car, no insurance, no money, substantial debts, poor health, physiologically drained, CONVICTED FELON!

The label "Convicted Felon" might as well be tattooed on your forehead! I couldn't imagine trying to enter any relationship hiding a burden like that. This is not to say that I was even remotely interested in getting in any kind of a serious relationship, I still had a bad taste in my mouth from the perils of my marriage. However, some female companionship would be nice. How did I go about it? How did I search for and go about asking a woman for a date? After 30 years of marriage, I was extremely out of practice. But then again, I guess it is kind of like riding a bike, Huh? However, who would be interested in an upper middle class man with my current credentials. Plus, the social skills taught by the ADOC would be of no benefit in the dating game. Later, after I was officially divorced and I did start dating, I discovered that I didn't even need training wheels. It was like riding a bike. You have heard the saying that women like the "Bad Boys." Is it true?

Although I looked forward to diving back into life, I knew that I needed to stay grounded so that I could address the obstacles that lay ahead. I needed to take the lessons of life that I had learned and try to use them to my advantage.

During the final weeks of my incarceration, in a pre-release program, we had studied the book "The Seven Habits of Highly Effective People" by Stephen F. Covey. This book came to mean a lot to me and I would recommend it to everyone. Although I generally don't like "self-help" books, a lot of Covey's paradigms or assumptions made a great deal of sense to me. I'm not sure that my interpretations and applications of his writings are exactly what he had in mind when he wrote the book, however I am prone to taking other people's philosophies and blending them with my own thoughts, to form my own assumptions. My ego and the bitterness still bottled up inside me would prevent me from qualifying as a total disciple, however I have taken much of the message to heart.

One of Covey's key and foremost 'habits' in the book is to "Start with the End in Mind." I thought on this concept a lot. In my mind, I could picture my goals, as well as those individuals that I would have to deal with on the way to them. With the mountain in front of me, I was going to have to become an extremely pro-active person to reach my quest. Could I overcome the anger?

As I thought back to how I got myself in this position, I realized that I would need to search for a new mindset. I needed to be a "New and Improved Mike." As I charged ahead, I would need to rid myself of the stressed, tired, embarrassed, and angry man that I had become. I had to find a determination to "overcome" and to pick myself up from the ashes.

As I moved forward, I would confirm what I had discovered during my confinement. The biggest obstacles to recovery were the very individuals who had put you in confinement and held you there. It was in their best interest for you to not succeed. If you were to succeed, then you might present a challenge. In their Kingdom, they didn't like challenges. There, everything was scripted and enforced by the "Court" and her merry band of Jesters. Thus begins my long and winding road.

Against the Wind

"I guess I lost my way, there were oh so many roads. I was living to run, and running to live, never worried about paying or even how much I owed."
—Bob Seger, "Against the Wind"

Las Vegas 2007: Sin City is appropriately named. Although the new Vegas is supposedly being geared toward family entertainment, this is still Sodom and Gomorrah West.

My good friend and supplier, Jeff, and I arrived in Vegas for the Marble Institute Show and Convention. Jeff's company had paid my way and the trip was the opportunity I needed to shop for new equipment to expand my business. New competition had started moving in on my little empire and it was time for me to beef up and run them off.

My little company, ArcStone Inc., had grown by leaps and bounds over the past few years. This was due to a booming economy and a reputation for doing good work. Virtually all our business was by referral. However, in my mind we weren't big enough to hold off the incoming invaders and it was time to pull out all the stops. We were making preparations for a new building and state-of-the-art equipment to move to the next level. Little did it cross my mind that most all the profits we had earned during our growth, had already been spent on previous growth and that we needed reserve working capital for any potential slow periods. Business had been too good, but, when in doubt—sell more!

Despite always juggling money for cash flow and dealing with daily work related stress, 2006 and 2007 had been good years for ArcStone. In 2007, we installed over 600 sets of kitchen countertops. The phone never stopped ringing. I was daily juggling our schedule and herded 26 employees to keep up with the demand.

I was on top of the world in my personal life as well. The previous year my wife and I had celebrated our 25th wedding anniversary with a trip to Hawaii. We lived in a beautiful home that we built on a golf course and were living the American dream.

Upon arriving in Vegas, Jeff and I checked into the Venetian, a truly magnificent hotel and casino. To walk into the lobby of the Venetian, unlike many Vegas hotels, you don't have to wade through hookers and barkers handing out sex flyers. The decor is beyond belief. The Venetian is also the Vegas home productions of *Phantom of the Opera* and of the Blue Man Group, the latter of which we attended. Not crazy about casinos, I really enjoyed the shows.

During the days, Jeff and I commuted to the convention center to the stone show, where he made the rounds with his customers and I shopped for equipment. Over the next couple of days, I looked at endless pieces of equipment before settling on two. I made arrangements to purchase a stone cutting bridge saw from a company out of Chicago. The Polish born rep for the

European manufacturer thought initially that I was competition scoping them out because I kept coming back to their booth so many times asking questions. The other machine that I made arrangements for was a small computerized sinkhole cutting machine from a Minneapolis-based company, run by a guy named Joe. I was to be receiving one of the first of these off the production line. Altogether I spent about $100,000, a lot for my little company. Add this to what I was putting into the lease purchase on my building, vehicles, and other equipment and I would spend the better part of half a million dollars in a short period of time.

The day before leaving Vegas, we were carried on a tour of a large granite countertop producer in North Vegas. I was shocked at how much my little group produced in comparison, with virtually no equipment and a quarter of the manpower. I left feeling great about the future.

After the tour, I made a quick jaunt through the streets of Venice (the Venetian Hotel Mall—canals and gondolas included) to buy souvenirs for the family. At the Bayberrys of London store I spotted a scarf that I knew DJ would love (personal joke between us) but then choked at the price. I ended up getting her a T-shirt just like I did the kids. I felt empty about it later because I'd always enjoyed getting DJ nice things. I once had joked to her that if she had married Bill Gates, she would make a millionaire out of him in a week.

Our final night in Vegas was one of the funniest experiences of my life. Jeff's company carried us out to dinner at Pieros, an old Vegas institution. After a great meal, one of the young salesman, JJ, was set up by one of Jeff's bosses and the waiters. They bet him that he couldn't eat two whole pieces of the restaurant's chocolate cake. He took the challenge. When the cake arrived, the slices turned out to be "quite large," meaning two half-cakes. To keep JJ from balking, a $200 incentive was thrown onto the table. Halfway into the ordeal, JJ was struggling and everyone started chanting and urging him on. Before long, the waiters and cooks were gathered around cheering. Even the hookers and musicians from the lounge soon joined in. Two of the hookers started massaging his shoulders and giving him pecks on the cheek as encouragement. Additional funds were collected from around the room and before long there was close to $500 on the table as the winner's prize.

JJ struggled but he finally got down that last bite. He was as green as the Incredible Hulk. I bet he hasn't touched any more chocolate cake to this day.

The following morning, we were off climbing into the sky from the Vegas airport. Harry was heading back to the next stage of ArcStone's existence. As I looked out over the Grand Canyon, stretching into the distance below me, I remember thinking about what an adventure my new business plans were going to be. Little did I know what was ahead of me. "I wish I didn't know now, what I didn't know then."

The Perfect Storm (Fall 2008)

"As individuals, groups and businesses, we're often so busy cutting through the undergrowth, we don't even realize we're in the wrong jungle."

—Stephen R. Covey
The 7 Habits of Highly Effective People

The year 2008 started out much like 2007. ArcStone had its nose to the grindstone, working countless hours of overtime, trying to keep customers happy. Our bridge saw arrived in the spring and was an instant success. I couldn't have asked for a simpler, more efficient, and durable piece of equipment. ArcStone was "moving on up!"

The sink machine, however, was a different story. After countless delays and put offs, the machine that finally arrived looked nothing like the prototype that I had seen demonstrated in Vegas. It was supposedly a new and improved design. By summer and after numerous tech calls, it had not produced a single acceptable sink cutout. Joe, the owner of the company, continually avoided my calls and eventually when I did reach him, he in effect cursed me out and told me to sue him. Upon investigation, I found out he had numerous lawsuits and judgments against him. After consulting an attorney, I decided that it was going to be more costly to go to Minnesota to sue him than it was worth. That's the way the legal system is set up. Chalk one up to experience.

Even with work booming, I was constantly having cash flow problems. The extra expense involved with the new building, equipment, and training was a huge burden on day-to-day operations. I was constantly overextended and fighting overdrafts. The solution? Well, just sell more!

During this time, I repeatedly resorted to floating funds from one bank account to another to cover bills and payroll. Banks call this kiting and it is not an approved practice, although a lot of bankers sometimes look the other way with what they consider good customers. This is a punishable act and a terrible business practice. In my mind, as long as I got the checks covered, what did it matter? I had always gotten away with it in the past during slow cash flow periods.

Additionally, we continued to feel pressure from our new competitors. One, owned by the uncle of a former employee who had left us to join them, was targeting our best contractors. I was furious and dropped my price to whatever I had to in order to get a job that we were both vying for. I couldn't stand the thought of them taking any potential jobs from me. After all, this was my territory and they were the ones infringing.

In retrospect, I remember the words of an old gentleman named John Sharp who had worked for me years before. John had said, "Mike, you don't need every job. Let them have some of these profitless jobs. Some jobs are better not had. Taking losses on every job can't be made up with volume." I wish that I had listened to these words of wisdom from this man that I had admired like a second father. Maybe if my Dad or John had still been around in 2008, they could've helped keep the reins on me.

Also during this time, I had employee problems. Besides losing a key employee to my competition, my right-hand man, Brad, was going through some serious personal problems after the unexpected death of his sister. The problem spilled over into work and extra stress was thrown on yours truly. As well, my accountant, Lisa, was constantly preaching to me about my business practices and about my putting things off. As a self-proclaimed "hip pocket operator," I kept giving her assurances that I would soon be to a point where I could set back and get these things straightened out and caught up. I promised her that I would become more organized. Although I was a great salesman, it turns out I was a terrible manager. Later, prior to my trial, Lisa stated that because of my poor business practices, her testimony would probably do more harm than good. Then came August!

The 2008 economic downturn hit like a bomb! It was like someone turned off a switch. One day the phone was ringing off the wall and my sales people were rushing in with orders. The next day, all the work seemed to vanish. Prior to the collapse, my little company was producing and installing 15 to 20 orders a week, a lot for granite companies much bigger even than mine. Afterward, we were scraping for four to five jobs per week. In no time, our backlog plunged from 185 jobs, and a 12-week backlog, to just over 60, cut by two thirds. The collapse of the housing market was like a tidal wave. To blame my downfall strictly on the economy, however, would be a lie. Years of bad business practices, unchecked growth, and freewheeling, had left me with my pants down. Better managerial skills could've possibly saved ArcStone. But as it stood, the Golden Touch was gone. Stress took over and I continued to make one bad business decision after another.

With no working capital and virtually no new business coming in, cash flow was an even bigger nightmare. Overhead doesn't reduce proportionately with the reduction in sales. To compound this, we had existing jobs to finish with a depleted bank account. The overdrafts, along with slow payments to vendors, started mounting. Although my bankers worked with me as best they could, I was constantly rushing to cover bounced checks, including payroll checks.

By the end of 2008, the stress was getting to be too much. I started looking for options. Over the previous couple of years, I had a couple of different individuals that had approached me repeatedly about investing into the business. At the time, I'd felt like I had no need for a partner and I didn't like the idea of consulting anyone else on how I did business. Now though, I was desperate and approached both parties looking for help. My hopes were soon dashed when I was told by both individuals that they had lost so much in business investments and in the stock market that they were not in a position to come aboard. My bubble burst, but I continued to look for options.

In a conversation with one of my contractors, Robert Eaton, I mentioned the possibility of trying to sell the business. Although ArcStone was in bad financial shape, the name, the customer base, and the reputation was still worth something. These assets, along with the knowledge of the industry and the market that I possessed were still marketable. In addition, besides the sixty plus jobs still on our books, we had been assured 68 high-end condominiums in Mississippi for which we had already completed the model homes.

Robert expressed an interest, saying that he was looking for something to help his son and his son-in-law to get into. As I gathered numbers for Robert to look at, I was once again ridiculed. This time, Robert himself did the ridiculing, and deservedly so, for my poor bookkeeping and management. Robert is the consummate professional. His success, even through the housing collapse, proves it.

The analysis of my business by Robert was very humbling and really drove a stake through my heart. He brought me to the realization of just how poorly I had managed a potential gold mine. Bottom line, however, Robert was interested in buying the business. He said that the price that I had quoted him was quite fair. Basically, the price I had asked for was just enough to cover the refunds of customers' deposits currently on the books. The customers were my major concern. I needed this to minimize embarrassment and to retain my reputation. From there I would work with him for a period of time to make a transition.

Robert asked for a little time to make the final analysis and decision. He wasn't interested in my current building and locale so he started looking for a better situation for his needs. This delay went on for about three months, but I was told that we "would make this happen."

As this wait stretched on, anticipating what I knew would be my salvation, I continued to struggle mightily. I kept going on hope. During this time, I asked for and was given "bridge loans" from my brother-in-law and from my aunt. The loan from my brother-in-law would prove later to be a severe strain on my marriage. The pressure and anger from my wife was unrelenting. Although I got a large portion of the loan back to him before the company collapsed, I still came up short.

During the time that I was waiting on word from Robert, production punctuality suffered. This was from having been put on COD by most of our suppliers and struggling to make payroll. Several refunds were given because we were unable to get jobs out on time. We were struggling for cash. Writing a refund check is one of the hardest things you'll ever do, especially when you're hoping to get the refund check covered before it bounces.

Just as I was entertaining hope, another arrow was shot through my heart. The new Toyota plant in Mississippi, which was tied to the condos that we were working on, was being put on mothballs. As a result, I was told the condo project there was stalling. They hoped to continue, but all future work would be done with no deposits and all billing had to go through bank draws (90-120-day turnaround). There was no way I could carry a job this size without upfront money.

When the call finally came from Robert, it was not the news that I had been waiting for. He had decided not to go through with the purchase. I was devastated. Although I am not sure how much the Mississippi loss factored in, Robert told me that he just didn't feel like his son and his son-in-law were ready to take on such an undertaking in the current economic conditions. I nearly blacked out during the conversation.

I don't blame Robert for his decision. I feel that, as a friend, he went above and beyond in looking for a way to help me. In the end, though, his business sense and devotion to what he felt was best for his family prevailed. If I had approached my business and put everything to God first, as Robert always does, maybe I wouldn't have been in this predicament.

The date was April 7, 2009. That night I went and drank my mind into oblivion and cried my eyes out. Then, I made up my mind, I couldn't go any deeper. The next morning, ArcStone was closing.

Titanic

"The ultimate measure of a man is not where he stands in times of comfort and convenience, but where he stands in times of struggle and inconvenience."
—Dr. Martin Luther King

The ocean liner RMS Titanic took three years to build. On April 15, 1912, after hitting an iceberg, she sank in less than three hours. ArcStone had hit an iceberg as well. That, along with a faulty substructure, had doomed my little company just like the famous ship. I felt like I had been bailing water with a pork-n-beans can for the last eight months.

The morning of April 7, 2009, I arrived to work at my usual time. However, I was not looking forward to my day. As my employees arrived, I asked them to gather around. The looks on their faces told me that most knew what was coming.

As best I could, I explained to everyone where we stood. "I'm sorry, I've failed us all," I told them, "I can't go any deeper."

Many of them consoled me, telling me it would be just a matter of time until we reopened. I knew differently. As one after another of my old faithful employees patted me on the back, they showed concern for me rather than for their own circumstances. The shame in me continued to swell because of all the people whom my poor leadership was affecting. There was more to come.

Artie, my lead salesman, had arrived that morning with a deposit check for a job that we had been after. That deposit would probably have kept our doors open for a few more days while waiting on a miracle. The deposit check was returned to the customer. There was no need to keep delaying the inevitable. Without a buyer, we could not survive.

The majority of my employees eventually left. I told them to check with me later in the week about payroll. I hung around the shop and the phone, contacting everyone possible to let them know what was going on. It didn't take long for word to get out.

If you ever wondered what Emperor Valentinian III felt when Attila's hoards were threatening Rome, or what the defenders of the Alamo felt as Santa Anna's troops stormed the walls of the old mission, I think that I felt some of that emotion as concerned and angry customers started showing up en-masse at my door. I made up my mind that I would stay and face the fire. It was the honorable and proper thing to do.

The stress was unbearable. I didn't know if I were coming or going. I was swarmed. I couldn't finish trying to explain that I was going to attempt to liquidate and take care of everyone to one customer before another stepped in or another call came in. Several of my old faithful employees had hung around and were trying to help.

Pleasing the masses under such circumstances was impossible. No explanation was good enough. The next thing I knew some angry customers started demanding immediate satisfaction and started scavenging my shop, saying they were going to take something in exchange for what I owed them. Out of my mind with grief, I went along as much as I could.

Trucks were backed up and between my guys and me, we loaded large amounts of stone and tools on them to appease whom we could. One angry customer, who we owed only one small bar top, remaining from his large order, backed up and hooked to one of our work trailers, loaded with stone and worth several times more than I owed him. He promptly drove off with it. I wasn't in the frame of mind to argue.

People can't see what you are going through in such situations. The grandmother of one customer later expressed openly in Walmart, I found out, that she couldn't believe that I had tried to rip off her grandson. Her son had shown up the day of the closing and loaded stone slabs worth well above the price of the job that I had sold. She also didn't happen to mention her pleasure at the previous work that we had done for her. This fact didn't seem to mean anything at this time. Bottom line however—I hadn't fulfilled my contract.

As bad as the situation was at work, trying to formulate a plan and calm customers, the situation at home was worse. My wife was beyond understanding and put me through a living hell. Besides the shame and fear that she was going through, her biggest concern was the money that I owed our brother-in-law. I took dozens of ass-chewings about this. She made the statement that I had in effect violated "her" family. I guess that after 28 years, I still didn't officially qualify as a member of that family. Later, I found out just how true that statement was.

DJ also, and rightfully so, chastised me for allowing irate customers to take compensation at will and I was immediately banned from making any decisions on reimbursement or to touch a checkbook. Maybe with this kind of help on other financial decisions and hurdles through the years, I wouldn't have been in that position. However, I was too numb to argue.

Within two days, we had put our house on the market. Even with two mortgages, there should have been enough equity to make a large dent in what I owed to customers. I also continued to go to the shop daily to meet anyone who showed up and to answer the phone, explaining that we were formulating a plan to correct everything. I had no idea of the blow that I was fixing to receive from left field. If I already was standing on the deck of a sinking ship before, I was fixing to have a torpedo slammed into her side. The unsinkable ship, was sunk.

Jailbird

*"If your parakeet knows the phrase "Open up, Police!",
you might be a redneck."*

—Jeff Foxworthy

The next couple of weeks were a whirlwind, listing the house, fielding one call after another, trying to formulate the liquidation plan, and trying to console and assure irate customers.

Upon answering one call, I found that I was speaking to an investigator from the Muscle Shoals, Alabama, Police Department. He said that he had a complaint and asked if I would come in and talk to him. I was stunned, but I agreed and drove over to meet him at the Muscle Shoals police station.

The detective told me of the complaint and then I tried to tell him what was going on. As the meeting reached a point where I expected it to wind down, the detective started reading me what I recognized as my "Miranda Rights."

"You are arresting me?" I asked.

"Yes," he replied as he continued.

The detective said something to the effect that he wasn't sure what was going on and that I seemed like a sincere guy, but that he had to address the complaints from his constituents and a warrant for my arrest had been issued. Stunned, I slumped down in my chair, with tears running down my face.

Another officer joined us in the detective's office. This officer was my youngest daughter Jessi's Sunday school teacher. He tried to console me and told me that everything would work out. He also told me how much Jessi loved and talked about her dad.

As I got up to leave with the second officer, the detective handed me some religious tracts and wished me luck. I was walked to an unmarked patrol car. The officer said he wasn't going to cuff me and that I could ride in the front. He then drove me to the Colbert County jail. To my recollection, this trip was my first ride ever in a police car. It wouldn't be my last.

As we rode, the officer continued to console me. I pretty much just stared out the window, numb. He kept telling me how much he liked Jessi and that she really looked up to me. He said that this would soon pass, but I wasn't so sure.

Getting booked in at Colbert County jail was a humiliating experience. Shortly after my phone call, answering a questionnaire, being fingerprinted, and having my mug shot taken, my mother and my daughters arrived and posted my bond. I asked where DJ was, and they told me that she said that she couldn't leave work.

Upon leaving the jail, Jenni and Jessi told me that I had sounded hysterical on the phone and that they were taking me to Eliza Coffee Memorial Hospital's ER to have me emotionally checked out. ECM has a mental unit attached to it. I pitched a fit but was told that I had no choice. I eventually relented when I realized that I was shaking uncontrollably. I generally hold a low opinion of shrinks, but I agreed to see one at the ER. I was evaluated, given some "happy pills," and sent home.

Over the next 24 hours, the mountains of stress that I had felt was intensified as my mug shot and a one-sided story was released in both the local newspaper and on a local TV news program. I was knocked down as to how news can be reported without even an attempt to first investigate both sides of the story. The reports made me sound like Al Capone.

Over the next few days, I was in a zombie like state. I continued trying to liquidate anything of value to pay bills and to build up a fund to start repayment of my customers. Besides having the house on the market, we sold our furniture, the piano, my golf cart and clubs, and anything else that could bring in quick cash. DJ, who was exceptionally cold during this time, took control of all the money to disburse. Visits from customers and constant phone calls continued throughout this time.

A few days after the initial publicity, I was tricked into going down to the local City Hall to read a report faxed to them. I was promptly arrested again and shipped to Lawrence County jail, where I spent my 49th birthday. That night, after mom and the girls posted yet another bond, we were informed that there was a hold on me in Marion County. Obviously, with the media publicity, customers were panicking everywhere and following the example set in Colbert County. Eventually, I was booked into six County jails total: Colbert, Lawrence, Marion, Lauderdale, Morgan, and my home county of Franklin. The money for bonds stretched my mother to the limit.

Marion County Jail was quite an experience. I spent the first ten hours in a holding cell with a sick drunk who had puked and shit all over the cell floor. There were no toilets in the holding cell, just a hole in the floor. Flies were everywhere. I was berserk and banging on the cell door. I had been transferred to Marion on a Thursday. For some reason, the judge there decided not to set my bond that day and then took Friday off, prior to a holiday weekend. I couldn't get a bond set and get released till the following Tuesday.

Marion County Jail's men's dorm was extremely overcrowded (the women's side had been vacated due to black mold). I had to sleep on the floor. Fighting a head and chest cold, I coughed my head off all weekend. A couple of times I thought that I was going to have an aneurysm.

On Sunday, DJ came down for visitation. We stood several feet apart from each other, on opposite sides of the fence, and cried, saying very few words. This was the first and only time that DJ would ever visit me during my time of incarceration.

Stress never seem to elude me. Not long after I had made bond and returned home, I was replacing a light bulb in the garage when I started having severe chest pains and nausea. DJ said that I was pale and should go to the doctor. I refused, telling her that I was going to use the bathroom and that I would be all right. Once in the house I realized that I was about to black out. I told DJ that I did need to go to the hospital and that I needed to go immediately. She opened the passenger door of the car for me and she was getting in the driver side when she said that my eyes rolled into the back of my head and I went down.

I don't know how long I was out. When I came to, DJ was over me screaming "don't you die on me!" I remember thinking that this was the first thing that she had said to me to make me think that she really did love me, in a long time. That thought was short-lived.

I recall extreme pain in my leg and my wrist. I wasn't able to get up, but in a few minutes the police and an ambulance arrived. I was transported to Helen Keller Hospital and admitted. It turned out that I had broken both my leg and my wrist in the fall. Multiple tests showed that I had the heart of an 18-year-old, according to one doctor. The only explanation that I was ever given for my chest pain and blackout were possible esophageal spasms caused by stress. Over the next year, I was in multiple casts and went through three wrist surgeries while trying to perform any kind of work that I could. I had no choice, I had to try and help buy groceries.

My friend Rob invented work for me, but I refused to work by the hour because of my slow speed working left-handed, and because I was creeping around on crutches. I performed odd jobs for him, by the job. I did everything from paint, to clean gutters, mow grass, clean shrubs, and so forth. After work, I'd usually go by Rob's or another good friend named Buzz's, and drink myself into a state of "comfortably numb." Buzz is a car wholesaler and he occasionally hired me to deliver cars for him.

During this time, my mother also had a fall and broke her hip. I stayed with her for a while after her surgery and hospital stay. Later, as she was able to get out again, we looked hilarious racing around Walmart together on the handicap scooters.

I was constantly sending out work applications and resumes during this time, but the non-responses and rejections just drove me deeper into a state of depression. My depression was well warranted because a storm was brewing just over the horizon.

Plea Jockies

"Make crime pay, become a lawyer."

—Will Rogers

During my first couple of semesters in college, I had toyed with the idea of a pre-law curriculum. As I researched my potential in the legal profession, I decided that if you didn't have the "Name" in advance or enough money to buy into a good firm, then you would ultimately wind up being an underling, doing all the grunt work for those who did have the name or the money. One alternative to this predicament would be to become a public defender.

If you are a good litigator and a salesman, you can become a successful and wealthy criminal attorney, selecting your clients and setting your fees. If not, you become a "Plea Jockey," claiming most of your business from court appointments. These are the lawyers who are not smart enough to be a successful corporate attorney, not dedicated enough to be in high demand, and are too damn lazy to be an ambulance chaser. Let me note that most courts require all their registered attorneys to take on some appointed work. These cases have fees set by the State and are not nearly as lucrative as other legal work. In this case, loyalty to the client is not necessarily required, despite what the BAR claims. Loyalty comes down to who's paying the bill, and with public defenders, at least on the surface, it is the State rather than the client. Research might show that the State is going to bill the clients' families, in hidden ways.

The oath required of attorneys in Alabama is as follows: *"I do solemnly swear (or affirm) that I will demean myself as an attorney, according to the best of my learning and ability, and with all good fidelity, as well to the court as to the client; that I will use no falsehood or delay any persons cause for lucre or malice, and that I will support the constitution of the State of Alabama and of the United States, so long as I continue a citizen (or legal resident) thereof, so help me God."*

BULLSHIT!

As you may have noticed, the word fidelity appears in the oath. The definition of fidelity is 1) the strict observance of promises, duties, etc. 2) loyalty 3) conjugal faithfulness 4) adherence to fact or detail, and 5) accuracy; or exactness.

As the Bible says, you cannot serve two masters. Make no mistake about it, court appointed attorneys work for the court. Their work load and which cases are assigned to them depends on the good graces of the judge. Public defenders want to keep the judge happy. Their main goal is to serve up pleas and save the court time, money, and accountability. If you are unfortunate enough to be broke and having to put your life in the hands of a Plea Jockey, it's kind of like having Adolf Hitler appointing Heinrich Himmler to represent a Hebrew candidate for Auschwitz.

Over the next year, being broke, I would put my life into the hands of a number of Plea Jockeys, some better than others. Realizing the risk in this, my Mother and I had looked into hiring an old family friend to represent me. After stretching me out for a while and eventually setting me down with one of the firms "young guns," I was quoted a price so high that if I had had that much cash I could probably have walked away from the problem by buying my way out of it. I found it amazing, throughout my experiences, the various levels of legal effort and concern that different monetary amounts would buy if available.

Colbert County—Welcome to Alabama's equivalent of TV's Hazard County, (of Dukes fame) a real-live Peyton Place. If you are looking for Podunk—Good Ole Boy justice, you've come to the right place. After my arraignment, watching the various appointees and the lack of professional enthusiasm that they seemed to bring to the courtroom, it was unsettling. It reminded me of an experience where I had carried one of my former employees for his daily "fix" at a methadone clinic and watched the addicts and the counselors huddled around with stoic faces drinking coffee, smoking cigarettes, and chit chatting, prior to their "professional" consultations. Then when court began, they came across as a bunch of arrogant taskmasters overseeing a beggar's banquet.

I was appointed an attorney whom I will call John McClueless. John was a very large man and appeared to have some trouble getting around the courtroom easily. Sometimes he appeared to have trouble even breathing. Eventually, he made his way back to me and introduced himself. He seemed like a nice enough guy and we made an appointment to meet at his office the following week.

When the meeting day arrived, I sat across from John as he thumbed through one of his law books. Reading from a section he stated that, according to Alabama law, although indebtedness occurring during the closing of a business was regrettable, it did not constitute a criminal act. "There seems to be no evidence of intent involved," he said, "so this should be a civil matter." You don't know how many different attorneys said these words to me over the next several months. I wish someone had remembered to tell the DA.

Upon stating his definition of the law, John's conversation somehow turned to motocross bikes and kayaking, a recurring conversation in each of my meetings with him (I really couldn't picture a man of his size on a dirt bike, or especially in a kayak). I interrupted to ask when he would like to start interviewing any of my potential witnesses. He stated that would come later, but for now that he needed to file for a continuance to allow us more time.

I said to him, "I'm anxious to get this behind me. Is a continuance really necessary?"

He assured me that it was common procedure and that the DA was wanting one, too. Did that make it the thing to do, I thought? Months and two continuances later I'm not sure that he had done a single thing to prepare for trial other than to provide time for the DA to invent a case against me. I was assured however, that this should be a civil case and I was up on my motocross bikes and kayaks. Where was Erin Brockovich when I needed her?

Around the other counties where I faced charges, similar processes were taking place. In each of them, I applied for indigent status and was appointed an attorney. In Lawrence County, I was able to scrape together enough money to cover the debt and it was quickly dismissed.

In Lauderdale County, a young attorney named John Odem was appointed to me. John impressed me from the beginning. Unlike all the other lawyers that I was given, he wasn't a Plea Jockey. Working out of a firm founded by his father, he came across as a real lawyer. He was young and energetic and seemed to take a sincere interest in my case. Once again, I was told that this should be a civil matter but that did not necessarily mean that the DA would look at it that way. John took on my case with the zeal that I would have expected out of all my attorneys. Over the next year, I would come to consider John as not only my lawyer, but also a friend.

In the remaining counties, I was appointed additional attorneys. I was given John McJimmyhoffa, in Franklin County, (John is obviously a very popular attorney name and this one was generally very hard to locate) and, for lack of a better name, Jim Lawless was appointed to me in Morgan County. An old golfing buddy, Shane James, came to me and offered his help in Marion County. He went to work and my charges there were promptly dismissed. Shane refused to take any payment, saying to remember him when I got back on my feet. It's hard to use Shane's name in vain and refer to him as a lawyer. Shane is a fine human being.

The big battle, however, was Colbert County. The Colbert County DA was Vice Mayhem, a second-generation fixture in local politics. To get an appropriate mental picture of Mayhem, imagine Larry Fine, of the Three Stooges, with a swagger. A friend of mine who was at court told me that when Mayhem took stage, he reminded him of a cross between Jimmy Swaggart and the prosecutor in "My Cousin Vinny." Don't underestimate him though, he is a tough and ruthless prosecutor.

My case had been assigned to assistant DA, Angelnott Hussey, a real Stepford Wife. Later in court, I would see firsthand just how accurate that description would be, for she was quite stoic and almost robotic in her presentation. She and Vice Mayhem would tag team me for four days.

Concerned over the lack of preparation by my attorney, John McClueless, I decided to meet with Angelnott Hussey. In a short meeting, I attempted to plead my case to convince her that no criminal intent was involved. I might as well have been talking to a lamp post. Ms. Hussey was all about the numbers (conviction rate + popular opinion = votes for her boss).

Also during this time, I was served on a number of cases that were processed in civil court. In each of these cases, I gave a consent judgment. How could I argue? I had not fulfilled my contracts. Boy, was I shocked later when some of these same names appeared in the criminal proceedings against me; obviously, they were recruited. I guess double dipping is allowed in the judicial system. Go ahead and kick a man when he is down.

I'm told that everything in this world has a purpose. Even maggots contribute by eating dead carcasses. I guess plea jockeys would be considered maggots, in that they are assigned to get rid of the refuse. After my meeting with the assistant DA, I went to circuit judge Tacky Snatcher's office to see if I could be appointed a different attorney. Although I didn't get to speak to Judge Snatcher herself, a court clerk informed me that the judge would not agree to the change, saying that the one I was appointed was the one who would be there for the duration of the trial. I am glad airlines don't look at faulty aircraft in the same manner.

Finally, my court date was arriving. My nervousness about this was somewhat tempered by the other stress in my life. I had constantly been in and out of the hospital and doctor's offices with my wrist and leg. Also after several months of trying to keep up payments, DJ and I had lost our dream home. Needless to say, the lifestyle change created a big rift in our relationship.

The week before trial, I had to attend a settlement hearing. At that time, I was offered a plea agreement. If I would plead guilty to two counts, (I had 19 counts in Colbert after the recruiting season was over) the DA would not object to probation. "No" I said, "none of this was intentional. I would be lying!" I felt like Monte Hall was offering me what was behind door # 3 or to take a chance on the consequences. In retrospect, that was a pretty good synopsis of how the plea system works. Still, I held to my convictions.

Court: "Do you solemnly swear to tell the truth, the whole truth and nothing but the truth, so help you God?"

Defendant: "No, your honor, instead of telling the truth, I would like to take a plea."

GET REAL!

John McClueless relayed my refusal to the DA and then said to me, "Well, I'll see you on Tuesday." Tuesday was the start of my trial!

"John," I said, "Aren't you going to interview any of my witnesses?"

"Oh yeah," he replied, "Call me on Monday." I fired him in my mind on the spot, despite having been told by the court that I couldn't. Later that day, I called John Odem and asked him what he would charge to represent me in Colbert County. John gave me a very fair price and my mom and some friends scraped up the funds to pay for his services. John told me that he would notify the court that I had released John McClueless and would ask for a continuance so that he could prepare for a case. "This should be granted," he said.

John was shocked when Judge Snatcher denied the continuance. Her reasoning for this decision was because John McClueless had already been granted two continuances. These are two continuances that I had not wanted, but the DA had wanted them to prepare for me. Upon John's protest, saying that he needed time to prepare and interview witnesses, Judge Snatcher basically told him to interview them on the way to the stand. I guess this was her show of contempt towards me for casting off the "appointed executioner" whom she had assigned to me.

What was going on? Is this the way the system is supposed to work? Can it really be this one-sided? The answers depend on which side of the table you are on. Over the next week, the answer to a lot of these questions would become obvious to me. I was up against a stacked deck.

Playing God

"The jury consists of twelve persons chosen to decide who has the better lawyer."
—Robert Frost

On the morning of March 30, 2010, I moved around in a state of numbness. D-day had arrived. My brain was still pondering why the judge had denied John time to prepare for the trial. Her reasoning about the previous continuances didn't hold water with me. She had to know that her appointed flunky wasn't prepared for trial. Yet, she denied my new attorney to make sure that he was unprepared as well.

Also, why was I being tried for each different "victim" as a separate case, with all of them being tried simultaneously? If I was guilty of one case, I was guilty of them all. This method was like a "birdshot" approach. The DA had multiple chances of shooting me down, while at the same time tainting the perceptions of the jury on the other cases. Were there hidden forces stacked against me? As time passed, the answer to that question became clearly—YES! However, with the cards stacked against you, being able to prove it would be difficult, if not impossible.

As I got ready to leave the house that we were now renting, CNN aired a piece on businessman Bernie Madoff's scandal and trial. I remember hoping that no potential jurors were watching and might associate my situation with Madoff's. I shouldn't have been surprised when the DA brought Madoff's name up during the trial. DJ mumbled a quick, "Good Luck," and I was off. I had asked DJ, my mother, and my girls not to attend the trial. I assured them that I would be exonerated and that I didn't want the extra pressure of them being there. Everyone, except DJ, protested saying that I needed support. I put my foot down and they reluctantly accepted my request. DJ said she was working a new job and didn't need to miss work anyway.

An hour or so later, an eerie feeling swept over me as I entered the courtroom. I wasn't here to just observe the happenings in court, this was my life on the big screen. John went over the rules for jury selection with me and asked me to jot down notes on any pros and cons that I saw among them. As the judge entered, I recalled the reviews and opinions of her that I had been given as being harsh and quick to throw out a heavy sentence. Later, I would, on several occasions, hear her referred to as Judge Roy Bean, the hanging judge of old west fame.

As the members of the jury pool filed in, I noticed several familiar faces in the crowd. Among them was an old friend, the wife of a golfing buddy, and a contractor whom I had done work for. All of these were short lived as potential jurors, as I expected they would be. There was no chance that I could have someone on the jury with a real knowledge and experience of me.

The first question asked by the DA was if anyone knew me. Appropriately, each of the aforementioned persons acknowledged acquaintance with me. Knowing they would be struck, John O asked each of their opinions of me and each gave positive reviews. Things were going well so far. It was the next question posed from the DA that caught me off guard and really shocked me. The DA asked if any of the pool had ever been self-employed or had any association with a small business, along with some referral to influencing their opinions (which was obviously made to cover his ass in the minds of the jurors). Needless to say, the 15 or so people who raised their hand were dismissed as well. So much for a jury of my peers. After the dust settled and we had a jury seated, I was basically at the mercy of a group consisting of homemakers, school teachers, unemployed laborers, and plant workers who picked up a check every Friday, regardless of the weekly economy. To the DA, this was not about right and wrong, it was simply about winning or losing.

The United States Supreme Court has ruled that a black man cannot be tried with a jury that excludes minority members (not that Alabama feels obligated to consistently follow this ruling). Why then should a businessman be tried by a jury that includes only those trained to follow instructions and one that excludes other risk takers and decision makers?

I was at the mercy of a hand selected group, which Vice Mayhem felt that with his grandstanding, he could influence. It would basically be like I was at the mercy of June Cleaver, Aunt Bea, Archie Bunker, Marge the manicurist, Kramer, Ralph Malf, and the late-night phone buddy of Jake from State Farm. Where were Bill Gates, R.H. Macy, Colonel Sanders, Henry Ford, Soicharo Honda, James Dyson, Walt Disney, Stephen King, Dr. Seuss, Stephen Spielberg, Oprah Winfrey, and Harrison Ford?

All of these people had been through business or career failures and setbacks. Would they not have a better view of business situations and be more likely to be peers than someone who doesn't understand risk and the resulting chance of failure versus reward.

The end result was a group that the DA felt he could manhandle. There is an old saying in legal circles that if the evidence is not in your favor, just yell and scream a lot. These folks would get a big dose of Vice Mayhem's theatrics over the next few days.

Also, I had to constantly worry about my own demeanor and keeping my cool under fire. A couple of years later, I would see an episode of Dateline, where an individual who was on trial said that the click of a pen or biting a nail could be the act that influenced a juror. This particular man was convicted of murder and later proven innocent when the real perpetrator was caught. However, lack of constitutional evidence had not slowed the DA down in obtaining the initial conviction.

The legal system and the legal profession are basically a practice in legal extortion, you are squeezed from every angle. The level of justice you receive is what you can afford. If you can't afford it, then the system turns its enforcers loose on you. Enter Vice Mayhem! I had been surprised when Mayhem had pretty much taken over the trial, for Angelnott Hussey had handled everything to this point. I guess the execution team felt like they needed his charisma, in lieu of her plastic courtroom manner. Make no mistake, as low as Vice Mayhem's ethical and moral reputation is locally, both in and out of the courtroom, he is a formidable opponent. He could probably convince a jury that Mother Theresa was more heinous that Charles Manson. He can also manipulate the jury selection to his full advantage. He can select and play a jury like a Maestro. I was probably convicted with his second question to the jury pool, which eliminated any potential business people. To quote author Michael Connelly in his best seller *The Lincoln Lawyer*, "To them it's not about justice, it's just a game, a batting average. They like to keep score and to see how far it will get them in the office."

In the movie *The Devil's Advocate* (which would be an appropriate title for many prosecutors, as well as defense councils), the attorney played by Keanu Reeves was hired by a huge law firm simply because of his ability to select a winning jury. Obtaining justice was not a factor, only winning. This frame of mind is all too present in many courtrooms.

Watching Vince Mayhem select a jury was kind of like watching the show *Shark Tank* with the roles reversed. Mayhem was the lone Shark selling himself to each potential juror and deciding who could give him the best returns.

The closest that I can describe to being put on trial, would be to go through a weeklong root canal. The emotions are gut wrenching. There were times that I thought that I would throw up right there in the court room. Do all people facing a superior and ruthless foe have the same fears? Did the infamous 300 Spartans at Thermopylae feel dread as they faced the overwhelming armies of Xerxes? It took every ounce of gumption that I could muster to walk into that courtroom each day, knowing that I was being painted as a terrible person.

During his opening statements, Vice Mayhem made the remark to the jury that "there is a high burden of proof in this case." To this day, I am still trying to figure out where that proof was. One by one each of the "victims" were called and questioned by either Vice Mayhem or Angelnott Hussey, as they became a tag team. Many of these were the people that had been recruited out of the civil cases, in which I had given consent judgments. This was done just so the prosecution could make the overall scope of the situation better for themselves. They went over their contracts with me and the amounts of money owed, none of which was in question. For the most part my attorney, John Odem, was quiet during the prosecution's examination, for there was really nothing to object to.

When John took his turn, he questioned each of the *victims* about how they had heard of me and my company. Virtually everyone stated that they had been referred to me by family members or friends. When John questioned them about whether the people referring me were happy with the jobs that I had done for them, the prosecution immediately yelled out, "This is hearsay." The judge would then promptly sustain the objections.

What was going on? My character was on trial. The DA certainly didn't hesitate to make referrals to Bernie Madoff in relation to me. (Note: Isn't it ironic that I later discovered that some courts don't put opening and closing statements in the official court transcripts? This basically gives the D.A. a free rein to attack your character without scrutiny of appellate judges.) Should the Madoff referrals not be considered impermissible speculation or as hearsay, if the opinions of other customers were? If opinions of the very people who had recommended me were not evidence, what was? John repeatedly tried to rephrase the questions and in none of the cases was there a theme that we had done improper work or tried to deceive anyone. Some of the "victims" testified that we had even done previous work for them.

John also questioned each of these witnesses as to whether I had tried to avoid them when they found out that I was closing the business. All but a couple said that I was easy to reach and did not try to avoid them at all. The two who did state that I had avoided them, obviously felt that this statement was what they were supposed to say. Upon further questioning, they talked about conversations that they had with me. I faced all their questions, yet I was avoiding them?

Several of the witnesses stated that I had answered the phone when they had called my shop or that I had contacted them first, telling them what was going on. One "victim" testified that she had run a business and knew how hard it could be. When John asked her if she thought that I had intended to take her money, once again there was a swift objection, which was sustained. If the very people from whom I was accused of stealing from could not answer this question for the jury, what chance did I have?

Later, as John was calling our witnesses, my former employees consistently stated that I was a fair and honest person. They, as well as some friends who were involved in businesses and with whom I had had conversations with during the time of ArcStone's demise, talked about how hard the economy hit us all. Artie, who was my second in command, testified to the fact, that in hindsight, I probably had held on to some of my employees too long, simply because I had a good heart. He stated that although I obviously made some poor business decisions that my heart was in the right place. He even testified, that he had seen me replace an entire set of kitchen countertops, just to satisfy an unhappy customer. Not a single one of these witnesses, people who had been around me daily, offered any hint that I was a dishonest person or had intentionally tried to deprive any of these people of their money. Did this testimony, along with the fact that I had been in business for twenty years prior to the collapse of the housing market, not mean anything?

Robert Eaton, who was a well-known local contractor and who had been the potential buyer of ArcStone, testified that he recognized that I had made some bad business decisions and that he and I had been in negotiations for a while, until situations with his son and son-in-law, caused the deal to fall through. This news came the day after we had learned that a large condo project we were expecting to do had been shelved because of the economy. I had then shut down the day after I learned that the potential sale of the business was canceled. A deposit check that had come in that morning was returned.

When Vice Mayhem cross-examined my employees, suppliers, and other business acquaintances, he totally avoided anything that they would have to say about my integrity or honesty. He repeatedly just screamed about the fact that taking people's money is stealing. He totally avoided the testimony of these people and the situation at the time. All the testimony about the economic conditions and the company collapsing around us were ignored.

Wikipedia says that the 2008 financial crisis is considered by many economists to be the worst financial crisis since the Great Depression of the 1930s. It resulted in the threat of total collapse of large financial institutions, bailout of banks by governments, and the turndown of the stock markets. Housing markets suffered, resulting in evictions, foreclosures, and prolonged unemployment. The crisis reached its peak in September 2008, just months prior to my closing ArcStone. Major institutions that failed, were acquired under duress, or were subject to government takeover, included Lehman Brothers, Merrill Lynch, Fannie Mae, Washington Mutual, Wachovia, Citigroup, and AIG. If the bailouts, takeovers and sales of these companies had not taken place, would their leaders have been compared to Bernie Madoff? Would they have been prosecuted as criminals?

Small businesses were not bailed out like the major banking institutions. There was no stimulus or FDIC to bail out the little businessman. Also, the banks did not reciprocate to the little guy after receiving their bailouts. Loans were virtually impossible to get. Foreclosures did not slow down a lick. As of 2012, in the US, a large volume of troubled mortgages still remained in place. It was impossible for most homeowners facing foreclosure to refinance or modify their mortgages.

In 2008 to 2009, over 170,000 small businesses were claimed by the recession. This figure is over twice the number of failures in any of the previous years. These factors, however, were not taken into consideration in my trial. Maybe if I could have hidden behind a bankruptcy or a bailout, none of this would be happening to me. Because I didn't hide behind bankruptcy and because I had made bad decisions and got caught up in a perfect storm, I was now Bernie Madoff in the eyes of the prosecutor. My situation was no sweat off his ass. The financial crisis did not seem to have affected the "legal" business. Politics was still going strong and using me as a sacrificial lamb looked good to the voters.

Despite the DA's stereotype of me, I was delusional about what was really taking place and what the outcome would be. I guess that I trusted the court to do the right thing and not the popular thing. In my mind, the one factor that I still had going for me was the law itself. The law stated that I had to have intent to do harm for it to be a criminal act.

> **in·tent** (in-'tent): The design or purpose to commit a wrongful or criminal act.
>
> *Merriam — Webster*

Would this law be properly defined by the court and instilled in the jurors' minds, or would this proceeding be a Salem witch trial in which I would have to jump into the river and drown, proving my innocence by not floating? Maybe I could have proved my innocence by going the Wall Street route and committing suicide. I should have guessed my ultimate fate by the simple fact that this *conjured intent* went to trial. In reality, politically induced reasonable doubt trumps right and wrong any day of the week.

I really thought that, between John's examination of the witnesses and my own testimony, we had done well and that we would win, however, after the closing arguments I wasn't so sure. Prior to the trial, I didn't realize that in criminal cases the DA gets both the first and last chance to influence the jurors. Is this fair? It was my ass on the line!

For his closing argument, John used a text book — law school, reasonable doubt argument. NOLO.com's free dictionary of law terms states that reasonable doubt is:

> *The standard of proof used in criminal trials to find a defendant guilty of a crime. When a criminal defendant is prosecuted, the prosecutor must prove the defendant's guilt "beyond*

a reasonable doubt." A reasonable doubt exists when a juror cannot say with moral certainty that a person is guilty.

I remember thinking in French terms, "This ought to be a no-frickin'-doubt-argument." I think that the monotony and the impersonal nature of the approach used lost some of the jurors. Still, the charm of the closing argument shouldn't have mattered. There was no proof or hint of any intent. If I had stashed these people's money away, I could have afforded an "OJ dream team" of my own to get me out of this mess! Hell, I would have been in the Caymans sipping Margaritas!

As ineffective as our defense was, Vice Mayhem's was prepared and in-your-face. You would have thought that he was vying for an Academy award. Going back to the old law school adage: "If you are lacking in evidence, just yell and scream a lot." Mayhem yelled and screamed—A LOT!

Vice Mayhem probably deserved an Oscar. He spent his whole time discrediting and mocking Robert Eaton by sneering the words "bad business" and by repeatedly calling me a thief. He stayed well away from questions of intent or character. This approach was all about the ability to influence people. SCREW right and wrong!

What do they teach in law school now? Instead of law degrees, maybe they should be issuing degrees in theater. It seems that instead of arguing facts for the sake of justice, prosecutors want to dramatize and present theories as fact, just for the sake of winning.

Some prosecutors envision themselves as crusaders. In the process, their crusades can develop tunnel-vision and be influenced by the wrong motives. The Crusades of the middle ages claimed a multitude of innocent lives in the name of Christianity. The same thing happens today with this modern brand of crusader. They beat their chest and pretend to be the watchdog of the public, when many times it is just a win/loss ratio and good publicity to them. A prosecutor's job should simply be about what is right and what is wrong, as defined by the Constitution. If prosecutors would follow this path, their job as crime fighters would take care of itself. Instead, many of them take advantage of the situation, grandstanding and presenting their hypothesis as facts, while performing a character assassination on the defendant.

As the jury filed out, I felt hollow. Would these folks fall for the antics of this kangaroo court? Would the Jerry Springer theatrics of the DA outweigh the definition of the law?

YOU BET!

A few hours later the jury returned. I stood as the judge started reading the verdicts of the 18 remaining counts one by one, the nineteenth was vacated for some reason unknown to me. As it turned out I was found guilty on seven counts and innocent on the remainder. The judge, the DA and my attorney all looked around puzzled. The judge stated that maybe it had something to do with the dates.

As it turned out, I was found guilty on only the most recent of the cases. In the cases involving the original people to bring charges against me, I was found innocent, but in the cases happening within a short time of the failure to sell the business and its ultimate closing, I was found guilty. This verdict made no sense. I had no intentions of taking advantage of any of these people, but if I was guilty of one of these charges, I was guilty of them all. I guess that the jury just felt like they just had to appease the District Attorney's Office with something and pulled a business cut off date out of the air. I wonder if they considered what the judge could possibly have in store for me. Then again, I guess that that was not their concern.

After the judge set my sentencing date for a couple of months down the road, I was released on my current bond. As we left the courtroom, John was telling me that he was sorry about this decision and that he felt that the verdict was not just. The DA and the assistant DA mumbled something to me about wishing me well, but I just stared back at them. I was numb! What was the jury thinking? Could they not see through the charade? How could this nightmare be happening? Was common sense unconstitutional?

I dreaded my sentencing hearing strictly based on the arrogance and reproach for me that showed in the judge's eyes. I didn't know the woman and had hardly said five words to her. Was this treatment simply because I had challenged her kingdom? John told me he felt that with no criminal history I had a good chance of getting probation to go with court ordered restitution. Something about the contempt on the judge's face told me different. Still, I held out hope. However, it really didn't matter at the moment. I couldn't believe what had just happened! I was a convicted felon! Even worse, I was being perceived as a bad and dishonest person!

Debtors Prison

"What lies behind us and what lies before us are tiny matters compared to what lies within us."
—Oliver Wendell Holmes

If I was numb before, there are no words to describe the feelings and the emotions that were going through me now. On top of that, I had a couple of months of speculation ahead of me as to the fate that the judge would bestow upon me at sentencing. As a convicted criminal, I was about to enter the world of Bernie Madoff, Enron CEO Kenneth Lay, Leona Helmsley, Jeffrey Dahmer, John Gotti, Al Capone, and John Dillinger. Did any of the members of this jury not take note about how the country was struggling? Did they not notice how many businesses that didn't receive General Motors bailouts were going under? Did they not see that the same banks that repossessed small businessmen's homes received government assistance to stay afloat? Maybe over the next couple of years, as the hardships possibly filtered to them, they would then understand. By then it would be too late for me.

I, although a convicted criminal, was a victim of economic fallout. I was cast as a criminal because of my own lackadaisical management practices and from being publically stereotyped. In July of the next year, I watched as Congress debated on raising taxes to keep the Federal Government from defaulting on its debts. I wish I could have just sent out supplemental invoices to take care of my shortcomings. My customers would not have understood this practice, nor would they have fallen for it.

To build up my ego, in case things didn't go well at sentencing, I tried to think of all the people who had been unjustly incarcerated at some point in history: Martin Luther, Dr. Martin Luther King Jr., John McCain, Galileo, Nelson Mandela, William Wallace, and Mary Queen of Scots. Also add to that list: Victor Frank, Anne Frank, Sir Walter Raleigh, Geronimo, Salmon Ruskie, Gandhi, Susan B. Anthony, Joseph, Daniel, The Apostle Peter, John the Baptist, and of course Jesus Christ. Guilty or not, other popular ex-cons that came to mind, including Johnny Cash, Merle Haggard, Tim Allen, Charlie Sheen, Lindsey Lohan and Robert Downey Jr. (one of my favorite actors). Plus, we can't forget Rambo, Papillion, Cool Hand Luke, The Shawshank Boys, as well as Curley, Larry, and Moe.

Additionally, as I weighed my chances, my mind turned to the judge and then to the other people of power that the world had allowed to judge others before me. These included Pontius Pilate, Hitler, Stalin, Papa Doc Duvalier, Fidel Castro, Pol Pot, Saddam Hussein, Nero, Caligula, Nebuchadnezzar and the Pharaoh of the Old Testament. Just because someone has a title like King, Lord, Your Honor or Judge doesn't necessarily make them a fair and moral person. What I was about to get hit with, and what I would find out later, certainly has left me with a low opinion of Judge Roy Bean Snatcher.

Months later, my opinion would be solidified as I listened to the abdication of responsibility in the Domenic Strauss Kahn case in New York. By proper interpretation of the laws of the State of Alabama, should the judge not have issued a directed verdict if there was no evidence of intent? Should she have not accurately interpreted the law concerning intent and not thrown it upon the jury? Would she do the right thing or the popular and most marketable thing?

If you want to see how media hungry Alabama prosecutors can be, search for the TV accounts about the Alabama man tried for his new bride's murder following her scuba related death on their honeymoon on the Great Barrier Reef. The state Attorney General himself decided to prosecute the case. Bad move! When the presiding judge threw the case out, without letting it go to jury, citing lack of evidence, the Alabama Attorney General publically criticized the judge and the decision. The state's head prosecutor was obviously embarrassed and didn't like having the tables turned on him.

Media coverage and public perception can convict you without you getting a chance to say a word to defend yourself. Throughout the early process, I read about the charges against me and the statements of the DA and the victims in The Daily newspaper. Not once was I approached for a statement. After I found out that another article was online, I finally decided it was time for me to make a statement. I called The Daily newspaper to speak to the writer but was told he wasn't available. Not one to give up easily, I tracked down his home phone number. "Barney, this is Mike Harrison. I believe you have another article on me coming out in the paper tomorrow." There was a stunned silence at the other end of the phone.

"I didn't call to cuss you out, I know you're doing your job. I was hoping to just give a little of my side of this story," I said. This statement relaxed Barney and I proceeded to give my statements, a few of which made the following day's paper.

As well as their daily news rag, The Daily also has an online forum where people could write in anonymously and say anything that they wanted in a special heading on me and my charges. I read that some thought I was a cocaine addict, a drunk, and a high rolling gambler at the casinos in Tunica. Who were these people? They obviously didn't know me. Sure, I'd have a drink with friends and have a small, friendly wager on a golf game but nothing like what I was reading. In addition, I've never tried cocaine in my life, unlike many well-known local politicians (winkwink). Were these people on the forums just getting off on stirring the pot or did they think that I had a bundle stashed in the Cayman Islands? I wish I had!

Fortunately, several people, whom to this day I still don't know who they are, came to my defense on the forum and rebuked every charge, stating that I had done work for their family and friends and that I was an honorable person. Whoever you are, I thank you for standing up for me. Eventually, because of pressure from my daughters, the forum pertaining to me and my case was dropped from The Daily's website. My girls had come to my rescue.

Seeing how public opinion can be formed and shaped because of one sided media slant and political correctness gave me great respect for celebrity human rights activists who go against the grain and bring needed attention to government or judicial misconduct. Musicians Eddie Vedder (Pearl Jam), John Mellencamp, and actor Richard Gere come to my mind as champions of the mistreated.

During my summer, while waiting to learn my fate, I had the last of three surgeries on my right wrist, my dominant hand. After two unsuccessful attempts to help me gain some movement in the wrist, the doctor finally gave up and inserted a steel plate. I would never be able to bend my right wrist again. I had been working the last several months left handed. It would be even longer before I could even stand to shake hands with my right hand.

I continued sending out resumes and going to any interview I could get. In every case, when the disclosure of felony was made, I was out the door in a heartbeat.

It really didn't matter anyway. I should have seen what was coming. The judge basically gave away her contempt for me during her previous lecture. I had tried to shake the tree when I had fired her "Plea Jockey." You don't mess with her preordained system.

Much to the dismay of my attorney and myself, I was sentenced to a 7 split 1, meaning that I was to serve one year in prison followed by probation for failing at business and ultimately owing money. Was my lack of any criminal history not taken into account? Was this sentence strictly a vendetta for challenging her system?

John O apologized to me, saying that he never expected her to give me time. As I was cuffed, the DA and the assistant DA came over and once again "wished me luck." I again just stared at them in dismay. Someone made the statement that I would be home in a couple of months. Whoever said that either just wanted to make me feel better or really didn't have a clue how this cesspool that calls itself a legal system, actually works. Blinking my eyes, I still couldn't wake up from this nightmare. I was going to prison!

PART II:
SALT IN MY WOUNDS

Rants and Raves

"Trial. A formal inquiry designed to prove and put upon record the blameless characters of judges, advocates, and jurors."
—Ambrose Bierce

To describe Judge Snatcher's scowl and her demeanor, imagine what the offspring would be like if you mated Nancy Grace and Bill O'Reilly. During the lecture that I received from her at my sentencing, she kept pounding on me that I had known that my business was in trouble. Sure, I did! That's why I had been looking for investors and had been in negotiations to sell it. Otherwise, I would've kept going without looking to bring others in. What was the message? Business should not involve risk. How many businesses do not incur risk? Does Wall Street not have losses caused by risk? Was the embarrassment of failure not enough?

The judge went out of her way to justify the actions of the court and of the jurors. Was there a need for this since I had already been convicted? Probably so. Maybe she needed to convince herself so she could sleep at night, or maybe she just has no feelings or morals. Personally, I do have feelings and morals. I was ashamed of the fact that I had drifted away from my business focus and failed. It cut me to the bone that I had let down my customers and owed some of them money. Instead of being allowed to go to work and attempt to take care of my problem, I was instead lectured and sent away to prison.

Throughout the trial, the DA had criticized me for putting our customers' deposits in our general operating fund, as most businesses do, instead of earmarking individual dollars towards specific customers' materials. In hindsight, maybe that would have been a great thing to do. However, as was testified by others, this earmarking is not typical business practice in most industries. I wonder if the DA has to answer for any and all investments into his office by his constituents. I imagine, it depends on who you are. I guess if you carry enough influence your deposit will mean something.

On August 2, 2011, less than two weeks before my release from prison, the United States of America was facing financial default for the first time in its existence. Fortunately, the government has options at its disposal that I didn't. First, they (the Government) are able to create their own money, either by printing it or by using forced sales (taxes) upon their customers (the citizens). Secondly, they have the option of extending their own debt.

For the sake of argument, let's say that the USA was just like me and millions of other small businesses and didn't have these options. Let's say that they had defaulted. The government had known for some time that their business was in trouble. They had continued to collect both tax deposits and Social Security deposits. Were all those Social Security deposits earmarked for the individual citizens who paid them in? Or were they perhaps put into the government's general operating budget to fund everyday business, including all kinds of "pork" projects for the Congressmen's obligations to their lobbyist? Surely not! If the same criteria was considered for the Federal Government, Social Security would be exposed as the biggest Ponzi scheme of all time!

Because of this default, would the president have been arrested and sentenced to prison? Would a group of deputies have been waiting for the budget and finance committee members on the Capitol steps? I think not. Just because they are politicians, what makes them different from me? Are they not citizens just like me? The same laws that apply to me should apply to them. Should double standards apply just because I was the little guy?

Another recurring question: should circuit court judges, who basically play God over people's lives, be elected officials? Does anyone think that public opinion or the opinion of prominent citizens doesn't affect their decisions when votes and reelection are to be considered? Should the marketing prowess of a campaign fund qualify these people to hold other people's lives in their hands? In 2011, the Supreme Court Chief Justice of the State of Alabama resigned. Although she cited family reasons, she stated that she had been frustrated that she had been unable to persuade the legislature to change the way Alabama elects judges. She had also cited that Alabama's prisons were operating at 195% of capacity.

Some of my clientele were the more influential and connected of the local community. One particular "connected" individual, to whom I owed money after ArcStone's failure, appeared to be the driving force behind the court's entire crusade against me and pushed a lot of buttons to have me prosecuted. Did any of these people's opinions change the meaning of "intent" in the laws of the state of Alabama and the Country, as pertaining to my case? I have admitted to obviously being a poor businessman in many regards, but are the people running our country making better business decisions than what caused my downfall and arrest? Obviously, they subscribe to my old "when in doubt—sell more" philosophy.

People who call the fallout from the 2008 economic downturn a recession, obviously don't have a clue what they are talking about. In the construction trades, it was an outright depression. In 2011, folks in the construction trades were still hoping for recovery to come. It took better than four years for all the spin doctor rhetoric of the government to actually convert into housing starts and the decrease of unemployment rates.

One day in 2007, I stood in the front yard of a house that my crew was working on in Madison, Alabama. In the three developments that I could see from my vantage point, I counted 32 houses in some stage of construction. Three years later, driving through the same area on my way to the doctor's office, I counted only three houses under construction and three vacated foundations in a ten mile stretch.

Another double standard in this country, is the preferential treatment of big business and the financial institutions. According to Pro Publica, the government committed a total of $634 billion dollars to 926 recipients in the financial bailout. As of this writing, almost $580 billion had been dispersed and only $276 billion returned. Among the recipients of this bailout were AIG, General Motors, the Bank of America, Citibank, J.P. Morgan Chase, Wells Fargo, GMAC, Chrysler, Goldman Sachs, and Morgan Stanley. Although several of these companies have now returned their free money, the government-sponsored enterprises, Fannie Mae and Freddie Mac were given a total of $169 billion and as of this writing, have yet to return a dime. Were the executives of these organizations, with their maverick lending practices, any less incompetent in their business practices that I was? Were they criminals because of their poor sense of business direction and lack of foresight?

Those who think that the financial institutions trickled down their relief to the little man and the small businesses suffering around the country are sadly mistaken. In most cases, they used the money for their own reserves instead of using it for the purposes it was reported to be for. That is why most of them have come through the economic times unscathed and richer, if nothing else. They accomplished this while small business America has greatly suffered.

Countless other Americans were like me and saw no relief as we lost our businesses and our homes to foreclosure. So, who does our government really work for, Average Joe the citizen or for Fat Cat corporate America? Is this view the way Uncle Sam looks at things? Maybe they took their distorted views from small town, good-ole-boy politics. Look out America, Colbert County wants you!

The Colbert County Hilton

"If it's illegal to rock 'n roll, throw my ass in jail!"
— Kurt Cobain

Orange is NOT the new black for me! As a rabid Alabama Crimson Tide fan, I become nauseous around orange. I get a rash when I come in contact with it. LOL! Most of our biggest rivals—Auburn, Tennessee and Florida all wear orange. The old joke among Bama fans is that the reason Tennessee fans wear orange is so they never have to change. They wear orange for the ballgame on Saturday, and then on Sunday they will have on the required orange for hunters. Come Monday they don't even have to change for their job on the county jail's road work crew.

This old joke didn't seem so funny to me anymore, but Southeastern Conference fans will always be ribbing each other. As a retort to the orange joke, Tennessee fans say that the best thing to ever come out of Alabama is Interstate 65 North, which leaves Alabama heading to Nashville. I would gladly have donned even this sacrilegious color and headed up I-65 if I could've done so. Anything to escape the idea of being jailed in Colbert County.

Although I had briefly experienced incarceration at Colbert on several occasions during the previous year, the first startling thing about becoming a resident of Colbert County jail was the language and manners of the jailers. I guess that I expected this from inmates, but not from those hired to oversee them. I hesitate to call the inmates criminals, because who knows how legitimate the reasons are that have some of them in Colbert County jail. Also, it's sometimes hard to see the line where the term criminal differs between them and their keepers.

The worst of these was the head jailer. Every other word was "fucking this" or "God damn that." If everyone in life is labeled, he would have smart ass or white trash stamped across his forehead.

After being processed, I exchanged my clothes for a nasty orange jumpsuit (YUUUKKK!!!), issued minimal toiletries and a nasty blanket, towel, and bed mat. Sheets were not issued.

I was then assigned to the northwest cell block of the jail. The only bunk available in the cell block was a top bunk. With three fused vertebrae in my back, the only way I could get on it was to use the toilet as a step.

Colbert County jail is a dump. Much of the plumbing doesn't work. Most of the lights don't work either. The facility, which was probably built around the same time as the Pyramids, was supposedly condemned in the 1990s. It is a damp and dismal place. The windows are shuttered up, allowing no sunlight, and no yardtime is given. It is my understanding that the living conditions at Colbert County jail are a probable civil rights violation. Living there was like living in a medieval dungeon.

Shortly after I arrived, I was taken downstairs to see an old friend, Anthony, who had been assigned as jail administrator. The head jailer's demeanor changed drastically with me after he found out that I had grown up with the administrator. Anthony apologized for the conditions in the jail. He told me that he had inherited a nightmare and that he would do what he could to expedite my stay there. I thanked him, and after the brief time that I was allowed to visit with my Mom, I was returned to my cellblock.

Unfortunately, my visit with Anthony was prior to my experiencing the "extended stay" conditions of the facility. They will flat-out try to starve you. The portions for a 250-pound man were the same as those for 100-pound inmate. The portions were tiny. If you liked bologna, Colbert was your place. Sometimes it was served every meal for several consecutive days. It also took a while for me to get used to drinking diluted Kool-Aid at every meal.

Regardless, I adapted the best I could and made several friends in the process. One of the bunkmates in my cell was a guy named Jay. We shared a lot of common interests, specifically football, baseball, books, and religion. Another guy, named Billy, had never learned to read well and I volunteered to help him. We worked on his reading skills during my short stay by reading the Bible. He improved dramatically, despite the fact that I realized he was probably dyslexic, even though he said that he had never been diagnosed as such while in school. I also worked on reading with a young black guy whom everyone called Teenager. Teenager was the only black guy in our cell block. For the most part, the jailers kept the jail population quite segregated. I guess that they felt like segregation was necessary to keep order, even in the New South.

Not long after my arrival, a young, white, gangsta wannabe was put in our block. Although I'm not ordinarily very aggressive, after a couple of days of listening to his mouth, I backed him into a corner and advised him that if he kept running his gums that I was going to plant a fist in it. Although temporarily shutting up, he was constantly into it with all the inmates. The day after my altercation with him, he got into a fight with another inmate and was then transferred elsewhere in the jail.

Inmates are not the only ones punished during incarceration. Their families are as well. Missing their loved ones, families will pay anything to talk to them or to try to make them more comfortable. The system takes full advantage of this. They bid out phone and commissary services to companies that rape the families financially. To place a call to my mom or to my daughters, just 15 miles away, cost an average of around eight dollars for a 15-minute call. Snacks that you could buy from the jail store were also ridiculously overpriced.

During one call home, I became furious when I found out that DJ had moved all my clothes from our bedroom closet and moved them to the workshop. I hadn't even been gone a week yet. Well, I guess that she did need the room. Imelda Marcos and her shoes had nothing on DJ and her clothes.

Visitation was also terrible. This took place through a four-square inch piece of scratched and clouded glass, between our cellblock and a hallway, where families were brought once a week. Meanwhile, the inmates across the hall yelled obscenities and whistled at my daughters, with many of the culprits trying to talk to them during my short visit time. You couldn't get to them to see who it was or to do anything about it. The guards seemed unconcerned.

The guards at Colbert County would've been hard to tell from inmates if it hadn't been for the uniforms. In real life, you find very few "Andy Taylors" from Mayberry wearing a badge. Besides the excessive cursing, bad manners, and hostile dispositions, on several occasions I smelled alcohol on the breath of some of the officers. One particular guard on night shift, routinely kept the glazed over eyes of a pot smoker. There were a couple of exceptions. Two guards, one named Corey and the other named Kyle, were respectful and polite. Corey was an Auburn football fan. As I mentioned, I'm a lifelong Alabama football fan. Corey and I joked around a lot about football. Conversations about football have no boundaries in the state of Alabama.

Once a week, two different church groups were allowed to visit our cellblock. One of these was a group from a local African American Baptist congregation, the other a Gideon group, led by a gentleman named Brother Tom. Both groups were inspiring and brought some uplifting during a difficult time. Sometimes, they also brought candy and toiletries.

On the morning of August 25, I was awakened early and told that I was transferring out to State. My old friend, Anthony, had succeeded in getting me out of this dungeon in record time (11 days). Jay convinced me that I needed to let them cut my hair before I left. He told me that if I waited to have it cut at State it would be a nightmare (Later I was thankful for the advice). The guards brought us some clippers and Teenager, who was being shipped down as well, and I were sheared like sheep. I had never been a skinhead before and had always boasted a thick head of hair. Now, I looked like Mr. Clean!

Around 7 AM, Teenager and I were loaded up and shipped to Kilby Correctional Facility. I was now the property of the state of Alabama.

273811

"I'm not a number. Dammit, I'm a man."
      —Bob Seger, "Feel Like A Number"

Kilby correctional facility, located near Montgomery and in a community called Mount Meigs, is the processing center for all inmates sent to the Alabama Department of Corrections (ADOC). If you ever happen to attend a cattle auction and walk through the entire process, you might get some idea what this facility is like. If you have never experienced the Heebie-Jeebies, a trip through there could be your indoctrination.

 The first two hours of processing is one of the most humiliating things that you could ever go through in your life. After being made to strip, inmates are marched through a line about 50 at a time, deloused, sheared, and forced to shower and shave. I had been fortunate that Jay and the guys at Colbert had shaved my head prior to leaving. Many of the other incoming inmates left this stage with their scalps bruised and bleeding. I was ridiculed about the shadow on my chin and made to attempt shaving three times, with what resembled a disposable razor. Using their razor was like trying to shave with a plastic butter knife.

After the shower and shave, your property is ransacked by the processing officers and they decided what you can keep and what is thrown away. I was told that I couldn't keep one photo, of me as a youth with my dad, because it showed us hunting with shotguns. After much argument, I was allowed to put it in an envelope to be mailed home. It never arrived. Also, the guards and trustees eyed and raved over photos of my daughters, but certainly not in an appropriate way. You have no choice but to take all their taunts and remarks because you are constantly threatened with violence. Through this whole process, you are herded naked like someone in a Nazi death camp.

After finally getting through the initial phase of processing and having been issued "state whites" and "bobos" (uniforms and shoes), I was photographed for my state ID and issued my AIS (Alabama Institutional Serial) number. For the next year, my name would be 273811. This drove home the meaning of the old Bob Seger hit, "Feel Like a Number."

After processing, I was assigned to M dorm. There I stayed for the next week in what the ADOC referred to as isolation. Isolation here certainly didn't mean being private. I bunked with about 100 others in a single dorm room. During the next few days, we were tested for any physical or mental problems, the latter of which appeared to be an epidemic there, regardless of the color of the subject's uniform.

Among the correctional officers (COs) running our dorm was a female officer whom we referred to as "Colonel" Crenshaw, not because of rank, but because of demeanor. She was a short, plump, black woman with a loud bark. It was her job to teach us to keep our bunks in compliance and to welcome and orient us to prison rules. It was an adjustment for me just learning to shower or to use the toilet with a strange woman walking around the room.

Kilby was run like a military camp. We were marched to each test or appointment and had strict rules and lines to follow. The main hall was usually patrolled by Officer Harris, or "Michael Jordan" as the inmates called him, because he resembled MJ, although his scowl looked like he had eaten a sour persimmon. "Michael Jordan" is infamous in the Alabama Department of Corrections. You won't find an inmate in the ADOC system who doesn't know who MJ is and very few who haven't experienced his demeanor. This man is one of the rudest, most foulmouthed, and most disgusting human beings that anyone could ever meet. Few Marine drill sergeants could touch him. My first personal experience with him was later on in pill call line. Not realizing that I had to open my mouth wide to let him confirm that I had swallowed my aspirin, he screamed, "Open your pussy, mother fucker!" at me. It took all the self-control that I had not to lash out. Later, when I was moved out of isolation, I witnessed him yelling from a tower, rifle in hand, threatening an inmate for walking on the recreation yard with his shirttail out.

Word had it that MJ had a job for life from the ADOC, because he had been injured on the job. Supposedly, he had been thrown off the top tier at the West Jefferson facility during a riot. Through the fence, you could witness him alternately driving several different luxury cars to work. Maybe this ritual was to confuse any ex-cons who would like to trash his vehicle. Officer Harris was not a pleasant or respectable individual.

The opposite end of the spectrum from MJ was a young lady in the pill call window whom I came to refer to as Miss Sunshine.

A short, attractive black lady, she was a ray of light every day with her kind greetings of "Hello Mr. Harrison, how are you today?" You didn't expect this kind of civility in the ADOC. Over the next year, I found out how very little of it existed there.

The chow hall was run like a high-speed drill. We were marched single file through a line to get our tray of food and our daily dose of Kool Aid. If you were lucky, you might have enough time to eat half your food before an officer was screaming for you to get up and clear seats for the next group. I probably ate as much food on the way to the dishwasher window as I did at a table. The food at Kilby was fair, although it was there that I was first introduced to the dreaded "mystery meat" patties that the system feeds ADOC inmates. I decided very quickly that I might need to become a vegetarian. The meat patties were basically ground beef hearts, etc. We could see veins and gristle all through them. Online, on the menu that the families see, they would refer to the patties as meatloaf, pepper steak, and so on. Bottom line, as one inmate told me, "In the end, road kill is road kill." Many inmates claimed that the packaging the patties came in was marked "not for human consumption." Later I was told by a former kitchen worker, whom I trusted, that he had seen this label on some of the fish products that had been served. Having seen the old sci-fi classic *Soylent Green*, I was very leery of the mystery meat. Witnessing all the inmates wandering around the exercise yard, looking like a scene from a zombie apocalypse, it made me suspect some very bizarre things.

Apparently, because I indicated that I had previously been on an antidepressant, the medical staff suspected that I was crazy. While I was begging for some additional pain relief for my back and wrist, because of my multiple recent surgeries, they were more interested in me being evaluated by a psychiatrist. I was seen by four different psychiatrist/psychologist in all. I was then prescribed an antidepressant or something that knocked me out for the better part of two days. I refused to keep taking it and had to go through an act of Congress to keep from being forced to take it, including signing off on my refusal.

After a week of medical tests and physical evaluations, I was moved to K dorm to await transfer. There, I made a number of friends, if there is such a thing in prison. One guy named Russ, who was from a place back close to home, tried to show me the ropes of prison life so that I could avoid trouble. Russ, as well as my bunkmate, Ben, were S.B.s (members of the Southern Brotherhood—a white prison gang). Although many S.B.s were tattooed up with swastikas like the A.B.s (the Aryan Brotherhood), they seemed to cohabitate as well as could be expected with black inmates, although they didn't take a lot of crap.

Every night that I could, I went to chapel services. There they had a great band and good speakers. I made a friend at chapel that everyone referred to as "Big Mike" (think Ving Rhames), a huge black guy, from a tough background, who had decided to take his faith to heart. All the inmates either looked up to Big Mike or were scared of him; I'm not sure which. Regardless, he always acted like a gentleman.

In K dorm, I also met a Cajun gentlemen named Marvin. Marvin shared my passion for literature. Every day we went to the chapel library where I worked on my attempt at writing a novel that I had started prior to my trial. Marvin had been released by the time of my writing this account, but I hope to someday make contact with him to see how life is treating him.

Two weeks into my stay at Kilby, I was rousted up and prepared for transfer. I had been rated and recommended for the facility at Limestone County, I had been told, which was much closer to home. Limestone had a reputation, among the informed inmates, of being one of the better places to be assigned. I also learned that I was rated—level IV, no custody, which meant that I had to wear cuffs and shackles during transport. This rating was apparently due to my pending cases.

Soon, a group of other transferees and I we were all crammed into a transport van, packed like sardines. Many of the guys transferring with me had been through the gates at Kilby more than once. Therefore, upon our departure one officer remarked, "We hope you enjoyed your stay! We will leave the light on for you!"

Hellmore

"Of course they sometimes make mistakes, and jail innocent people, and they often use the system to pay off personal grudges, and so on; but nothing in life is perfect, is it?"
—Ken Follett, *Jackdaws*

I had settled into the crowded transport van ready for the long ride to Limestone. To my surprise, 30 minutes later the van pulled into another camp that appeared to have come straight out of Hogan's Heroes. As we pulled to the back gate, I noticed a cardboard sign was posted on the wire that said, "Welcome to Hellmore." Although I was hoping that we were stopping just to drop off some other inmates, my bubble was soon burst when an officer yelled, "Harrison, off here."

I had been sent to Elmore Correctional Facility, the bottom of the barrel. Its reputation preceded it as one of the dirtiest, nastiest, and roughest camp in the system. Short of the Super Maxes, which housed death row, this camp was the destination for many of Alabama's most violent criminals. I felt like throwing up!

From the word go, Elmore was a real clusterfuck! At the back gate, things were so disorganized it was like a Chinese fire drill. The correctional officer (CO) who was processing me was so illiterate that he had to get an inmate trustee, called Radar, to read him every question from the entrance form.

Radar is a common name in prison. It is generally tagged on any inmate who takes care of the clerical work that is above the guard's intellect level. This particular Radar reminded me a lot of the Radar character from "MASH."

A really nasty CO, who was called Big C, ran the back gate. He constantly cursed at everyone and everything and got practically nothing accomplished. What should have taken minutes took a couple of hours. Even then, I was not given a mat to sleep on. I later found out after several trips to court, that upon each return, we were practically on our own to come up with a mat.

Also, every time we entered or exited the gate, we were required to go through a strip search. My first time into Elmore I was quite the novelty. The guards had apparently seldom seen an incoming inmate with no tattoos. Trust me, I was not the typical candidate for a level four prison camp.

I was assigned to C2 Dorm, Bed 94A. C2, or the Thunder Dorm, as it was referred to, was a big dose of chaos. Talk about keeping Bad Company! Here, in one big room, resided 195 rapists, murderers, arsonists, crack heads, pedophiles, drug traffickers, and now one convicted debtor! I kept expecting to run into some Klingons!

Elmore would serve me up a big dose of Humble Pie! There was certainly no Starbucks here. What happened to the nice little private cells that you see on TV, complete with personal television sets? "Hey Toto, we're certainly not in Kansas anymore!" For that matter, I was not in the Alabama that I knew, either. I don't know if any of you truly understand what misery is, but one night at Hellmore will certainly enlighten you.

When I went to the guard cubicle to try to get a bed mat, I was given a plastic mat cover with no stuffing. The guards said that it was all that they had. This situation was extremely disheartening for a guy with three fused vertebrae and multiple screws in his back. The guards didn't seem concerned at all but said that I would have to catch someone transferring out and steal his mat.

Later on in my first day, I was sent to see my classification officer, Ms. Minniemee, to go over my status. This act turned out to be a routine that prisoners went through each time that they returned to camp, from court or for whatever reason. Routine is the key word here. A classification officer is supposed to keep up with all aspects of the prisoners' current situation and to assist in any programs and transitions available. In reality, expecting assistance or even getting viable information from my classification officer turned out to be an exercise in futility.

Classification officers at Elmore were people who filled in the ranks of program job quotas. I decided very quickly that the primary part of a classification officer's job description was to shine a seat with their ass and to collect a check on Friday. Before my time at Elmore was up, I would find out just how true this statement was. These people were not social workers, but rather they were anti-social workers!

My first night in C2, the CO on duty sent me to the shift office after I complained about my mat, or the lack thereof. There the short, fat, female 3rd shift Sergeant called back to the dorm and had my entire bedroll (empty mat cover, sheets and blanket) brought up for her to inspect. "You have a mat," she snapped, holding up the plastic cover. She then cursed me and said, "You'll be happy with what you've got" and promptly threw my sheets and blanket out in the dirt. I decided right then that I had rather pull hen's teeth than to have to go back to the shift office for anything. In retrospect, I'm sure that was by design. It was over a week before I finally got a real-mat and only because I swapped with someone who was transferring out.

Years later I would watch a YouTube video, taken from a hidden phone camera, of this same female sergeant repeatedly hitting a restrained inmate. Under public pressure, she was suspended. In reality, her actions are common in the ADOC. I doubt that any suspension would have been handed down if this incident had not been made public.

I had heard a terrorism expert on TV say that if you were ever on a plane that was hijacked, to try not make eye contact with the terrorist. This rule applies in prison as well. Here, I lived in the world of the Crypts, Bloods, Gangsta Disciples, Black Disciples, Aryan Brotherhood, Southern Brotherhood, Latin Kings, and MS-13. Talking about culture shock! Then there was the most dangerous gang in Elmore. They called themselves the Correctional Officers!

Shortly after I arrived, I was sitting on my bunk smoking a roll up cigarette that someone had given me when half the dorm started whooping like a crane. Puzzled I looked around and someone motioned for me to put out my cigarette. Apparently, this whooping meant that a CO was on the floor. This ruckus was heard frequently in the dorm. A short while later I was offered a hit on a joint, but already knowing how most of the marijuana came into camp, I told them I didn't want to smoke anything that had come in stuffed up a sissy's ass (Sissy was the term generally used for homosexuals). It had been a lot of years since I had smoked pot anyway.

Another quick shock from the first day was witnessing many of the black inmates running to the window and "gunning" as a female CO walked by. I'll let you use your own imagination as to what that involved.

Modesty was nonexistent at Elmore. Once again, this wasn't the prison of TV with two people sharing a cell. I slept in the same room with 196 other people. I used the toilet sitting beside several others, hoping not to get hit in the knees by the guys using the lavatories, while the guys taking a shower were rapping. The noise was sometimes deafening. The condensation was so bad, it was like taking a shit in the rain. Let Gene Kelly make a song out of that one!

If we didn't wash off well after being exposed to the shower room rain, small lesions would sometimes appear on us (fungus?). Getting used to living in filth day in and day out was a challenge. Also, there was never an absence of offensive odors. Scents of sweat, farts, halitosis, tobacco, and marijuana were always in the air. Then there was Blue Magic cream (similar to ladies Nair) that the blacks used to remove hair. They would apply it to their faces, heads, and sometimes to their chests and legs (sissies). Then they strutted through the dorm till it dried. This smelled like the worst—something must have crawled up your ass and died—sulfur fart that you have ever smelled. The only thing that overcame that odor was the smell of the camps compost. More on that momentarily.

Incarceration was the first time in my life that I was a minority. The ratio when I arrived at "C" dorm was probably 75% black to 25% Caucasian/Hispanic. I was a WASP in the ethnic jungle of the ADOC. Here, social and racial power meant a lot. We were governed by a different constitution. Where were all the civil rights activists when I needed them? For the most part, blacks were very rude to new whites. If you were in line for chow, canteen or whatever, the line eventually became all black in the front and all white at the rear. They made no pretense about breaking line in front of a "cracker." It was like an embarrassment to them not to show dominance in their world.

If you ever lit a cigarette, several inmates would be in your face to "get some fire." Rarely did you ever get any word of appreciation, so being the smart-ass that I can be, I facetiously started telling each one "thank you" for allowing me to give you a light. It took a while for me to realize that some of these guys couldn't afford matches and for me to tone down my smart-ass ways.

I made a few friends in C dorm. Among these was a young black guy who was transported from Kilby with me: everyone called him "Bakin' Soda." Soda was a 6' 4" guy from Pritchard, AL who obviously got his name from being a drug runner on the street. It was my understanding that they took baking soda and use it to cut down cocaine and to make "crack." Soda, a product of a difficult background, was caught between two worlds. He was intelligent and had a good heart, however he was just born in the wrong place at the wrong time. Soda would eventually start calling me "Pop" and referred to me as his "white daddy."

Another neighbor of mine was Robbie. He was a "Maytag," meaning he was a dorm laundry man. He performed this hustle for items such as pastries, chips, and so forth. He washed items of clothing in a plastic bag to keep us from the hassle and likelihood of losing them by sending them to the camp laundry. I nicknamed Robbie the *Artful Dodger* after the infamous Dickens Character. I had laughed at his story about being chased, running bow legged through a Walmart parking lot, with a chuck roast stuck in one pant leg and a ham in the other. Robbie was only about 5' 3" or 4" and I often asked him, "How's the weather down there?"

Another inmate I befriended at Elmore was Glen, a 61-year-old-black ex-Marine. He was one of the few in C dorm older than me. I referred to him as the *Ancient Mariner*. I joked with Glen, saying that he was the only person in C dorm with the letters BC behind his birthdate.

One of my best friends (if there is any such thing in prison) was Chad. He was a young white guy serving a life sentence on the habitual offender act. Although he was a "lifer," Chad hoped for parole soon and to someday open a ¾ house to help prisoners readjust to society. I hope that Chad is someday released and is successful with this goal. He is a great guy, as well as intelligent, and could be very successful in this role. Chad did not come across as a criminal. When other long-timers were establishing their dominance, smoking dope, and so forth, Chad stayed mostly to himself. He did however give me lots of pointers on how to survive in prison.

Most of the correctional officers were given nicknames by the inmates. There was Birdman, Loo, Bevis, Butthead, Tweety Bird, Gangster, Jamaica, Mini-me (not the classification officer) and Family Guy. A few were cool, but most were complete assholes. Some were sociopathic and dangerous!

We had two TV's in C-dorm, one in the bunk room and the other in a separate designated TV room. The TV room showed only sports during operating hours. I discovered very quickly that a Kracker never had possession of a remote control. The dorm TV was usually on something like "Cops." Why in the hell a bunch of inmates would want to watch a show glamorizing a bunch of self-righteous, gung-ho cops was beyond my understanding. Much of the other late time viewing was devoted to soft porn on Showtime. This is something a bunch of locked up criminals didn't need to be watching. They weren't going home to their spouses that night. If you can understand the ADOC's explanation for this policy, please explain it to me. "Gigolo" and "Diary of a Call Girl" were regular features. Also, everyone would be fighting for space to see Dexter and who would be his next victim. This is prison, folks! These are criminals! Give me a break! What kind of reform is the ADOC providing!

Note: Prisons and jails would be much more humane if they would filter the food and restaurant commercials that the inmates were exposed to. This is an inhumane form of punishment to people who are hungry!

When I first arrived, football season was getting underway. I had to get into the TV room early and hoped to get a seat before it got packed. Secondly, I had to hope that "the thugs in charge" wanted to watch a game of interest to me. Unfortunately, a lot of the powers to be at Elmore turned out to be Auburn fans. Not gracious and polite Auburn fans, but arrogant, in your face Auburn fans. *This was not good!* Auburn games were watched uninterrupted, while Bama games were constantly flipped to and from (so goes the never-ending feud in football crazy Alabama).

Around my third week of stomaching this situation, I had about all I could take. Being a rabid Bama fan, I voiced an objection. I was promptly backed into a corner by several thugs and instructed as to who was in charge. This moment was my first lesson in Elmore style humility. The firsts didn't end there. Afterward, I experienced the first occasion in my life to ever fantasize about having another human being (?) in the crosshairs of a rifle scope (chalk up one for the ADOC—that's a wonderful state of mind)! Regardless, we take our football seriously in Alabama!

Some of the COs played constant mind games with us by using the accessibility to the vent fans. When it was 100 degrees outside, they sometimes refused to turn them on for whatever reason, and later when winter hit they sometimes ran them all night long, sucking all of the heat out of the dorm. This act was done to punish us for whatever reason they decided the group needed to be punished.

During the late summer and early fall, it was sweltering in C2. I'm sure that it got close to 120 degrees inside the dorm on some days. Most mornings, I woke up in a puddle of sweat. Then there was the compost! Elmore had a compost facility just outside the camp fence where food waste was reprocessed. The augers were turned on each evening at sundown and the stench drifted through the camp. It was like trying to sleep in the middle of a garbage landfill. For those of you who have never carried trash to a garbage landfill, the smell is a mixture somewhere between a skunk and the worst public toilet that you have ever been in. Oh well, its prison in the middle of Bomb Fucked Egypt, so who really gives a shit?

We did have the good fortune of having a lot of wildlife at

Elmore. That is, if you liked watching rats the size of cats, and dive bombing pigeons and seagulls. Interestingly enough, we always seemed to be missing a lot of pigeons on chicken day at the chow hall (LOL).

The most abundant wildlife present were the hordes of flies, cockroaches, and spiders. A man with a flyswatter could go on safari. It was unbelievable the number of spider bites that were written off by the medical staff as insignificant. After one guy had returned in misery from seeing the nurse, with a hand that looked like a boxing glove, I watched another inmate lance the wound and squeeze enough puss out of the bite to fill a Styrofoam cup. I kid you not!

One of the more interesting terms that I learned in prison was "Babymama." This is a reference to a girl or girlfriend who has given birth to an inmate's child. Only a small minority of the inmates that I came in contact with had wives, but most had babymamas. Is this really the United States of America? One guy that I bunked near kept referring to "my other babymamas."

I asked, "How many children do you have?"

"Seven," he replied.

"How many babymamas?"

"Six, I got one set of twins."

Seriously, is this society what Lyndon Johnson had in mind?

Conversations with many of the "kids" that were in Elmore led me to realize that a significant number of them had mothers who were children themselves. The lack of age differences between some of the mothers and their children was almost unbelievable. This country and this state seriously need to take another look at some of our social programs.

I guess this situation lends credence to an old joke that I was once told about my beloved state from a Yankee when we were joking around. It goes like this:

"What is the definition of a virgin in Alabama?"

"What?" I asked.

"An ugly third grader," he chuckled.

At the time, coming from what is obviously my sheltered social background, I didn't take the joke too kindly. In retrospect, maybe he had statistics to back him up. Maybe this scenario was more accurate than I would have ever imagined.

Cigarettes, coffee, and other items are the monetary system in prison. Those who can afford to buy extra from the commissary, break down the goods into "top balls" (cigarette tobacco) or coffee balls. They then sell these items to those who could not afford the high prison prices for full containers and make enough profit, in items, to keep themselves in snacks, toiletries, etc. Some even ran Dorm Stores, offering credit. Those were the guys whom you had to watch out for. It is not advisable for a newcomer to get in debt. The repercussions are severe. A lot of young, naïve guys wind up getting "whored out" because of debts.

There was an abundance of drugs in C2. What kind you ask? What kind do you want? C2 was like a drug store, only most of these were either illegal drugs or ones that required prescriptions that I don't believe that most of the local population had. I watched men smoke, snort, ingest, and inject everything from pot to cocaine, to Suboxone or Soma. Most of these drugs were either smuggled in up a trustee's ass when he was on work assignment, or obtained through the Black Market controlled by some of the guards. When a new shipment of pot arrived, there would be a L.A. (Lower Alabama) smog in the dorm for a couple of days. I remember ending a letter to Jessi, my baby girl, by saying, "Hey, I've got to sign off now. I've got the munchies from the second-hand smoke in here. I've got to go find some cheese curls!"

A.D.O.C.
(Alabama Department of Corruptions)

"If you want to see the absolute scum of the earth, go to any prison in the US during shift change."
— Paul Harvey

The title Alabama Department of Corrections is an oxymoron. Perhaps no greater contradiction of terms has ever existed. Elmore doesn't rehabilitate or correct. They teach hate and disrespect for authority. A more accurate title would be the Alabama Department of Corruptions. The COs seem to be recruited from the "hoods" and the nearby redneck bars. There's a fine line between many COs and the criminals they are hired to oversee. In many cases, the only difference is that they are wearing blue uniforms, instead of white ones.

One such example is CO Focker. From day one, I was warned that Focker, a large muscular black man, was racist and that he liked to "put his hands on you" (meaning that he liked to use physical force). I figured that it was normal for some black guards not to like white inmates, but before my vacation at Elmore was over I would get a full dose of Focker. Trust me, he is one psycho bastard with a chip on his shoulder, a real piece of shit to use redneck terms. His actions toward inmates should warrant for him to be locked in a cage. I have always tried not to hate people, but this man, or animal, or whatever he is, really pushed my limits.

Paul Harvey once had a segment on a visit that he had made to a prison facility. He stated, "If you want to see the absolute scum of the earth, go to any prison in the US during shift change." A similar statement is attributed by many to Eleanor Roosevelt.

The ADOC basically institutionalizes its "guests." It teaches them to be criminals and how to scavenge to survive. Sure, everything needed for absolute minimal survival is supplied, but these provisions are certainly not far from that of a kennel, and certainly not resembling that of any all-inclusive Sandals resort, as many people joke. It is better described as one step up from Auschwitz. Prisoners are constantly subjected to punishment for things that they had nothing to do with. If someone completely on the other side of the dorm was caught doing something against the rules, the entire dorm would many times be locked down and privileges taken away from the entire group. Administration would stretch the definition and use of the term "privileges" to justify this behavior. A good parallel is having your electric power cut off because your neighbor didn't pay his bill.

Many of the inmates were simply unlucky enough to be born on the wrong side of the tracks, and grew up in bad environments. Instead of trying to rehabilitate them and teach them something useful so they could make a positive contribution to society upon release, they were taught that they were useless and deserved to be punished for simply existing.

Many prison programs showcased for the benefit of the interested public are a farce. One such program was the SAP (substance abuse program). It was lip service for the public. It didn't slow drug abuse down. There are as many, if not more, drugs behind the fence as there are on the outside. Many of the participants of SAP came back to the dorm during their breaks from class and got high. This practice seemed so stupid to me. Their main objective should have been trying to get home, not taking a chance of an extended stay! One young guy in my dorm was within days of his release when he failed a piss test. It added months to his time. I looked at him and said, "Way to go, Einstein. Go ahead and smoke another joint." He did!

The ADOC rapes the families of those unfortunate enough to be spending time in the system. Among the injustices are ridiculous phone use prices and extra charges to send money for store/canteen use (a big prison system windfall). The cost of the phone calls created a big black market, run by crooked guards, by creating a demand for illegal cell phones. Many of the phones sold to inmates would be confiscated during shakedowns and then resold, by the same guards, to another inmate.

Also, many guards took bribes to look the other way when tattoo artists were at work. If not paid off, the guards confiscated the artists' tattoo guns. Soon afterward, the tattoo guns would be sold to another artist who understood penal mafia extortion rules.

As uplifting as the chapel was at Kilby, the one at Elmore was equally depressing. Occasionally, an outside group such as Pastor Carmen's ministry group or a traveling family ministry from Nebraska came in, and they were a treat. Normally though, outside of the Muslim services, things were sporadic and unorganized.

Although the menus across the ADOC are supposed to be the same, I can't stress enough how bad the food was at Elmore. The resident cat that hung around the yard wouldn't even eat the meat patties! In the few months that I was there, I lost 70 pounds. Don't get me wrong, I certainly needed to lose some weight (I had packed on a lot due to my physical problems and during my trial), but this wasn't my idea of a health spa. Some inmates tried to keep their weight up by consuming a combination of doo-wops, made with honeybuns and peanut butter, and shams, a concoction made with coke, candy and coffee. A health nut would freak out if they weighed the calories and the caffeine levels of this prison cuisine!

Many inmates who didn't receive any outside money came up with a "hustle." Some became laundry men or "Maytags," some rolled cigarettes for a cut of the yield, some smuggled extra food from the chow hall and some just whored themselves out.

Some of the store workers hustled by shorting random inmates on their orders and then selling the spoils to others. I caught this happening to me and immediately called it to the attention of the observing CO and the woman in charge of the store. I was stonewalled by the woman. It took persistence, ten days, the business manager, and raising a lot of hell to get the balance of my order. This scenario was typical of the way things worked at Elmore. Who else was getting a cut?

In a letter home to a friend I included a list of some of the things that I had learned so far in prison. These included:

1. I learned how to eat spaghetti with a spoon.
2. I learned that the root word of the modern Ebonic-English

language is Muthafucka (I used to think that this was two words, but now I know differently).
3. I learned that to be an ADOC corrections officer you have to be able to count to 100 by 2s (sometimes this is optional) and you have to be able to use Muthafucka twice in the same sentence.
4. I learned that Darwin was right! I used to wonder that if the theory of evolution was correct, where were all those in between the start and the finish? Guess what! I found every damn one of them!
5. I learned to hate!

During this stretch of time, I had started experiencing problems again with my lower back (I had major back surgery just a few years previously). The process of filling out a sick call form and waiting for a "stop up" call was frustrating. Then after seeing the nurse it usually took a couple of weeks to be called to the prison hospital at nearby Staten Correctional Facility, a half mile up the road. On three different occasions, I was transported to Staten for a doctor's appointment. During those three trips, I spent over 20 total hours in a holding cell but never once saw a doctor. Your guess is as good as mine as to why. Your health and well-being are not a high priority for the ADOC. Obviously to them, being healthy is highly overrated.

In conversations with the girls at home, I learned that DJ had removed all my pictures at the house and was talking about selling her wedding ring. Although I was furious, I continued to pray that God would soften her heart. How could someone who had professed to love me for all those years be so cold? I started to believe that there wouldn't be a yellow ribbon around the old oak tree when I was released. DJ did send me a couple of letters during this time, but they were very self-righteous and basically just chewing me out for exhibiting self-pity to the girls. Many days, the words to the old Billy Joel classic "She's Always a Woman to Me" wandered through my brain:

And she'll take what you'll give her as long as it's free.
Yeah, she steals like a thief, but she's always a woman to me.

Fortunately, I could always call my mom for uplifting. However, at the time, I think she was starting to blame herself for convincing me not to leave DJ years before, after some tumultuous times in our marriage. At that time, I had decided to stay to preserve harmony for the kids.

Months later, I would read Stephen R Covey's *The Seven Habits of Highly Effective People*. In it he stated:

> "We might even have some degree of success when the sun is shining. But when the different times come—and they will—we won't have the foundation to keep things together… And until we stop treating the symptoms and start treating the problem, our efforts will only bring counterproductive results.

I thought long and hard about what Covey had to say. These observances were true in both my personal and business lives.

At midnight one night, I was awakened and told to pack up for court. The checking out process took most all night and then I was sent to a holding cell to wait for transport. Somebody missed the boat and I spent ten hours in a holding cell and missed two meals before it was decided that Colbert County wasn't coming. I was then sent back to C2 to start the long search and debacle of trying to find another bed mat.

The next day, I was finally picked up. I later found out there had been about 50 people at the courthouse the previous day to support me at a community corrections hearing (DJ wasn't among them). For some reason, the judge or one of her cohorts had fumbled the ball, but I was brought in quickly the next day, unawares to many of my friends. I still had a few family and friends in attendance, but I would have loved to have had a full house. I struggled to hold back tears when I saw my mom and my girls.

The hearing was requested by my attorney and friend, John Odem. It was an attempt to get me away from the dangers of Elmore and put into some kind of supervised work-release type of imprisonment. I was promptly denied community corrections by Judge Snatcher, obviously because of the danger that I posed to society. I was also denied an appeal bond.

Upon my return to Elmore, the County deputy who brought me back was shocked when one of the COs working the back gate was drunk and fell into him. He looked at me, bewildered. I simply shrugged my shoulders and said, "Welcome to Hellmore."

Returning from that court trip, I found that I had a new neighbor in "The Hood." He was a 6'5" acknowledged sissy named Felicia. Think Lawrence Taylor in drag! Why the sissies were allowed to get away from the dress codes that applied to the rest of us, I don't know. However, maybe I could guess. Certain immoral favors were reported to go a long way at Elmore.

Felicia pranced around a lot of times in a pink thong. Although I was careful to keep a certain distance with Felicia, because of our differences in moral philosophy, he was basically an okay guy, excuse me—gal. We both shared an appreciation for reading and I started loaning him/her, books. Although many of the young guns in the dorm showed basically no respect for an OG (old guy) like me, they showed lots of respect to sissies for some reason.

Years later, I was told that Felicia had died the day before his release of a reported overdose at St. Clair correctional facility. St Clair is another camp with a notorious reputation. This facility has been in the national news quite a bit recently.

Note: because of some sense of reasoning, many long-term inmates justified that if you were on the giving and not the receiving end of a male/male relationship, that it didn't make you a homosexual. I don't agree with this philosophy. One night, one of the guys, who we called light skin Rico, woke me up and propositioned me. I promptly screamed at him to, "Get the hell away from me or one of us is going to die." I had no more problems with Rico. I am not homophobic and respect someone else's space. In return, I expect for my space and values to be respected as well.

I received some bad news from home around this time. A lifelong friend of mine, named Bill, had died. I had gone through 12 years of school and played many rounds of golf with Bill. He had been fighting poor health for a while. I asked my mother to send a card to his family.

I fought depression over the news about Bill and for being unable to attend his memorial. I thought back to golfing with Bill and to memories of our school days. Bill was a jokester and had a dry sense of humor. He could always interject some sly quip into a conversation to lighten the mood.

As I was mourning Bill's loss, the only depression and stress relief in prison is to roll and smoke another cigarette, so I smoked a couple in honor of Bill. You know—after you smoke enough roll-up cigarettes, fresh air tastes like shit! LOL. Bill would like that one!

"A Made Man"

"Nothing can be more abhorrent to democracy than to imprison a person or keep him in prison because he is unpopular. This is really the test of civilization."
—Winston Churchill

A lot of the young bucks in C2 strutted around like they had accomplished something by having made it to prison. Maybe because of where they had come from, incarceration was an accomplishment. Maybe to them it was equivalent to receiving a college degree. I guess that many of them viewed it as similar to making rank in the mob. Was I now a "made man?"

In prison, you have to adhere to the old proverb: *Though I walk through the valley of death, I will fear no evil, because I'm the meanest SOB in the valley!* If you didn't come here with this mentality, you had better develop it quickly in order to survive.

One day in November I discovered that being a part of the prison fraternity could be dangerous, even if you just tried to blend into the woodwork. That morning I was told to go quickly to the shift office and see Sgt. Coe. I immediately got dressed and reported to her office. Upon being told to enter, she looked up at me and said, "I guess you don't want to go to the honor dorm."

"Ma'am?" I replied.

"I had you down to go to the honor dorm, but then you come to my office without having shaved first, so I guess you don't want to go."

I had skipped breakfast that morning, and had an early morning shadow on my chin. I had rushed to her office not knowing what was going on. Although I would've loved to transfer to the honor dorm, for it had a reputation of being less dangerous, her smartass attitude infuriated me. I thought about arguing and explaining the situation to her, but knowing her reputation I decided that I would be wasting my time. I held my cool and in a sarcastic tone simply replied, "Well, I guess I don't."

The thing that I hated most throughout my incarceration was being told what to do by ignorant, smartass idiots with a chip on their shoulder. Fear, however, will humble you in a hurry. I wasn't afraid of her as much as I knew what would have been done to me if I had argued. I turned and returned to the dorm without pleading my case further. I would regret this action very shortly.

About an hour later, while I was sitting on my bunk reading, a pair of shoes appeared in my vision. Before I knew what was going on someone hit me in the side of the head. Shaken, only for an instant, I jumped up, threw off my glasses and gave chase. Rounding the end of my bunk I ran into four assailants. When you have fists coming at you from all directions, you are basically swinging at any movement. I had a lot of difficulty swinging with my bad right wrist, apparently my subconscious was hesitating to allow me to reinjure it. My left was pretty useless; however, I did deliver at least one solid elbow into a thug's nose. Blood flew everywhere. What seemed like minutes was probably only a few seconds, but to my credit I kept my feet. I could tell that I had taken one hard shot to my right eye and my ribs had taken some hard licks. One on four is tough. The tide had turned out of my favor.

Then, thank God, came the Calvary, or maybe I should say the Lone Ranger. My friend Bakin' Soda, with whom I had ridden up with from Kilby, grabbed me, pulled me away from the fray, and confronted my attackers. I was still pissed off, but as I charged back past him, Soda grabbed me and threw me on my bunk, yelling, "Cool it, Pop, before you get your ass killed! I'll handle this!" Soda is 6'4" tall, 225 pounds, and ripped. I didn't argue.

As it turned out the four guys who attacked me were pledges in the same gang that Soda was pledged to. I was attacked because some old white guy over near the windows had snitched on one of these thugs to another inmate, because that thug had broken into the other guy's bunk locker and stolen his store items. I was the wrong old white guy. Soon, it was realized and acknowledged that I was the wrong target, a case of mistaken identity. This fact really didn't make me feel any better. My right eye was swollen shut and my ribs felt like they were caving in.

As I took inventory of my condition, I realized that besides my swollen shut right eye and sore ribs, that my lips, gums, and elbow were all bruised and bleeding. My head throbbed and my eye felt like it was going to pop out of the socket. But I had survived. In retrospect, I can relate to Gen. George Armstrong Custer's famous last words when he shouted, "Where'd all those fuckin' Indians come from?"

Soda watched over me like a hawk for the next couple of hours, making sure that no one else bothered me. During this time, I was informed by some other inmates who had witnessed the attack that there had been a fifth man with a "shank" lying in wait, but he had pulled out when Soda came to my rescue.

Then early in the afternoon, I was called to the shift office.

I was ushered into the captain's office where he and some smartass female officer started grilling me about what had happened in the dorm. Apparently, a snitch had told them of the situation. I had an idea about unwritten prison rules and knew that I had to go back and live in that dorm. I refused to talk to them. The captain said, "You will talk to me or I will take away your store privileges."

I replied, "Do what you think is necessary."

After a few rounds of insults from the female officer, the captain stated, "Harrison, you're always going to wind up being a victim in here."

I answered, "I was a victim the moment that they assigned me here."

Finally, they gave up trying to get me to talk and sent me to Staten Hospital to see a doctor for a body chart, which was some bullshit documentation designed to cover their asses. Oh boy, here we go again. As soon as I arrived, my blood pressure and temperature were taken and then I was put in a holding cell again to wait for a doctor. Five hours later, tired of the process, I slipped into a line of Elmore inmates leaving this cell and returned by van to my dorm.

Upon entering the dorm, I immediately searched for and found the leader of the gangstas that had jumped me. He was called "Soldier."

"You run nothing but a group of damn cowards," I said to him.
"What did you say, OG?" he shot back.
"I didn't stutter," I replied. "If it takes four of them to jump an old man, then they are cowards. Teach them to fight like men!"
"You're either very brave or very stupid to talk to me this way," he said.

After about a 10 second staring match, I turned and walked to my bunk, wondering the whole way if I would make it without being shanked. I did not sleep that night.

I was called to the shift office four more times over the next day with the captain and the assistant warden trying to pressure me into giving a statement. In the meantime, they had locked up the culprits who had attacked me and told me that they were giving statements. I wasn't buying the captains ruse and continued my refusal to talk. Also, I was asked if I had been to Staten for a "body chart."

I replied, "Yes."

I didn't really lie, I had been there for one. It wasn't my fault that the place was a clusterfuck, and that the doctor never saw me. Later, I always wondered what the administration came up with for my body chart, because I had found out that they are required to make one in such circumstances. I guess they just winged it.

My dad once told me stories about a friend of his who had fought on the front lines in the Korean War. I remembered him using the phrase, "Sleeping with one eye open." The meaning of this phrase became very clear to me over the next several days. Of course, at the time, I only had one eye I could open, but I had also basically learned to sleep half-conscious.

A few days later, I was once again called to the shift office and was yet again confronted by a group of officers about the altercation. This time, MJ, who was the young gangster who had first hit me was present (not the CO named MJ at Kilby). Although I still refused to talk, MJ had admitted that he alone had attacked me. Keeping my mouth shut I played along and didn't rat out the other culprits. Later, I found out that because of the group factor, if I had given a statement of what really happened that all of the other parties could have received very stiff penalties and additional time for assault. Although maybe they deserved it, that's not the way things work in prison.

In the end, MJ and I were made to sign a "living agreement," stating that there would be no more incidents. Any future problems between us would result in severe punishment. We signed and I returned to the dorm. Later, after MJ was released from lockup, he came to me and apologized, saying that he knew he had attacked the wrong guy. He stated that he felt bad about jumping me. This statement and apology surprised me coming from a gangsta. He then also thanked me for not getting him more time.

Later in the day, Soldier, the gang leader, sat down on the bunk adjacent to mine. As I warily eyed him he said, "Pop, you are all right. You could have got my guys more time added on their sentence if you had talked. You don't have to worry anymore about my guys or anyone else as long as you are in this dorm. You are off-limits."

I had no more problems of this type during the rest of my stay at Elmore. As a matter of fact, several of the gang members gave me soups, Cokes, and even a padlock for my bunk locker, as a sign of their respect for the way I stood tall. And, although he was constantly in confrontations with others, MJ and I got along from there on out.

During the fall and early winter, I received letters and cards from many of my friends and family members. The same theme was repeated over and over, trying to build me up and telling me that this hell would be over before I knew it.

In one letter back to a group of friends at the country club where I had lived, I mentioned that a lot of the guys in here received letters splashed in perfume. Because DJ and I were not on the greatest of terms, I asked if someone could please splash some Old Forester Bourbon on their next letter. They did, so in my next letter, I asked if they could possibly sneak some chicken fingers from the Speedy Pig, my buddy Vic's restaurant. I'm sure that got some laughs.

Every day in Elmore was just another day in paradise, another dose of reality. Each morning you had to put your game face on and play the hardened criminal. I guess if there was an anthem for the place it would be Nazareth's *Hair of the Dog*. "Now you're messing with a-son-of-a-bitch."

Regardless of how careful you were or how tough you were, some kind of daily difficulty always awaited you. One time, it took me better than two weeks of attempts to get a document notarized for DJ for tax purposes. When I finally managed to get it done, on third shift at 5 AM, I received my daily dose of hazing. My ID was taken and I was made to stand in line outside in 20° weather waiting for a haircut. Once the 1/16 of an inch was taken on my scalp, I was allowed in the office to get my papers notarized. If the administration and the COs at Elmore stressed rehabilitation a fraction as much as they got off on enforcing cropped haircuts and shaves, it would be a much better place. Some COs would almost scrutinize you with a magnifying glass while you were standing in chow line. If you had any sign of a shadow, you did not eat. Shaving was sometimes an adventure when your only razor was dull. It's hard to imagine how an adult can get his rocks off about such matters.

One day as I was leaving the chow hall I was confronted by a young smartass cadet, who was a real dick-with-ears. The cadets (COs in training) were daily stationed at the exit door of the chow hall to prevent us from smuggling illegal contraband (apples, biscuits, etc.) back to the dorm. The cadet smirked at me and said, "You need to learn how to shave, OG. You missed a spot on your chin."

This statement really pissed me off because this kid had probably only shaved twice in his life and just wanted to show off in front of the other cadets. I calmly looked at him and said, "Son, I was shaving before the best part of you ran down your mama's leg."

Speechless, the kid dropped his jaw. The other cadets started howling with laughter. I quickly exited the chow hall and returned to the dorm. I was lucky. If that had been a seasoned CO, my ass would have been grass. I needed to learn to bridle my mouth.

Somewhere around two months into my sentence, I was notified that the judge had finally appointed me an attorney for my appeal. I was thinking, "That took long enough." A month later I was notified that the attorney had filed to be relieved because of conflict of interest. It took three months to figure all of this out? And now we were still at square one! Was this county court really that incompetent or was something else going on here? How much longer would it take to appoint someone else?

As the holidays approached, I was really depressed. I had never been away from my family during special occasions. This situation was gut-wrenching. To pass the time I started tutoring some of the guys in the dorm for their GED. I primarily worked on reading and math skills. If you teach anyone to slow down, take their time and go one step at a time, they can master basic geometry. I had a lot of success. The tutoring helped to lift my spirits.

On multiple occasions, guys told me, "Man, OG, you sure are smart. You sure do know a lot." I thought about their remarks. After reflecting on where I had been and where I currently was, I started giving this basic reply to that statement: "I know a little about a lot, but I don't know a lot about shit!" I certainly don't consider myself smart, but my disdain for the ADOC has certainly made me a smart-ass!

Hurry up and wait!

*"They cannot take away our self-respect
if we do not give it to them."*

—Gandhi

You have probably heard the sarcastic expression, "Everyone in prison is innocent!" Whoever coined this phrase insinuated that all criminals, or accused criminals, being incarcerated claim to be not guilty of whatever crime that they are serving time for. I found this observation not to be the case at all. Are there those who proclaim their innocence? Sure, but the vast majority admit to their guilt. Some are even proud of it. I believe that the statement that all prisoners claim to be innocent was fabricated by someone in the legal system to camouflage the fact that innocent people are convicted.

    A majority of the prisoners that I met, especially those in for selling or manufacturing drugs, would tell you that once they hit the streets they would be right back to doing the same thing again. A large group of inmates consider prison their home away from home and acted just as inhumane, or worse, behind the fences as they did on the street. About two thirds of the sons of bitches that

I was locked up with, I wish would never be released. I don't want them on the same streets with my children and grandchildren. In fairness though, if these inmates were put through a proper and effective correctional process maybe their attitudes and net worth to society could change. Rather, they are only reprocessed.

One statement that I remember from C2, came from a guy named Rick who was a jailhouse barber. Rick had been incarcerated for some petty violations and he had nowhere to go and no one to go to when he was released. He had been trying for a while to get sent to work-release (he qualified) so that he could build up some money for when he hit the street. He told me, "All they give you on release is $10 and a bus ticket. If I don't get work-release first, I'll have to stop and rob the first convenience store I come to, so that I can survive." I don't know how Rick's release turned out.

The holidays rolled around and we actually had very good Thanksgiving and Christmas meals served to us. We were even allowed to carry them back to the dorms and eat them at our own pace. For at least those two days, the administration didn't have the COs, or "police" as we referred to them, constantly harassing us about something. I guess they didn't because the administration wasn't there. They were home for the holidays.

During this time, I received an extremely facetious card from my mother-in-law stating that their family had been embarrassed by me, but for me to "put everything in God's hands." The card didn't go over well with me. I already knew that they were embarrassed and didn't need her driving the point home. Soon after the holidays, all the letters from my in-laws stopped. I figured that DJ had put a halt to them.

I was notified by Mom that another attorney had finally been appointed to represent me on my appeal. Mom started leaving messages for him to call her after I informed her that he had not contacted me. After a week of no return calls, she drove over and caught him coming out of his office. After my mom questioned him on the status of my case, he replied, "It will be after the first of the year before I'm able to look at it, and then it will take me probably a month to review the transcripts. He's really making a big mistake by appealing his case."

"What?"

How could this man make this statement if he had not attended my trial or already read my transcript? Who had put a bug in his ear about my case? Had he predetermined whether or not he was going to properly represent me on my case?

This statement and situation infuriated me. The Colbert County Circuit Court and their stable of plea jockeys take care of their own. I decided that maybe I should look toward other options. The only question was how to do that from where I was.

My mom called a friend of ours who had connections to the current outgoing governor Bob Riley's office. We waited to see if they would look at the case for a possible review and pardon. I really wanted to beat this case on appeal, rather than pursue a pardon, but I was getting really suspicious of the integrity of the Alabama appeals process. The governor's office responded that I would first have to get my pending cases resolved and then they would take a look at it. This message was relayed per my connection. I knew that a new governor would be in office in January and that would decrease my chances of any attention.

Meanwhile, back at the ranch, my bunkmate, Gabe, who slept

on the top bunk above me, was going home. He had EOS'd (end of sentence) his time. The day before he was to leave he hit me up to loan him some items to pay for a new tattoo. He said he would call his sister and have money wired to my account to cover it and took the info to do it. I felt like we had developed a trust and I loaned him the items. Gabe left and I never received the money. Turns out, prerelease loans are one of the biggest cons in prison. If you don't have an enforcer on the outside, there is a slim chance of getting repaid. I felt foolish.

By January I had decided to take a different approach to fighting my case. I made inquiries to see if I could use the media to my benefit. To this point, all the media coverage had been one-sided against me. I intended to turn this around. I drafted a letter to the local daily newspaper. I hoped to voice my complaints about the court system and Colbert County. I also drafted a letter to the newly sworn in governor, Robert Bentley.

There's an expression in prison that goes, "Hurry up and wait." Anywhere you're told to go or anything you try to do you were hurried (meals, shift office, laundry, court, etc.). Afterwards you wait endlessly for them to get around to you. Now I was creating my own waiting game as I drafted these letters. I anxiously awaited Barney's response.

Uncomfortably Numb
(Reflections on all the socially redeeming factors at Elmore Correctional Facility)

> *"In my country we go to prison first
> and then become President."*
>
> —Nelson Mandela

The potato chips in the camp commissary were not that bad.

Deaf Ears (S.O.S.)

"Politicians—that's like a step below child molesters."
—Harlan Coben, *Drop Shot*

With a lot of time on my hands, I did what research I could into my situation and my possible appeal. The prison library at Elmore was like everything else there, designed to frustrate and discourage. Scheduling time and trying to wade through disorganization was a nightmare. The freedom to Google needed information and research was not in the cards. Jailhouse lawyers were abundant, but like free world lawyers their services were costly. You could drain your commissary account in a hurry by taking a chance on their self-proclaimed expertise. Once again, the system was designed to prohibit an appeal.

As mentioned, just after the first of the year the new governor, Robert Bentley, was sworn into office in Alabama. I eventually wrote two letters to Gov. Bentley, explaining my situation and hoping to stir up some interest in my case. Although I really didn't expect the governor himself to see the letters, I expected to get some kind of response from his staff. Alas, I never received any response. Of course, as a convicted felon, I had given up my voting rights; therefore, I was of no value. What was I thinking? A politician was not prone to give any heed to a creature that his state had locked away. Maybe if I could have afforded a campaign contribution, I might have at least warranted a response.

Also during this time, I sent another letter to the daily newspaper at home. I addressed it to Barney, the same journalist who had covered my trial and whom I had previously spoken to on the phone. Once again, I received no response; however, phone calls to Barney from my daughters received a promise to meet with me when I went to Lauderdale County for court. This promise got me excited. Maybe I could sell Barney on the idea of telling my side of the story. Big city journalists jumped on stories like this, so why not a small town one?

Attached are portions of my letter. As you probably have already figured out, I can be long-winded and tend to have plenty to say. I have tried to limit the repetitions in my babblings. This is an abridged version of my 15-page letter:

> *For the first 50 years of my life, I held a typical view of the Alabama legal system. As an extension of our great American justice system, I maintained that our state ran a court and penal system that was void of political and prejudicial influences and that upheld everyone's civil rights. That was my opinion until I lived it.*
>
> *As a convicted felon, this is not about my innocence or guilt—because I'm guilty. I'm guilty of failing at business. I'm guilty of stressing out and making some terrible busi-*

ness decisions and blunders during a trying economic period. Finally, I'm guilty of owing a number of people money due to the failure and closing of my business.

This story is about the misconceptions that I had with our County and state courts and their correctional facilities. It is about how everything is stacked against you as you go into battle with them. Also, it is about the double standards set in the name of the law and, as a result, the grave and flagrant violations of many civil rights.

Having always heard about inmates being in a "country club" environment and having seen modern movies about prison, I wasn't prepared for what I've experienced inside the walls. As an inmate, you basically have no rights. Any conveniences available such as books, TV, phones, yard time, etc. are considered a privilege rather than a right and can be taken away at any time. This usually happens in instances of group punishment. Basically, this is when one of a few out of a cellblock or dorm act up and the whole group is punished. It's comparable to having the power company turn off your lights because your neighbor didn't pay his bill.

Most people would be appalled at the language used in both the Colbert County jail and the state penal system. Mother F----r seems to be used in almost every sentence, both as a noun and as a verb. The inmates curse a lot, also. However, the language and attitudes of the "correctional officers" really took me by surprise. To Lauderdale County's credit, the officers use much less profanity and are somewhat more professional. In all fairness, even Colbert County jail had one officer who showed some professionalism — an officer named Corey, who *although he did his job, he did it in a courteous and decent way. Most of the others will snap at anything you say as they glare at you out of their bloodshot or glazed over eyes.*

While on the subject of Colbert County jail, our local elected officials should be asked to look into the living conditions there. These living conditions hold true not only for the convicted but also for the accused. Besides being an old, nasty, cold, dark place, most of the shortcomings are due to institutional neglect and lack of compliance. As an inmate at Colbert County jail, you are given no yard time. Many prisoners there have gone months at a time seeing the sun only when transferred to court. I know of no other jail where this is true. Also, you are fed just enough to survive. Sometimes it is bologna sandwiches for many days in a row. In Colbert, you are given no bed linens, just a nasty blanket and you have to fend for yourself many times for toiletries.

On to the Colbert county circuit court system. If you have plenty of money — no sweat. If you are broke — you are screwed! A good "paid" attorney and enough cash can get you out of most any situation. If you are in dire financial straits and have to have an attorney appointed to you, you are in a world of hurt.

Once they convict you, the Colbert County court makes sure to limit your resources for appeal. Since my conviction and subsequent file for appeal, it has been several months. During this time, my attempt to appeal has been dragged out.

How fair is it and how much sense does it make for the same judge that sentenced you to appoint you an appeals attorney and to rule on your chance of a new trial or an appeal bond? I guess it makes about as much sense as allowing the DA to ask if any of the jury pool had ever owned a business or been self-employed, so that he can subsequently strike them from the jury to assure that you don't have a real jury of your peers.

After finally having been appointed an appellate attorney, we only discovered this upon the investigation of my mothers and daughters. In the months that I had been incarcerated, I have been sent only one legal notice of any kind directly from Colbert County. This was the notice of receipt of my intent to appeal.

Another thing that really struck me in Colbert Court was at the hearing for a new trial. In her arguments against it, the assistant DA said, "We gave him chance after chance to accept the plea and he repeatedly turned us down." Basically, my case came down to "intent." Pressuring me to plead guilty to taking someone's money with no intent of performance was like sticking a gun to my head and asking me to renounce my faith in God. I've never intentionally tried to harm or take advantage of anyone in my life. But when you fail and in the process you owe people money, they understandably get very upset. I owe a number of people, scattered over five counties. This number represented what would have been two to three weeks of work for my business. This was what was left of approximately a 10 to 12-week backlog, prior to the national economic fallout and subsequent loss of business.

Back on the subject of finally being appointed an appellate attorney, after my mother finally found out who he was and contacted him to see when he would be contacting me, she was told by him that it would be sometime in the upcoming months and then it would take several weeks for him to review my transcript and to put together a brief period. He went on to *tell her that the whole process would probably take longer than my sentence and that he thought that I would be making a mistake to appeal. Interesting comments coming from an appointed appeals attorney who has not met me nor read my trial transcript. Has he been briefed and rehearsed on my case? I guess the bottom line in the Colbert County system is that I'm a "convicted by jury" criminal and basically out of sight and out of mind, and need to stay there.*

Now on to prison life. Sometimes telling the inmates from the correctional officers strictly comes down to who is in blue and who is in white. Many of the COs are only a narrow step from being in the opposite color uniform. Drugs are everywhere in prison. Marijuana, cocaine, pills, you have it all in here. Although they have the dogs in on us two to three times a week and regularly wreck our bunks searching, they seem to ignore the obvious hiding places. The director of Alabama's prisons should be ashamed of himself. It is hard for me to believe that he is unaware of what he is running. I sincerely hope that Gov. Riley, a man I voted for and supported, was unaware. Either he or his successor, Gov. Bentley, need to look into the shortcomings of the system. If they don't, maybe Anderson Cooper, Geraldo Rivera, Diane Sawyer, or some other journalists should look into it. Sometimes, looking from the inside out, I'm ashamed to be an Alabamian.

My father was a kind and compassionate man and would give you the shirt off his back. I'm ashamed of the fact that he has to look down and see where my shortcomings have gotten me. Also, spouses are victims in situations like this. Even a 30-year marriage sometimes can't survive the embarrassment and changes in-

volved when one spouse has let the other down. My biggest loss has been my reputation. For many years, I ran my business on my reputation. I ask God every day how I can regain it.

In closing, I would like to offer some apologies and some prayers. First I would like to apologize to my 26 employees. I'm sorry that I let you down. We tried to get too big—too fast. Also, I would like to apologize to my family and friends for the embarrassment and the hardships that I have caused you. Lastly, I would like to apologize to my customers. Although in my heart I know that I didn't set out to take your deposits and not perform, I nevertheless failed. For those who filed criminal charges on me, I hold no grudge against you—money is a serious thing. To those who file civil suits or those who didn't file at all, I thank you for your understanding and your patience. Although at this point I can't give a timeframe, I intend to make all this right before I leave this world. I would also like to thank all the other customers that I've had over the years. I apologize if any of your recommendations got caught up in my downfall.

I've experienced a lot of new emotions while incarcerated, including hate, self-pity, and fear. I pray that God will help me deal with these. I also pray each night for my family, my friends, those incarcerated with me, and those who are in charge of us and judge us. I asked that each of you will remember us in your prayers as well.

Sincerely,
Mike Harrison
AIS #273811
Elmore Correctional Facility

If you have never been in a desperate situation you have no idea what a small flicker of hope does to you. When you're incarcerated, I guess the term "grasping at straws," would apply. Every angle that I pursued would, in my mind, be the route to my freedom; however, it seemed that every door that I would try to open would quickly be slammed in my face. Still, I clung to the hope that I could get my story out to the public so that maybe I could shed light on the reality of the situation, and I would no longer be perceived as a thief. The very fact that many people viewed me this way, ate at my soul.

Food for thought: bureaucracy is present not only in government but also in the media. Whereas government is comprised of mostly non-elected appointees running the show, newspapers have a hierarchy of decision-makers as well. In both cases, many of these people make decisions that can aid or hinder other people's lives. In my case, I simply needed a chance to be heard. It would all come down to whether or not it would be a popular and marketable decision. This fact was true with both the newspaper and in the state government. Also, I would later be led to believe that sometimes, especially in the small-town arena, one institution would influence decisions by the other. I then wondered who pulled whose strings?

The Pillars of Southern Society

"Being defeated is often a temporary condition. Giving up is what makes it permanent."
—Marlene vos Savant

In the good ole boy parts of the South, judges and prosecutors are not really concerned about eliminating crime and injustice. The same can be said of their cohorts in the jails and the prison system. Courts and Corrections at this level are a business.

I know that you constantly hear about how much money counties and states lose on the enforcement of the law and the incarceration of criminals. If they are losing so much, how do they keep affording new toys for their departments? Look around and see who has new fancy uniforms and special Task Force vehicles. I'm sure that seldom does a judge, prosecutor, or jailer in Colbert County, Alabama ever miss a paycheck because times are slow. I'm sure the same can be said in the State Corrections System. If worse comes to worse, I'm sure that, if nothing else, they can find a way to suck a little more out of the inmates' families to help with payroll if need be.

If there were no crime, these people would not have jobs. In some cases, where there is not a crime, they have to create one to pay the bills and to justify their existence. The crime necessary for their paychecks is cultivated like crops in the system. Those who think that the system is set up to reform criminals are grossly mistaken. Rather, it reenergizes the criminal element to insure further business.

To make sure that this process happens, they must have the right kind of employees. Where do you find the kind of expertise to keep your business flowing? Easy, hire wannabe criminals! These are the guys who fantasize about a criminal life, but just don't have the balls to take a chance in public. As jailors, they have the ability to act out their fantasies without repercussions and have the blessings and permission of the court so that they will make sure that the courtroom has plenty of repeat customers. There's nothing like setting a good example.

A March 2014 article in Cosmopolitan Magazine reported on the gross misconduct happening in Alabama's Julia Tutwiler Prison for Women. Among the charges were repeated reports of sexual harassment and rapes (which have reportedly produced at least one child). The report states that at least a third of the prisons staff has been involved in some kind of gross misconduct. Since 2009, at least six correctional officers at Tutwiler have been convicted of sexual crimes. Women were reportedly sent to solitary by the staff for reporting the sexual misconduct. Of course, business is still good. Tutwiler is at double the capacity that it was set up for.

A clinical psychologist hired at Tutwiler in 2012 quit after two months, citing the horrific conditions. He stated, "We need to back up and look at it with fresh eyes. The people that are running it don't have the perspective to see what can change."

A Justice Department report gave credit to the allegations in the Cosmopolitan article. It referred to a "culture" of sexual abuse at Tutwiler. Nevertheless, Alabama state investigators found the complaints and charges "unfounded" and said that there was insufficient evidence. In response, the Justice Department accused the state investigators of often failing to use even "basic investigative tools and techniques" and of being guilty of closing cases prematurely.

The commissioner of the Alabama Department of Corrections shot back that their department thoroughly investigated abuse allegations and that the investigators work for the state rather than the prison and are therefore independent. Yeah, sure! I guess if my hands do something wrong, I can appoint my head to investigate it as an independent and impartial party.

The Justice Department report wasn't fooled. It stated that chronic abuses, including rapes, have been going on for at least two decades. The state bureaucrats cover their own asses repeatedly and laugh in the face of anyone who questions them. One department takes up for and lays a smokescreen for the other. My question is, why the Feds aren't doing something about it. We are willing to send troops to Iraq and Syria to stop human rights abuses. What makes Alabama any different?

The problems don't end at the gates of Tutwiler. This mentality is present throughout the Alabama prison system and in many of the city and county jails. In my home town, an officer was caught trading favors for blowjobs given through the bars. Was he any less criminal than the inmate? What kind of background check was he given prior to being hired?

I realize that there are bad elements in businesses everywhere, however, it is bad when the percentages are much higher in the very system that is supposed to uphold morality and the laws of decency. How can these judges and prosecutors sleep well at night, knowing the kind of criminal element that exists under their watch? How can they be so focused on their win/loss ratio and their vote tallies that they bend over backwards to send people, deserving or not, into this hell. Oh well, I guess it's just easy to pass the buck and consider that unfortunate fact to be someone else's problem.

In my case, the system went out of their way to interpret my situation as a crime. Intent can be perceived if the right courtroom "actor" is convincing enough. By small business standards, I was a big fish in their arena. Of course, I was vulnerable at the time and the media circus of the Bernie Madoff situation made me great fodder for potential voters. Play me up as a crook, to those individuals who loved seeing someone fail and be punished for it, just because they were not brave enough to take business risks themselves. It's good business for the legal profession to jump on an easy target and score some points with the voting public. Don't give him a chance to redirect himself. He's got to be just like Bernie Madoff! Let's throw him to the wolves and reap the publicity benefits from it. This crusade will look good on our resume. Who cares? Go ahead and kick a man when he's down!

Picture a man being called into the office of the manufacturing company where he has worked for the last twenty years and being told that he no longer has a job. The economy is bad and they are being forced to shut down. Also, all of the stock he had purchased in the company over the years was now worthless.

Imagine the shock he is in as he drives home to inform the family. As he pulls into the driveway, he looks around at the fine home he had built and wonders what he is going to do now. He had just refinanced the home to make improvements, having already used much of his equity, and he still had some of his contractors left to pay. They had deposited their time and materials in the project.

Upon discussing and lamenting over the situation with the family, the house is put on the market, as well as many of their possessions, after all, they had bills to pay. They decide to try to hold off on bankruptcy and see if they could liquidate and at least somewhat take care of the people that they owed that would be the most affected by the bankruptcy. But with the economy in shambles, nothing went as planned. The house doesn't sell, and the other possessions sell for pennies on the dollar.

Soon the contractors show up, demanding to be paid.

"The bank has cut me off," the man tells them. "I have no funds to give you. Everything is gone. I didn't prepare well for what has happened and I am broke. I am trying to come up with a plan to take care of what I owe you."

'Well, we want our money now," they demand. "We deposited our time and goods with you. We want them back."

Some of them scream, "You are a crook. You did this intentionally."

The man feels terrible. He allows some of the angry people to rummage through his work shop, taking anything and everything as payment to appease them. Others storm off angry.

Soon the man has lost his home to the bank. A wrecker takes away his car. A decent job is not to be found. His life as he had known it is gone.

One day the man receives a message to come by the police station to answer a complaint and he complies. There he is told that he has been accused of theft. He sits in shock as he is read his rights, cuffed, and carted off to jail. He is going to be tried for theft by deception.

His court appointed attorney does not take the case seriously and when he hires another one, the judge is pissed off and does not allow time for him to prepare. All the cards are stacked against him.

When his trial approaches, he is offered a deal. "Admit to just two counts of this and we'll let you off light," he is told.

"But I would be lying," he replies. "None of this was intentional."

"Have it your way then," he is told. "Don't act like you weren't warned."

In court, he is constantly labeled a thief by the prosecutor. "You meant to cheat these people," the DA screams time after time.

The man doesn't understand what was going on around him or how to handle the situation. How could this nightmare be happening?

As it is, the DA and the judge are going to show him not to cross them and their plan. He should have taken the deal. Sure enough, after enough courtroom theatrics, the man is convicted and sentenced to prison. To the court, this process was good business and a feather in the system's cap.

"Let's send him down and let our people reform this criminal," they gloat. "Our fine system will teach him a lesson."

Who was this man, this criminal? Who was this justice minded court? What prison would they send him to be corrected?

Could this man be someone like you or me? Could this Court be in Colbert County, Alabama? Could this reform system they referred to be the Alabama Department of Corrections?

You do your research and then you answer the questions.

"The Criminal"

"Arrange whatever pieces come your way."
—Virginia Woolf

One constant underlying theme with the occupants of the Alabama prison system was the fact that almost all were from a dysfunctional background. Single-parent homes, broken homes, foster homes, and so forth, provided the upbringing for most of my fellow inmates. Very few had the fortune to have been raised in a loving and caring family like I had.

Another recurring theme was making prison a family affair. You won't believe how many inmates have a father, a mother, a sibling, or multiple siblings who either have been or are currently incarcerated. This fact makes me wonder if in many of these cases it's in the DNA. Maybe it would help to come up with a plan to reduce prison overcrowding based on this fact. We could call it the "Bob Barker Plan," In exchange for being spayed or neutered, offer family affair offenders early release, a bag of pot, and A NEW CAR! You might be surprised how many would actually take the deal. The bag of pot and the car are the real teasers because prison is a second home to many of them. The prizes would be more enticing than early release. Who knows, maybe if this plan was implemented, after a while the reduction of the gene pool might significantly reduce crime and thus prison overcrowding. Oops! This would also mean a reduction in business for the legal system. Some would object to that.

One day during a conversation with an inmate named Shabazz, a revelation suddenly hit me. I was a criminal! He and I set down and wrote up a list that proved this fact:

- I had smuggled an Apple back to the dorm from the chow hall.
- I had smoked cigarettes inside the dorm.
- I had lined up my shoes toes out instead of toes in when getting my living area in compliance.
- I had taken a shower before regulation time.
- I had subliminal insubordinate thoughts aimed at certain Correctional Officers.

That proved it! I was a criminal! What was next? Would I become institutionalized? Would I become a repeat customer for the system? Not no, but hell no. I made up my mind. I would survive this cesspool.

The term "institutionalized" is not a term that most convicts, even long timers, apply to themselves. They are in denial. No matter how much they give in to the system, they don't feel that they are patterning themselves to it. Regardless, I for sure had no intentions of letting this pattern happen to me.

Manners rarely exist inside the fence. Although occasionally the young guns give some respect toward an old guy (OG), it is not because of manners, but because they think that the OG has enough survival experience or that he has the resources for severe retaliation. When a youngster does show disrespect and a complaint is made, his homeboys simply laugh and say, "Its prison, man."

Right after the first of the year, I was assigned prison duty as a third shift dorm cleaner. "This wouldn't be so bad," I thought. I wouldn't mind pushing around a broom and a mop during quiet time. Boy, was I wrong! This was a time that many of the sissies came out. I got so sick of seeing them fucking each other on the bunks in the back of the dorm that I could hardly work. Some hid under the sheets to hide their actions. Others simply didn't care. They would always have someone "hot railing" (standing lookout) for the COs. In reality, not that many of the COs gave a shit. These sights will haunt me the rest of my life. I'm not homophobic, however these were scenes from a different lifestyle that I had no business being exposed to.

Another group that came out heavy, late at night, were the tattoo artists. Although this hustle went on all day, it picked up at night (it was never extremely dark in the dorm). Some of these guys were amazing, real Bohemians. With ink from writing pens, matches, homemade burners, and contraband ink guns, they could create works of art that Da Vinci would be proud of. Arms, legs, backs, chests, torsos, heads, faces, eyelids, they applied their art everywhere. One popular tattoo was a teardrop under the eye for a fallen comrade (others say this is a sign that the bearer has killed someone). I wondered how the individuals with faces and necks tattooed, as well as full sleeves, ever hoped to get a good job. I saw tattoos ranging from elaborate crosses and quotes of Scripture, to swastikas and demons performing oral sex on naked nymphs. Of course, there were also some economy ink artists. I saw a few tattoos that look like a three-year-old had done them with a crayon.

Another form of self-expression was with "bones" or carved dominoes. This was especially popular with the Latin crowd. One of my neighbors whom we appropriately called "Amigo," was telling me about this process. They take the carved pieces of dominoes (hearts, etc.) Then they slit the foreskins on their penises and insert them before sewing it back up. Was this the Latin spin on a French tickler?

"You've got to be kidding me," I told Amigo. "That's sick!'

"Oh no," he replied, "the women love it."

I looked around and didn't see any women present to appreciate it.

"Wanna see?" he asked.

"I'll pass," I said quickly and changed the subject.

Later on, as I was heading into the showers, I heard someone say, "Hey, Mr. Mike, this is what I was talking about."

Without thinking I glanced that way. What I saw was one of the grossest things that I have ever seen. Why would anyone want to put a domino in his dick? Would this surgical transformation not come back to haunt them physically in the future? Did it not increase chances of infection? Someday when their abilities fail them, they will remember the old saying, "You don't fuck with Mother Nature!"

Killing time is an agonizing thing. Every day I got up and checked to see what was on the social calendar for the day. When

I realized that once again it was the same agenda as yesterday, I became further depressed. You become a creature of habit, a subject in a never ending and boring group therapy session. I wished that I had been allowed a dart board to pass the time. I would have pinned a certain judge's photo on it.

To get away from the Elmore experience, I constantly read. My daughters were allowed to ship me three books a month from an approved vendor. Three books lasted me about three to five days. Fortunately, there were several other readers in the dorm and we swapped books. I probably read 200+ books during my incarceration at Elmore alone. Although the prison library didn't have a very good selection, I sometimes was able to find something there to read. This privilege stopped though, when a member of the prison administration caught some sissies fucking in the library and closed it. The library remained closed the remainder of my time at Elmore. Remember the analogy of "the neighbor's power bill?"

PART III: ROCK BOTTOM

ANIMALS (The Goon Squad)

> "In reality they were, at best, guys who couldn't become cops and thus are that dangerous creation known as the 'cop wannabe'. Matt had seen plenty of wannabe's working as prison guards. The mixture of failing and imagined testosterone produced volatile and often ugly consequences."
> —Harlan Coben, *The Innocent*

The Alabama Department of Corrections has a program called SRP (Supervised Release Program) that I was told was for non-violent offenders nearing the end of their sentence. I decided to ask my classification officer, Ms. Minnimee, about the program.

Ms. Minnimee instructed me that prisoners had to be within six months of your EOS (End of Sentence), be a non-violent offender, and then have an application and home plan approved by the SR board. John Odem, my attorney, confirmed this info with her and also noted that we could get all the people we needed to write the board on my behalf.

Knowing that my other court dates and the six-month mark

were approaching, I set about making plans to pursue this SRP. *If I had known then what I know now.*

Also during this time, I was struggling to get a visitation list approved so that my mother and daughters could come to visit me. The female officer in charge of visitation got in no hurry to do her job. After this process had dragged on for a while, my youngest daughter, Jessi, who worked for another state agency, had her boss call the head of the ADOC to see if he could get anything done. He got something done all right. I was promptly called to the shift office, cursed out, and asked why I had caused them problems.

I explained, "This inquiry was not intending to cause anyone problems, my daughter was just wanting desperately to see me on the upcoming weekend."

"Well, it ain't gonna happen, I'll see to that," shot back the female CO. "You don't call people on me." As I left, I noticed that her in-house mailbox didn't look like it had been emptied in weeks. Another three weeks passed before I was able to receive a visit. She put me through the ringer to get approved. My mom and my daughters finally were allowed to visit me. It was the happiest three hours that I had experienced in a long time.

One night during this process, I was called to the shift office by Sergeant Waverly, the 2nd shift sergeant and an OK guy (compared to most of the COs). Jessi had called upset about not getting to see me and, as only she could do, convinced the sergeant to let me talk to her on the prison phone. We had a nice conversation. Sergeant Waverly, an older black man said, "Harrison, your daughter obviously loves your very much, I couldn't tell her no." This statement lifted my spirits.

During the early parts of the New Year I once again had a court transfer mix-up, this time from Franklin County. No big deal. I missed only one night's sleep getting processed, missed two meals, and stayed in a holding cell for around ten hours before the decision was made that I wasn't being picked up. I was again sent back to C-2. Then I was off to find CO Jameson to find another sleeping mat. I had learned that Jameson, despite being a smart-ass, would do his job and assist you on such matters when the other COs wouldn't.

I read a book during this time that in many ways related to much of my last few years in business. It was called *Cleaning Up* and was written by an ex-con and current minister named Barry Minkow. It chronicles his struggles and transgressions as a whiz-kid business man and his eventual downfall and incarceration. Although I didn't commit any of the intentional and deliberate criminal acts he describes, such as insurance fraud, I can relate to much of what he describes about struggling to keep a business afloat and the personal pressures involved. Much later, after my release, I watched an episode of *American Greed* reporting that Minkow had reverted to his old ways. This report, if accurate, changed my opinion of the book's author and his religious conversion.

A friend of mine in C-2 named John, (with a name like that he should have been an attorney), had been put to work as a clerk in the DOC central warehouse. With his custody level and his intellect, he was ideal for this type of position, however, shortly after his appointment he was accused of smuggling drugs back into the camp hidden up his ass. It was common for such patsy accusations to be made to divert attention from the real sources. John was kept in a holding cell for three days in restraints and repeatedly taped to a bucket to force him to shit the evidence out. No such evidence ever surfaced and he was eventually un-restrained and sent back to C-2, no apology, no nothing. John looked like he had gone 12 rounds with Mike Tyson.

Also down this stretch, I was amazed at the level of knowledge in certain fields that some of my comrades possessed. Two of my buddies, Red and Drew, knew enough about every drug known to man that they could be pharmacists. Of course, they did have something in common with pharmacists, they both sold drugs. At least they claimed to be crooks.

Drew was also a comedian. One day he stopped by my bunk and with a serious look on his face asked, "Pardon me, sir, but would you happen to have some Gray Poupon?" Drew could make us laugh even in a miserable place like Elmore.

Another buddy, Dill, shared with me his recipe for Jailhouse Julep (liquor). This concoction involved orange juice from the camp store, and scavenging for sugar, bread crust, apple sauce, and so forth. Some of the hiding places for his stashes were really quite Hogan's Hero-ish. When a stash around camp was discovered and poured out, the camp smelled like the Jack Daniel's distillery.

Life at Elmore slowly crept by. Although every day was one day less in my life, it was one day closer to freedom. I was settling into a routine. Then came the morning of January 20, 2011.

I had heard from other inmates about the riot squads or "Goon Squads" as they were called, and their shake-downs. I had brushed it off thinking it couldn't be any worse than going through processing at Kilby. Boy, did I have something to learn.

I was wondering why we hadn't already been called for chow

on this particular morning. Then I found out why as they burst through the dorm doors at 4:30 am yelling and cursing and banging their sticks off the bunks. Altogether, there were around 15 of them plus a good number of German Shepherds.

As they scattered around the dorm, they screamed at those who were still in bed to get their asses up. One inmate who was having a hard time getting his head clear was promptly hit across the face with a truncheon (baton) and the blood went flying. Another kid, whom we called "Crack Baby" had his nose bloodied also, because he reacted too slowly. It was clear to everyone in the dorm that Crack Baby was mentally retarded and should not be in a level four prison camp. He should have been in a mental hospital where maybe he could get some help. Instead, he was here at Elmore with the riot squad beating on him because he didn't understand what was going on. Hell! I didn't understand what was going on! Were these civilized Americans or the SS?

We were ordered off our bunks and instructed to strip naked. We were then marched into the showers, all 198 of us, and told to stand nose to back of head until we were individually called by bunk number.

As we were called to our bunks, they made us open our bed lockers and then they proceeded to destroy our property, ripping apart anything that they felt could potentially hide contraband (which the guards had probably already sold to start with). Afterwards, everything was simply thrown onto the floor. The spine of my Bible was ripped open and my Bible thrown down the aisle. The photos of my girls were also thrown onto the floor after they were thoroughly scrutinized. It looked like a tornado had hit the dorm.

Once each inmate's locker was searched and destroyed, he was ordered to lie face down, still naked, on the cold metal of his bunk (the bedrolls were being ripped apart and scattered around the floor). We were also ordered to cover our eyes with our hands, an attempt to limit vision of any physical bullying going on around the dorm.

I had attempted to see the nurse for my back pain during the previous day, and after about an hour on my stomach the pain became excruciating. I rolled part way over on my side, still partially shielding my eyes. You would have thought that I had tried to escape. Officer Focker started hitting me repeatedly in the back of the head with the palm of his hand, driving my face into the steel bunk. I started screaming that I was down in my back; however, he continued hitting me several more times. This animal, who is the size of a WWF wrestler, was a bona fide piece-of-shit. I'm not sure where he falls in the evolutionary chain. You don't have to be white to be a racist. Focker's reputation as a racist and as an asshole had, as I mentioned earlier, preceded him. It was well deserved.

Several of the other inmates started screaming at him to leave me alone. He yelled back for them to close their mouths and to cover their eyes or that they would get some of the same treatment. I was appreciative to them for diverting his attention.

After they had finished demolishing the dorm and all the inmates were back at their bunks, we were allowed to stand. I struggled getting to my feet. Then, in marched some huge guy in a brown suit who I later learned was the head of the riot squad unit.

He paraded up and down the aisles as if he were Papa Doc Duvalier or Heimlich Himmler, inspecting the spoils of the fray.

I don't remember him saying a word. Then he left as suddenly as he came.

Was this Haiti during Papa Doc's reign, or Pol Pot's Cambodia? Or had I been transported through a time warp back to one of the Nazi camps at Treblinka or Sobibor? Were we about to be marched to a bath house to be gassed?

Fortunately, we were not gassed. However, it was still very difficult to believe that I was in Alabama, the state that I had grown up in. My forehead was bruised, and I had a throbbing headache for a couple of days, as well as coping with the pain in my back and the still impaired vision in my right eye. However, some of the guys had been less lucky and had been beaten up badly.

My Mom and my girls, upon later learning of what had transpired, called the Elmore county Sheriff's office about it. They were told that they had no jurisdiction on state property. I guess that I was at the mercy of the State and its elite fighting force, "The Goon Squad." They should be so proud of themselves. These animals were very efficient against unarmed and defenseless subjects; however, bullies will usually shit in their pants when really confronted with a real threat. I wonder if any of these ultimate warriors would stand up in a real battle or would they turn tail and run? Perhaps we'll never know. However, the State of Alabama should be ashamed that Nazi police tactics exist within its borders and under its watch! Welcome to the third world, Harry! Welcome-hell! I was born here!

Hell's Bells!
(Will the real criminals please stand up?)

"You can knock me down and watch me bleed,
But you can't keep no chains on me"
— Kid Rock, "Born Free"

Most people who have read or watched a version of Jonathon Swift's classic *Gulliver's Travels* view it as simply an imaginative and comical work of fiction. In truth, however, Swift's work was a satire of the European political arena of his day. In the book, Gulliver is made both a hero and later a villain by the powers that be, depending on what their agenda was at the moment. In the end, Gulliver escapes Lilliput by sea. I have been to Lilliput. I'm still waiting for my opportunity to escape.

Although we don't have Jonathon Swift to satirize our current system of government, there are plenty of John Stewarts and Stephen Colberts who have performed this duty on Comedy Central. The only problem is that a large majority of our society view their opinions as simply entertainment and are either too complacent, too saturated into the system, or too uneducated to demand a change.

However, there are those who have tried to make a change in certain areas. Although my efforts to reach out to the Civil Liberties Union and the Southern Poverty Law Center were unsuccessful for me, (they had bigger fish to fry or rather to try to keep them from getting fried), I still respect the ambitions of their founders and those who sincerely devote their lives to the cause of civil correctness, instead of political correctness.

One organization that I have started to follow is The Innocence Project, for obvious reasons. Although my conviction would not meet their criteria for representation consideration, I strongly respect the work that they are doing. They concentrate on major crimes that can be disproven with the advancements of DNA technology. Their cause is one that is dear to my heart—the exposure of false or wrongful imprisonment.

The Innocence Project was founded in 1992 by Barry Scheck and Peter Neufeld in conjunction with the Cardozo School of Law located in New York, and named for Supreme Court Justice Benjamin N. Cardozo.

Scheck, renowned for his work with the notorious "Dream Team" representing and gaining acquittal for O.J. Simpson, serves as director of the project. Whether you agree or disagree with the O. J. verdict, Scheck's record of proving innocence in many high-profile cases is well documented. Among those defended or represented by him are Hilda Nussbaum, Dennis Fritz, and Ron Williamson, British au pair Louise Woodward, and wrongly accused Duke University lacrosse player Reade Seligman.

Fritz and Williamson were also the subjects of bestselling author John Grisham's first non-fiction book, *The Innocent man: Murder and Injustice in a Small Town*.

The Innocence Project is committed to exonerating wrongly convicted people through DNA testing. Scheck urges that if prosecutors can use DNA evidence as evidence of guilt, then they should also pursue it as evidence of innocence. He says, "Results are results." As I have researched the justice system, I was dumbfounded at the resistance of many prosecutors to review cases and test DNA results on old convictions. Are they worried about the score on their conviction record, or simply the bad press? Either way their egos should not stand in the way of the potential proof of innocence.

According to Innocence Project statistics, 76% of the wrongful convictions that they have exposed involved eyewitness misidentification and 50% involved invalidated or improper forensic science. I wonder what percentage was because of misperception of intent.

In a news release, Peter Neufeld stated, "These DNA exonerations show us how the criminal justice system is flawed and how it can be fixed. There is still a great deal of work to do to make our system of justice more fair, accurate, and reliable." I personally think that judges not allowing prosecutors to theorize on presumption would be a start.

To date, the innocence project has led to the exoneration of 353 wrongfully convicted "victims." A couple of these cases were in the state of Alabama. Ronnie and Dave Mahan were convicted of rape in 1983 based largely on identification by a victim in a lineup, saying she had gotten a look at their faces when they raised their masks. In 1998, the Mahans and their attorney were granted access to the biological evidence. DNA tests on the rape kit were performed and excluded them both. They were both released in December of 1998. Who were the real victims?

Jeffrey Holeman was convicted in Alabama in 1988 based on lineup identification of a rape victim. Although she said her attacker never removed his mask, she was able to give a facial description and tagged Holeman as the culprit.

In 1992, when Holeman first came up for parole, he was required to give a DNA sample as a result of a state convicted sex offender law. With assistance, he filed to have DNA evidence studied from the crime evidence and was subsequently exonerated on January 14, 1999, and his conviction was vacated.

Neither Holeman nor the Mahan brothers have yet to receive compensation for their wrongful convictions. A freed man with similar circumstances in Georgia was reportedly given a seven- figure apology by the state. Is Alabama beneath owning up to and trying to make up for its mistakes? Is Alabama so broke that it can't compensate these men for the State's mistakes? We always seem to be able to find money to pay football coaches. Is the State's honor not as important as winning on the gridiron?

These men all had a decade of their lives stolen by the state and the prosecutors involved. Did the prosecutors use theatrics and/or deceitful pressure and practices to produce a conviction and steal freedom from these men? Some say yes. If true, were the prosecutor, and subsequently the State, not guilty of "theft by deception?"

For the last 30 years or so, I have followed the chronicle of a man from my home region in Colbert County, Alabama, who was sentenced to death row. A locally high profile case, the conviction and impending execution of Thomas D. Arthur has been going on since 1981. Tommy Arthur was not by all accounts a nice man; however, that fact alone should not convict him to death. Having watched local news coverage and knowing what I know now, I believe the trial could have been choreographed by the prosecutors. I once felt sure that Mr. Arthur was guilty of the murder of Troy Wicker Jr, for which he was convicted. The media coverage made it look that way. He may very well be guilty, but the thing that stirred my interest was the fact that the prosecutors were so resistant to later performing DNA tests on certain evidence. After researching the case, I was amazed at how much evidence had been lost and how much witness testimony had been reversed or overlooked in order to get a conviction. If you don't believe me, do your own research. Make sure and read an article in the Atlantic by Andrew Cohen, dated Feb 27th, 2012 entitled, "Another Death Row Debacle—The Case Against Thomas Arthur." There has even been another man connected to the victim who has at one time confessed to the murder.

Like I stated before, Thomas Arthur does not appear to be a nice man and he may be guilty as charged, however, there is something in his trial and conviction by the court in Colbert County that stinks to high heaven. I've seen the way Colbert's court works. Don't trust a rotten apple. Personally, I had always been an advocate of the death penalty and I still believe that there are people who don't deserve to live because of the acts that they have performed. The problem is that I just don't trust our local judicial system to decide and administer it. Politics, votes, win/loss ratio, and ego should not come into play in the court system, however, in our world of social media, politics does come into play. Corruption and a win-at-all-costs attitude prevails in the good ole boy system.

If you carry the necessary clout or can afford the right lawyer, you have a very good chance with the courts, but if you are reliant on the court appointed plea jockeys, it's kind of like Christ hiring the Pharisees to represent him in front of Pontius Pilot.

I know that you may say that my case, and serving only one year, cannot compare to many of the cases detailed, however, everything is relative. If a prosecutor or a judge decides that he or she wants to convict someone of intentionally committing a crime, it is easy for them to fabricate a bogus case. Where there is no DNA evidence to consider, they simply go on presumption of intent. Then theatrics and theories come into play.

Barry Scheck stated in an interview that the overall system needs to be reformed; not just in cases tied to DNA. He asks in the interview, "With the great number of wrongful convictions being overturned with DNA evidence, what are the percentages of wrongful convictions in cases where DNA doesn't apply?"

"Soda"

"Who knows, he may grow up to be president someday, unless they hang him first!"
— Mark Twain, *The Adventures of Tom Sawyer*

Jonathan Walker: a.k.a. Bakin' Soda got his nickname from his previous employment. He was a low-level drug dealer, as well as a motorcycle thief. The nickname "Bakin' Soda" apparently came from cutting amounts of cocaine with baking soda to increase the yield. It is also cooked with coke to make the product known as crack cocaine.

I first met Soda on the ride from Kilby to Elmore, when we were both initially transferred there. My first recollection of him was the artwork he had drawn on his bobos, the arch-less, canvas, state issued shoes. He was quite the artist.

Soda and I had become acquaintances during the ride, and we were both assigned to the same dorm at Elmore. After his coming to my rescue during the gang attack on me, we became friends. He had taken a great chance by stepping up for me when no one else did. I never did really understand why he did, we didn't know each other that well at the time, but I was glad he did (so were my ribs). Soda had risked his standing with his gang brothers to do what he felt was right; however, Soda knew about risk and dangerous situations. He grew up in Prichard, Alabama. Prichard is Alabama's equivalent of New York City's Harlem, New Jersey's Newark, Chicago's South Side, and East LA. A suburb of Mobile, it is predominantly poor and black and has a reputation of being run by drugs, prostitution, and violence.

I remember years ago when my hometown high school, Russellville, was scheduled to play Blount High School, out of Prichard, for the state football championship. At the time, the State Athletic Association format called for title games to be played in one or the other of the cities involved, based on some crazy criteria. In this instance, it called for the game to be in Prichard.

The rumor was that the Russellville High School administration refused to play the game there, even if it meant a forfeit. Russellville, although having a significant number of black citizens, was largely white. Also, Russellville carried quite a crowd to football games. The old joke was that if you wanted to be a successful house burglar, go to Russellville on a football Friday night. The administration's concern, and rightfully so, was that they would be endangering not only the team but their families and fans by asking them to drive to, park, and walk to the stadium at Blount High School. There had been a lot of recent violence in and around the campus. The administration was concerned that this fact combined with potential racial prejudice toward the white fans, would create a potentially dangerous situation.

The game was ultimately moved to Ladd Stadium in Mobile.

Violence erupted there anyway when a Blount fan in the stands pulled a gun on a Russellville supporter. I'm not sure who started the confrontation. Rumor has it that the incident involved alcohol, and when confronted with the gun, the Russellville fan stuck his finger into the barrel.

As I stated before, Soda was a big man. Although trim, he was 6'4" tall, an athletic 225 pounds, and resembled Jimi Hendrix. Outwardly he was a 23-year-old man; inside, however, he was just a big kid. To describe his demeanor and personality, imagine a cross between Buckwheat (of Little Rascals fame) and Kramer (from Seinfeld) and you have a picture of Soda. He was always pulling pranks, wrestling, and cutting up with someone. Lots of times, it was me. He was just a big kid! I would play along for a while, and when I tired of the horseplay, I would tell him to cut it out before I kicked his ass. (Yeah really! 6'4" 225-pound guy who was ripped versus an old, out of shape, white guy with a bad back and a crippled wrist. Think I had a chance? Sure I did!)

Soda was constantly getting into trouble. He had a knack for it. He was continually getting disciplinaries for smoking in the dorm (Actually, he got the disciplinaries for getting caught; we all smoked in the dorm), being in the wrong dorm, fighting, or for just being in the wrong place at the wrong time. He repeatedly was put on restriction and many of his camp privileges were taken away.

Early on, Soda also stayed in trouble within the population of the camp. This trouble usually had to do with owing gambling money, a dope deal gone bad, or a cell phone that he had borrowed being confiscated. Cell phones were everywhere in Elmore, thanks to the black market run by some COs. I bailed him out of these situations more than once. On too many occasions, I saw young guys at Elmore get in debt with the wrong people and wound up being forced to whore themselves out to pay their debts. Even with Soda's size, there was still always some enforcer that was bigger and badder. Many times, these situations of indebtedness were set up intentionally. Although Soda was more capable than most in taking care of himself, I gave him store items to clear his slate and then chewed him out for being so stupid. Prison was not a place to run up a gambling tab and so forth.

Sometimes I got so frustrated with Soda and his continually finding trouble, but over time he started getting a handle on his habits. I kept telling him, "You can't keep running with everyone. You've got to decide if you want to be a thug or a decent human being." I think that despite his background, Soda had a lot of potential to make something of himself. He was bright, intelligent, and well-spoken when he is not reverting to Ebonics (black street language). I told him that with the right chance and direction, he could have been president of the United States. I urged him to get himself straightened out while doing his time and to get his GED so that he could try to get in a program and continue his education upon release. He promised that he would. I was thrilled later on to find out that he had kept that promise and received his GED.

Soda had little correspondence with the outside world. He was constantly writing letters to his mom, his sister, and his girlfriend, but he rarely got responses. To my knowledge, his father was hardly in his life. After a while, he concluded that his girlfriend had moved on (a common thing to happen to those incarcerated, I would experience this myself firsthand), and that his mom and sister just didn't seem to have enough time to write. I felt sorry for him and talked my mom and my girls into writing him so that he could hear his name called at mail call. They soon all became pen pals.

Soda referred to me as "Pops" or as his "white daddy." I referred to him as my long-lost prodigal son. When we were allowed yard time, I regularly walked on the dirt track running around our recreation yard. When he wasn't on the "weight pile," Soda walked with me. We talked about everything from cars and music to society and religion.

Soda claimed that he was a Christian and we discussed our beliefs. We also talked about what it meant to be a good and respectful person. I hope that I have had some positive influence on him. I know that he, as a young man from the wrong side of the tracks, was an inspiration to me with the way he aspired to rise above his background. He was a kid caught between two worlds. He wanted something better for himself. I feel confident that someday he will succeed, despite the efforts of the ADOC to institutionalize him.

Soda and I had become pals. We were Tom and Huck, one from middle-class America and the other from the ghetto. We watched each other's backs. Soda was always telling me that when we got out, that he was going to buy him a BMW with 24 inch wheels and a killer, booming sound system. He said that he was going to come pick me up, and we would go cruising. I told him that the BMW was all right, as long as it was not hot, as in stolen, but he'd better not pick me up in a pimp-mobile.

In other notes from this time: Several of my friends from home, including Rob, Alf, and Yogi, not only wrote me but also wired money to my commissary account. This windfall, on top of what my family sent me, allowed me to splurge and buy a small pocket transistor AM FM radio and a set of headphones. What a godsend. I know it's only Rock-N-Roll, but I love it! I spent much of the winter months escaping into some sorely missed music. When walking on the track, I jammed out. If I could have picked up 97.1, The River out of Atlanta, my time would have gone much faster, however, I made do with what I could pick up.

Besides the music, in the mornings I would listen to either "Rick and Bubba," a couple of really commendable Christian guys that have a syndicated show out of Birmingham, or I listened to the "John Boy and Billy Show" out of the Carolinas and laughed my ass off. My radio was a welcomed relief from the junk that the inmates watched on TV.

Although I had previously never been a big fan of Kid Rock, he released a song around this time called "Born Free." It became my personal theme song during my incarceration. It lifted my spirits every time it came on and I sang along.

I received a card in the mail, around this time, from friends in a Sunday school class from North Highlands Church of Christ back in Russellville. The card said that they were thinking of me and they voiced their hopes for my future. Among the signatures on the card were some old friends, Dan and Amy, whom I owed because of a deposit they had with me during the collapse of my business. Despite this situation, they had penned a side note that they loved me. This note touched me deeply. Also signing was a dear sweet lady named Dot, who was the mother of another one of my businesses casualties. However, they had offered sympathy and understanding to the situation and weren't a part of any action against me. Maybe everyone hadn't written me off as a criminal.

This card was the only such showing of support and well-wishing that I received from any of the churches that I had had connections with from back home. I did receive, along with all the other inmates, a handmade Valentine's card from the children at a church near Elmore. It made me feel good that these children took the time to think of people in our position. My thanks to them and to whoever was behind their show of love.

During a cold spell in February, sometimes we had to wear our state issued clothes to bed to try and stay warm because the dorm heaters didn't put out much heat. After a homemade phone charger (wired into one of the heater fans) was discovered by one of the sergeants during an inspection, he promptly had all the heat cut off to the dorm as punishment (neighbor's power bill!). It was miserable at night. Fortunately, the fourth day into this punishment, I was transferred out to Morgan County for the first stop in my "Magical Mystery Court Tour."

The Callous Palace

"A recent police study found that you're much more likely to get shot by a fat cop if you run."
—Dennis Miller

Decatur, Alabama—The first step of my mission to become eligible for early release on the Supervised Release Program (SRP).

Morgan County Jail was a newer, state of the art detention facility. It was clean and very well maintained, quite a change from the gothic dungeons at Colbert County. After arriving, I went through processing and inventoried my property. I was then required to take a shower and to be de-liced and disinfected like many jails require upon arrival.

When I had finished with this process, I found that my property had already been checked in. I asked what I was to do for underwear and socks. The jailer didn't want to have to retrieve my boxers and socks, so he instructed me to put on the ones that I had arrived in. I complied and was then given county issued coveralls and a pair of size 7 plastic shower slides (the only shoes that they allowed). To those of you familiar with construction terms, this was kind of like wearing 2x4s on your feet.

"I wear size 12," I told the officer.

"We are all out," he replied. "That's the largest size that we have left."

As I started to hand them back to him, he said, "No, you have to take those. It's required that we issue you shoes."

I walked to my assigned cell pod in my dirty socks, shoes in hand.

If you could see the guards at Morgan, you would think that you were in a right-wing militia camp. They wear para-military uniforms and slick combat boots. If they put as much time into doing their jobs as they did in dressing, they might be worth the county's tax money that they take up. As it stands though, they are a lazy and callous bunch of juvenile delinquent ass-holes. I repeatedly heard and saw a couple of them bragging about their army and martial arts experience and how tough they were. It is my experience, that if someone has to tell you how tough they are, they usually turn and run at the first sign of trouble. I definitely think t that assumption applied here.

Although Morgan County was a welcome break from Elmore, including the food, the jailers still drove me to a point that I almost snapped. Even after three days of asking for my property (undergarments, toiletries, etc.) so that I could take a shower, I continued to get one put off after another, not to mention that by this time my socks were black and my boxers stunk.

Finally, when I had again asked the night shift sergeant to help me out and received a smart-assed reply, it drove me beyond frustration. He later proceeded to instruct me, over the intercom, to help another inmate distribute food trays. After I politely passed on the opportunity to take orders from someone not willing to do his own job, he screamed at me to do as instructed. That's when I lost it. I ranted and raved and called him every name that I could think of, plus a few that I made up. He yelled back over the intercom that if I didn't shut it up that I was going to face serious discipline.

I replied to him, "Bring it on! But you better bring more than a stick and a can of mace. You better bring a whole fuckin' army, you lazy son-of-a-bitch!" The weenie-boy shut off the intercom and never came near the pod for the remainder of the time that I was there, nor was I ever disciplined. Sergeant my ass! Needless to say, though, I went on to day four without any shoes or clean boxers.

Of course, after I thought about my tirade, I was glad that he was such a wuss. In retrospect, if I had screamed what I did to the jailer to the COs at Elmore, I would have had a sure ticket to the infirmary, if not to Boot Hill. I had seen too many inmates learn this lesson the hard way. I knew not to be that brazen there, no matter how angry I was.

After my little episode with the sergeant, I was the big man on campus. The other jailbirds in my pod were mostly meth addicts and in on possession charges. After watching the dude that came in from State stand down and embarrass the sergeant, they treated me like a rock star. Besides the extra food and cigarettes sent my way, I was given soap and shampoo and a semi-clean towel so that I could take a shower. However, afterward I still had to put on the same boxers and socks.

A day or so later, I was pulled out of the pod to go to court. As I was going through the booking area to be prepared for transfer to the courthouse, the ranking officer at the desk asked, "Where are your shoes?"

I briefly, and for the hundredth time in four days, informed another officer of what had transpired at check in. Promptly and miraculously, a pair of size 12 slides was discovered, just in time for me to go to court. I'm sure that they looked great with my nasty ankle high socks.

I sincerely hope that Morgan County's newly elected lady sheriff has addressed the laziness and inefficiency of her staff. Maybe she can increase the professionalism of their job performance to match their wardrobe.

In court, I met with Jim Lawless, my court appointed attorney. I also got to see my mom in the courtroom, but at a distance. Jim had reached a tentative settlement with the assistant DA and the charges against me here were to be dismissed.

My wife had always accused me of having selective hearing, saying that I heard only what I wanted to. Honestly though, I do have trouble picking up certain tones when there is background noise present. As a result, I have become pretty good at reading lips. Using this secret power was handy in court. When my case came up I was able to read the assistant DA's lips as he conferred with the DA. I was able to make out the words "civil case." The DA looked in my direction with a puzzled look on his face. I felt a small sense of vindication.

My charges were dismissed "with prejudice," meaning that they could not be brought back up later and round one was behind me. I excitedly thanked Jim and blew a kiss to my mom. Shortly after court, I was picked up for transport to Lauderdale County. On to round two of the Magical Mystery Court Tour. Pending charges had now been dropped in three counties, Lawrence and Marion had been dismissed earlier. My quest for SRP was underway. I was thinking that maybe I would be back on the street by my birthday in May. I just didn't understand how the ADOC really worked.

The Dark Side of the Moon
(Lauderdale County Jail)

"We can easily forgive a child who is afraid of the dark: the real tragedy of life is when men are afraid of the light."
— Plato

This was my third trip to Lauderdale County jail. I had visited there a couple of times before for court procedures. After being processed and de-liced, I was escorted back to population. On the previous trips, I had been assigned to the "condo" units in A dorm. These were two-tiered units with four two-man cells per floor. This time I was assigned to an eight-man cell in B dorm. I was occupant number 10. I spent my first few days sleeping on the floor. When a couple of guys finally checked out, giving me a bunk, I had to sleep directly in front of the toilet.

The cell in B dorm was as drab, dank, and monotone as the dark side of the moon. It was an echo chamber, a cave. You could hear your thoughts echo back at you. Casual conversations or the toilet flushing were like going to a Ted Nugent concert. If my hearing was not good going in, I probably needed help from

Annie Sullivan before I left. The constant din of the noise was excruciating to me. Being locked in this cave made me feel like the Count of Monte Cristo.

Every time that I transferred for court, I had to go through the repeated process of filling out a sick call form to try to get some Tylenol or Motrin for my back and wrist. This process was easier said than done. Once again at Lauderdale County Detention Center, good health was considered highly overrated. The first nurse whom I saw at LCDC, after filling out the standard questionnaire, indicated that she couldn't give me anything for my pain. When I protested, she made the statement, "Hurtin' ain't never kilt nobody." I swear, that is exactly what she said. This particular nurse would certainly not win the Florence Nightingale award for compassion. If her statement was accurate, why was she even there? What need did the county have for her services? I guess she just figured every inmate was a lying dope head and that I wasn't worth her getting up off her fat ass to do anything. Trust me, she could have used the exercise.

A couple of days later, when a different shift was working, I once again put in for sick call. This time the new nurse once again filled out a questionnaire on me. I decided to soften her up with a little humor. When she asked if I was allergic to anything, I replied, "Yes, jail cells." She chuckled. I then informed her that my free world M.D. had prescribed me plenty of old Forrester Bourbon and a Tempurpedic mattress. Once again, she laughed. I was put on the pill call list and started receiving something to knock the edge off my pain.

I wound up staying at LCDC for a month while waiting for my court appearance. We were only allowed yard time twice a week for one hour each time. Occasionally the church service provided by the local Church of Christ was held on the yard. Other than this service, plus what sick calls and visits I had, I was confined to the cave the entire time.

Prior to my transfer from Elmore, Jess, my youngest daughter, had sent me a copy of John Grisham's *The Innocent Man* as an early Valentine's gift. To my knowledge, this book was Grisham's first work of nonfiction. I read it in a day. I really felt the pain of the main character featured in the book. I was starting to realize just how hard it was to take on the system. All the cards are stacked against you, whether you are guilty or not.

I had a number of visits while at the LCDC. These were usually uplifting even though they were done through a glass window, with a phone receiver in my hand. On one visit, however, I was infuriated when the girls informed me that DJ had dropped me from her health insurance. Here I was, 50 years old, with serious medical conditions and no insurance. How would I ever get a new company to take me without excluding pre-existing conditions or waiting an extended probationary period? What if my conditions worsened? Although DJ had made the statement to them that I was on the states healthcare plan now, surely she was not delusional enough to think that the state really cared about the health of its inmates, and even if it did, they wouldn't continue any healthcare after my release. I finally started to realize something that was very painful: DJ just didn't care anymore.

The girls also informed me they had received a letter from my buddy Chad at Elmore, saying that he had an altercation with my favorite CO, Officer Focker. Apparently, during a shakedown, another inmate had spit out some dope that he had been hiding in his mouth onto the floor near Chad's bunk. The other inmate was black. Chad was white. Focker accused Chad. When Chad objected, Focker and a couple of other guards had roughed him up. He filed a complaint and was currently awaiting a prison hearing on the matter. I was worried for Chad because I had heard how such things worked. Later, when I went back to Elmore, I would find out that Focker had threatened Chad and promised to make his life miserable unless he dropped the suit. Regardless, it just kind of went away.

The girls had called Barney at the paper to let him know that I was at LCDC. He set up an appointment and visited me for an interview. I asked him if they were going to print my letter. He told me that it was extremely political, and that he had to run it by his publisher for permission. He said that it was a great story and that they would probably print an article with excerpts from the letter and the interview. A couple of weeks later, when it still had not made the paper, Jess called and was told to look for it in the following Monday's paper. A lot of Mondays have passed since then with no story. I was extremely disappointed and never heard back from Barney. Did the editor reject the story because it was too political? Since when did things get too political for newspapers? Were they worried that they would lose sources at the Colbert County Courthouse? Or did, perhaps, news of the letter leak to the powers that be in the Colbert County Courthouse, who in turn pressured them to can the story? Does the local court run the newspaper? I will probably never know for sure.

One day shortly thereafter, I was carried to the front for an attorney's visit. However, when I entered the attorney/client room, there was a man that I didn't recognize. He turned out to be Bill

Meathauler, my court appointed appellate lawyer. Instead of an appellate attorney, they should call this position a "going through the motions-predestination-I answer to the same judge-routine attorney." After introductions, Mr. Meathauler proceeded to tell me that he could find no grounds for appeal in the transcript. Apparently, the way the law works in Alabama is that for a direct appeal on a conviction, the judge or prosecutor has to make some kind of legal error that can be appealed. Otherwise, you have to file a "rule 32" on grounds of ineffective counsel. This way, the court throws the appeal back on the defense attorneys, to cover their own asses.

I voiced all my objections to the way things had been handled in court, but he informed me that he had already prepared his brief. He didn't seem interested in anything that I had to say, citing that he had already read the transcript. He also said that upon submitting the brief, he was withdrawing as my attorney. Having already heard the statement that he had previously made to my mom about me making a mistake in appealing, it appeared to me that this meeting was just to go through the motions. His viewpoint was predetermined. I was furious with his position, his statements, and his callous, bureaucratic attitude.

I told him, "Go back and tell your boss, the judge, that I'm not going to quit."

"The judge is not my boss," he replied.

"Bullshit!" I shot back. "You're just another one of her court stooges."

We didn't part on very pleasant terms. When he came back later to bring me the copy of my transcript that I requested, I apologized for being belligerent. Although I was sorry for losing my temper, this fact didn't change the way that I viewed him, his effort, or the manner in which the system was stacked against you. The court cronies take care of each other. After I thought more about it, having Mr. Meathauler representing me would have been kind of like having Hannibal Lecter represent a case at the Donner's Pass Cannibal Court of Appeals.

My stay at LCDC stretched to a month. My trial date was approaching. During this time, I met several times with John Odem, who had argued my Colbert trial and who was appointed by the court to represent me in Lauderdale County. We started going over preparations for trial. I told John that besides the lack of preparation time, the thing that I thought had beat us on the guilty verdicts in Colbert County was the closing argument. John had used the standard law school reasonable doubt approach. I told him that this time we needed to pound on the "lack of intent" and use a no-frickin'-doubt approach. He agreed.

Also during John's visits, I shared several of my favorite lawyer jokes. John's pretty cool for someone in an occupation that I define as educated liars.

Do you know what's brown and black and looks good on an attorney? Answer: a Doberman pinscher!

Unawares to me, my mom, my Aunt Barbara, and Mike Waddell, a good friend of mine, had approached John about trying to work out a settlement to keep my Lauderdale case from going to trial. Mike and my Aunt Barbara had offered a significant amount of money to attempt this. I already owed Aunt Barbara, from a bridge loan prior to the collapse of the business; however, you have to realize that this was my dad's sister. She is much like him, a loving and loyal saint. She would have given her last dollar to help me. Mike and his wife Sandra, whom I had only known for a few years, had taken it on themselves to try to help me, too. Their son, Blake, was one of Jesse's old boyfriends. These are fine Christian people, the kind of good Samaritans that you hear about and read about in the Bible, but the kind that you rarely see in action.

After John made me aware of what they had all cooked up and proposed, I refused. When I got to talk to them personally, I told them to not throw good money after bad money. "Let me take my chances," I told them. I was so deep in debt to them already that it would be ages before I could pay them back. They all told me that the money wasn't an issue and they wanted to help me get out as quickly as possible. They said that we would worry about repayment in the future. I held my ground for a few days, but I finally relented.

The deal that John worked out with the Lauderdale DA, Chris Connelly, was in John's words a rare one. It was called a deferred plea. I would give a "best interest" plea of guilt. In return, the judge would then defer or postpone acceptance of the plea for an extended period of time. During this time, if I took care of the balance of the restitution of the cases involved, they would be dismissed. A best interest plea meant that although I was pleading guilty to the charges, I was only doing it for my best interest, in fear that I could lose and the consequences could be more severe. This form of plea is a very strange tool of the justice system in this country, primarily used to convince accused persons to plea and, as a result, taking the monkey off the court's back. It didn't even seem ethical to me.

My biggest concern with the agreement was the timeframe

of the restitution. I was currently incarcerated and had no source of income. It looked like a recipe for failure. John assured me that Chris Connelly was a good guy and would work with me. Also, he said that Judge Self, the presiding circuit court judge in Lauderdale County, was fair and trustworthy. Judge Self's father had been one of my instructors in college. If the son was anything like the father, he was a fine person. I trusted John enough to take his word for it.

I took the deal, but only after having John restate my concerns to the DA and getting assurances that he would work with me. I needed this to work. I needed for all these charges against me to ultimately be dropped. The relief of not going to trial was tremendous. I hoped that the faith that we put in my ability to come up with restitution, and also the fairness of the DA, was warranted.

My mom had also been working on getting me an unbiased and competent attorney to handle my appeal. Jim Lawless, who had so capably handled my case in Morgan County, gave her a very fair price and offered to take it in installments so that she could handle it. He told her that he believed in my innocence and that I was unjustly serving time. He also told her that he wished he could take my case for free, but he had to make a living also. Mom hired him. The economy had affected Jim heavily. He had been involved in some kind of real estate law, and the economic slowdown had hit them hard as well. Because of this common ground, I felt like he could relate well to my situation.

Soon after my settlement, I was rounded up for transfer. John Odem, who was concerned about me having to go back to Elmore, had called the court officials in Franklin County and made arrangements for me to be carried directly there, to await my trial in that county. This was my home county and I could remain close to my mom and to my girls. I also thought that with the proximity, I might get a visit from DJ.

When I was checking out to leave LCDC, the jailers took my copy of Grisham's *The Innocent Man* that Jesse had sent me as a Valentine present. When I complained, they told me that any books, besides the Bible, had to be donated to the jail. Obviously, this policy is how they stock their library. I objected, stating that this was a gift from my daughter. The jailer on-duty told me that he would talk to the administrator to okay it and hopefully my daughter could pick it up later. This effort turned out to be futile. Jess attempted several times over the next week or so, but ran into a stone wall with the administrator. LCDC had stolen my gift from me. Can I press charges?

As I made the ride to Franklin County, I was excited. If I could get my cases there taken care of swiftly, I would be SRP eligible! Maybe I would be going home soon! Then I could get to work and try to resolve some of this nightmare. A month later, I would still be wishing for the same thing.

M – I – C – K – E – Y – M – O – U – S – E
(Franklin County Day Care)

"The significant problems we face cannot be solved at the same level of thinking we were at when we created them."
— Albert Einstein

As I was booked into the Franklin County Day Care, also known as the Franklin County Detention Center (FCDC), I at first gave my address as Highway 43 Overpass North. I guess that I may as well make light of the situation because I now considered myself practically homeless.

I pitched a fit when I discovered that I would have to spend my first 72 hours in a 7 x 12 holding cell. This isolation, I was told, was a new policy implemented to allow time to get a medical clearance from the nurse. This policy made little sense to me as I discovered later that the nurse didn't get around to your physical and TB test until sometime several days after you were put into population. I wound up staying in the holding cell initially for four days.

After finally being put into population, I was assigned to the medium security pod. Whereas many of the jailers were okay guys and much different from the ego/psycho cop wannabes in the other jails that I had been in, I'm not sure how qualified any of them were for a physical altercation or a threatening situation. Think: Barney Fife. Welcome to Mayberry, Alabama.

One of the jailers always made sure that we got regular yard time because he always wanted to play quarterback for both teams in a makeshift tag football game. He would get so excited that we would have to tell him when he was being paged on his radio. The term Franklin County Day Care was quite appropriate. Most of the inmates were made up of dope heads and petty thieves.

Drugs were rampant in FCDC. Also, cigarettes were readily available, at extreme prices, despite it being a non-smoking facility. I always tried to buy my cigarettes through a trustee and to avoid the "Dinged Brand" tobacco brought in by the inmates on work detail. Defined, this was loose tobacco, wrapped in plastic, and smuggled in up their asses (dinged). Yes, this fact is true, and it grosses me out, too.

In my first week in medium security, I was involved in an altercation with a guy who had ripped me off for some cigarette money. I complained to him, and he took a swing at me. We started fighting. Despite my limitations, I held my own till his buddy jumped me from behind. Together they got me down and proceeded to start kicking me. I was kicked in the head several times and dazed. The situation was not good. I had to just cover up and try to protect myself as best I could, especially considering my back problems and the neck and eye problems that I had lived with since my altercations at Elmore.

Before the guards made their way into the pod to stop the

melee, I had taken quite a beating. My right eye was again swelling up and my head felt like it was exploding.

The guy who jumped me from behind was a real animal, possibly the missing link in the evolutionary chain. He was 6'4" tall with a tattoo on his forehead. He ran around like a hyper four-year-old, thinking that he ran the pod. When I was later sent to segregation (seg) because of the fight, I found out that half of the people in seg were there because of altercations with him. This guy was deranged. The guards were scared of him. He should be the poster child for birth control. He could even be a strong argument for abortion. Why the jailers kept sending everyone whom he caused trouble for to segregation, instead of him, was beyond me.

After I was moved to segregation, I refused to give a statement (jail house rules). However, I later learned that the two guys who had jumped me gave a statement that it was my fault. That would never fly if the punk assholes were sent to State. They said that I had started it. Nevertheless, the guard had to have seen the whole thing through the pod window.

In seg, I complained about my head. The nurse checked me out and said that I had no symptoms of a concussion. I was then transferred back to a holding cell for observation. I remained there for another three days. Healthcare at its finest.

During the fight, my glasses had been knocked off my head and stepped on. They were bent in half and a lens was knocked out. One of the jailers assisted me in replacing the lens and trying to straighten them out. Although they were badly warped, we repaired them the best we could. I had no choice. I couldn't read or function well without them. I wore them riding crooked on my nose through the balance of my incarceration.

During this second stay in a holding cell, I had a good view of the comings and goings at the booking station of the jail. If only the taxpayers of Franklin County could witness their money at work. The day shift at booking in FCDC usually had a handful of jailers huddling around the booking desk all day, some male — some female. Although a small amount of time was used for booking incoming prisoners, probably 80% plus of their time was used for flirting, horseplay, snacking, etc. Sometimes the flirting became groping. Jeeezz! Come on guys, get a room! The night shift had significantly fewer jailers who generally stayed busy and monitored the inmates.

When I was again taken out of holding, I was put in minimum security. Here I settled in and made the most out of what would turn out to be a month and a half. I didn't understand why it took so long, both before and after my hearing, but I was told (inmate speculation) that it was because of the daily state money that the FCDC was allotted for housing me. Supposedly it was enough to cover the budget to feed the whole pod during my stay.

Once again, I made a number of friends during my stay at this location. Among them was a guy named Snyder. Snyder's mannerisms reminded me a lot of the Snyder on the old TV sitcom "One Day at a Time." Alas, every time that I think of that show I wind up thinking about another character on the show, Barbara Cooper (Valerie Bertinelli). I think every guy my age had a crush on Valerie Bertinelli. I had a huge crush on her and I will still pause and even watch an infomercial that she is on. What was Eddie Van Halen thinking when he let her get away? Oh well, I'm losing my train of thought.

Another friend that I made while I was in minimum, was a

kid named Matthew. Although very cerebral, he suffered from some emotional problems and fought drug abuse. One day he read me a poem that he had written, and I liked it so well that I asked him to write it out for me. This is Matthew's poem:

There once was a saying,
this shall pass.
And through all the good and evil
my friend it will.
But don't let life hold you down too much.
You would have to realize it's just the
mere illusion of the truth.
Blind for the man to see,
but blinded more by evil things.
There will be a snake to cross your path but
let it pass from you like the blood in your body.
For the soul shall heal.
Now at the end hearts are prepared
For the final meal.

—Matthew Dylan Scott

I urged Matthew to go back to school and use his talents. He assured me that he would. He seemed excited that I thought he had potential. The last time I saw Matthew he was leaving FCDC for a drug rehab facility. I hope that he accomplished what he said he would.

Another young man I became acquainted with, named Lee, had multiple tattoos all over his head, including his eyelids. Without the tattoos, he could've passed for Steve Perry of the rock group Journey. Of all the artists whom I had observed during my year of incarceration, and I saw many great ones both with a pen and with a tattoo gun, Lee was by far the best. The depth and the life in his portraits and the murals that he drew on his cell wall were amazing. This guy was FCDC's version of Pablo Picasso, Vincent van Gogh, and Salvador Dali, rolled into one.

Overall, the food and the treatment at FCDC were okay. One problem that I did run into was that you were issued one roll of toilet paper per week, and if you needed more you were simply shit out of luck (pun intended). One week I threatened to rip up my sheets if they didn't give me another roll because I was out a day early. The threat didn't work. Luckily, a friend named James loaned me a roll of what he referred to as John Wayne Toilet Paper.

"Why do you call it that?" I asked.

"Because it's rough and rugged and don't take shit off nobody," he replied.

When you think of it that way, the sheets didn't sound like such a bad idea.

The Franklin County Detention Center was one of the newer facilities that I had the misfortune to stay in. But, considering its age, by far, FCDC was the worst maintained. I'll bet that more than half the plumbing didn't work. A water leak in the wall of one of the holding cells that I was in, ran across the cell floor to a drain in the center. A hot water leak in our pod's shower (not a drip, but rather a wide-open spray), I was told had run for months and months. I was told that every time that a plumber came he worked for a few minutes and was then whisked away to work on something at the Captain's house.

The Captain at FCDC was a real hypocrite. Although I didn't personally know him on the street, we had mutual acquaintances. I don't think that he was aware of that. The folks who listen to him sing in a gospel quartet on Sunday would be shocked to hear some of the things that come out of his mouth through the week. I guess correctional officers consider themselves out of sight and out of mind as well.

When my hearing date finally arrived, I was offered a similar deal to what I agreed to at Lauderdale County, a deferred plea. This idea was basically put together by John Odem, my mom, and my good friend Mike. John was not being paid to work on my case in Franklin County, but he is a great person and had become a friend. The deal was given to my Franklin County attorney, John McJimmyhoffa, to present to the Franklin DA. This was only the third time that I had seen McJimmyhoffa during all the weeks that I was at Franklin. John McJimmyhoffa was a hard person to find.

For his court appointed clients, it was extremely difficult to locate and confer with him. The first two times we met in FCDC, combined, had totaled maybe three to four minutes. When I walked into the first meeting, the first words out of his mouth were, "I've only got a minute to talk to you; I have to be somewhere else." The second meeting, which I requested, went very similar. I guess court appointed attorneys in Franklin County, Alabama are very busy. There is always a ballgame or some other social function requiring their time.

Many lawyers are very poor at recognizing faces as well. I don't know how many of the attorneys present during both my Franklin and Colbert hearings, I had gone to school with or had done work for. Yet, with the exception of my friend Shane, they all looked the other way and pretended not to see me. Maybe I then realized just an inkling of the disappointment that Jesus had in Peter after he denied him. Where was the courtroom Rooster when you needed him?

The Franklin County DA, Joey Rushing, is a very nice guy. I had met with him earlier, in his office, when I was first taken to the courthouse. He had told me that we had mutual friends who thought a lot of me, and he would try to work with me in any way that he could. He had stated that my case was a gray area and that from what he knew of me, he didn't think that I was a criminal. However, he said that the case was political and that he had to answer to his constituents. He jumped on the deal that John Odem had brokered through John McJimmyhoffa. He agreed to give me time to be released, go to work, and make good on my restitution. He promised to work with me. I once again considered this deal to be in my "best interest" because it would allow me to be eligible for SRP release. Then I could get to work on my restitution.

Of the six counties that I had been charged in after the initial publicity of ArcStone's collapse, three had dismissed the charges altogether (basically saying that they should have been civil charges), two had deferred everything to allow me to get back to work and start paying restitution, and one, Colbert County, had convicted me as a thief.

Colbert County must have become aware of the events in the other counties. Shortly after returning to FCDC, on the day of my hearing, I was surprised to be called to the booking desk. There I met my Franklin attorney, John McJimmyhoffa, who promptly put me on the phone with John Odem.

"Colbert County has offered to let you out today," John told me, "You won't have to go back to Elmore."

"Today?" I half screamed, my heart wanting to jump out of my throat.

"Yes," he replied.

"What's the catch?"

"They have two stipulations."

"Go ahead."

"Number one, you have to agree to pay restitution to the *victims* in Colbert County that you were found innocent on as well."

"No problem, I owe them the money. I had stressed that from day one."

"I know," John replied, "I told them that I was sure that you would agree to that."

"What's the other stipulation?" I asked.

"You have to give up your appeal rights."

"No way," I said. "They can shove that up their ass."

"I knew that would be your answer, too," he said. "Are you sure? I really want to see you get out of there."

"Yes," I said. "I could have possibly been free from day one if I had agreed to lie and take their plea bargain."

"I'll relay the message."

I stood firm, as did the DA's office in Colbert County. The way that I basically took their offer and the stipulations was that they were scared of my appeal being successful and embarrassed by the views and stances taken by the other counties. In the end, they basically threw their "innocent victims" under the train to protect their score. As it turns out, I discovered that they probably weren't too worried about an appeal either. They ran that show as well. Outside of an act of God or maybe alien interference, appeals in Colbert County were predetermined.

However, not knowing the script that was ahead of me, turning down an offer to be released was one of the hardest things that I have ever had to do in my life. But now that I had my pending cases off me, I should be eligible for SRP early release. We immediately began having people write to the SRP board on my behalf. Then all I had to do was get back to Elmore, get my application in, and wait. As it turned out, it would be a couple of more weeks before I even caught a train back to prison and then I was in for yet another rude awakening about the workings of the Alabama Corrections System.

Highway to Hell
(Return to Elmore)

"If you're going through hell, keep going."
—Winston Churchill

Meanwhile, back at the ranch: My return to Elmore was typical of my other times returning from court. Once again, obtaining a mat and a locker box was a nightmare. I finally got a piece of a mat that had been shredded by the COs during a shakedown, and a bashed-up lockbox. As quickly as I was allowed to, I made my way to my classification officer's office so that I could apply for SRP.

Upon telling Ms. Minnimee that I now had all my other cases resolved and would like to apply for SRP she said, "Oh, you're within 12 months of the end of your sentence. That's too close to your release to apply for SRP."

"That's not what you told me before," I said, "You told both my attorney and me that I had to be within six months of my EOS with no pending charges and no disciplinaries. We've already had people writing to the SRP board. Besides, I only had a twelve-month sentence to start with."

"Oh," she replied, "Well give me a couple of weeks to research this case and get back to me."

I would be transferred out before I received any attempt on her part.

Over the next few days, I became reacquainted with my friends, who were surprised to see me again. After two and a half months at court, it took a while to catch up on the camp news and gossip. Among the news was the fact that one of the COs had been arrested for shooting and killing someone in an incident away from the camp. Also, my friend Dill had been turned down for parole, supposedly in part due to flunking a "piss test." Dill was serving a life sentence for killing a judge's twin brother. I doubt that the piss test was the prevailing factor.

During my short return to Elmore, life was much as it was before. I'll bet that during the two weeks that I was there on this trip, "Twilight" was on Showtime at least 100 times (exaggerated). It played so much, many of the inmates could recite it word for word, reminiscent of crowds at showings of the 70s cult classic, "The Rocky Horror Picture Show."

Also during this time, I noticed continuous ads for correctional officers on the radio. I laughed at how glamorous and prestigious they made the position sound. I looked around at the COs in the dorm. I'm sure they were not what the marketing people envisioned in their ads.

My buddy Chad filled me in on his ordeal with our favorite CO, Officer Focker. According to Chad and others, Focker had basically dared Chad to keep pursuing his complaint against him. Intimidation was a regular tool for guards when they misbehaved. Their actions were basically unaccountable while they were employed behind the fence.

On April 27, 2011, a storm was brewing in Alabama. Seriously, an actual storm was brewing. I was praying that a storm would not hit our camp. Our dorm was one huge mass of sheet metal. If a big wind were to hit it, we would be basically dodging razor blades. The ADOC makes no provisions for such events. Required storm preparation in other State facilities did not apply to us. As we in C2 hunkered down and watched weather reports for the Elmore/Montgomery area, we were unaware of what was happening north of us in the state.

Sometime in the evening I was sent to the shift office. I was wondering what was going on. When I arrived, Sgt. Waverly, the same CO that had previously let me talk to my daughter on the phone, said that my daughter had called and wanted me to call her. He said that she had told him to tell me that everything was all right, but I still panicked, something had happened! Sgt. Waverly allowed me to use the office phone, something unheard of at Elmore. Upon reaching Jessi, she informed me that tornadoes had hit all around home, including one that destroyed much of the towns of Phil Campbell and Hackleburg, which were just a few miles away. She knew that if I had seen reports about it, I would be worried. She wanted to assure me that they were all right. We talked for a few moments before I had to hang up.

Upon thanking the Sgt. for getting me the message and for letting me make the call, he said, "Harrison, you have a sweet daughter who really loves her daddy. I may have to marry that girl someday." We both laughed.

More than 50 tornadoes hit Alabama and surrounding areas that night, including the one that ripped through Tuscaloosa, near the University of Alabama campus. More than 200 people lost their lives during this outbreak, 131 died in Alabama alone. Thousands were left homeless. It was a reminder of how fragile we as humans are, and how nature and an act of God can change our lives in an instant.

Right after the storm had occurred, and roughly two weeks after my return from court, I was awakened in the middle of the night and told to pack my possessions. I was transferring.

"Where am I transferring to?" I asked.

No one would answer me. Eventually, I found out from Radar, the clerk at the back gate, that I was on the list to transfer to Limestone Correctional Facility. Radar generally knew more about what was going on at Elmore than even the Warden did.

Limestone was much closer to home and had a much better reputation than Elmore. I was eager to go, although once again it was into another great unknown.

I quickly packed my belongings and around 5:30 AM was moved to the back gate, where I checked my gear in and was put in a holding cell with the other transferees. I would remain there all day, along with a small group of others. Once again, there was some kind of transfer mix-up and we were finally sent back to the dorms around 4 PM, rushing to make it to chow. We were not allowed to take our property back and were told to make do till the next morning.

Upon rushing to get to chow, I was turned around by my old friend officer Focker, because I hadn't shaved. I tried to explain that I had been in lockup at the back gate and didn't have access to my razor.

"Get the fuck out of my face," he snarled at me and didn't allow me out of the dorm to go to the Chow Hall.

One of my friends who had witnessed the incident, told the Sergeant at the Chow Hall about the situation and a few minutes later Focker received a radio call. Afterwards he yelled at me to, "Get my ass to the Chow Hall." He was really pissed. That fact certainly breaks my heart. However, I was certainly glad that I was leaving.

That night I scrounged around and found a mat. Also, some friends gave me some toiletries to take a shower with. I repossessed some clean boxers that I had given to another inmate upon my supposed departure. I knew it would be hard to sleep that night, partially from the excitement of the transfer and partially because I was leery of the fact that Fokker was pissed off.

My last night at Elmore was anything but uneventful. During the night, a fight broke out a few paces from my bunk. I witnessed a guy that I knew and liked named Herm stick another guy multiple times with a shank. Herm was carried to lockup and the blood quickly cleaned up. Herm was hastily transferred out the next day to Bibb County (I think). I was later told that Herm died from shank wounds incurred in another facility. Whether this was true or just prison rumor, I don't know.

Also during the night, my buddy Dill was busted with about 20 packs of cocaine in his lockbox. Although he said that he was holding them for someone else, they were in his possession and he wound up being slated for transfer also. I'm not sure where he wound up.

Later in the night, as I sat on my bunk, a guy we called Light Skinned Rico (one of the pimps in the dorm) came and set down across from me.

"Pop, I know you're glad to be leaving here," he said, "You don't belong here."

"I'm glad to be getting away from all of you sick fucks in here," I replied as I looked him in the eyes. I did not care for the creeps who took advantage of the young and hungry punks that came through prison, and I had voiced that fact to Rico before.

He didn't say another word, got up and left. I think my message was clear. The next morning, I was again rounded up and left on a transfer van heading to Limestone. I had 93 days left on my sentence.

Riding the Storm Out
(Limestone: A Breath of Stale Air)

"Never doubt in the dark what God told you in the light."
— V. Raymond Edman

As our van rolled through the entrance to Limestone County Detention Center (LCDC), the evidence of nature's fury on April 28 was quite evident. Subdivisions on either side of the prison, as well as the entrance to the camp itself were destroyed. The tornadoes had apparently jumped over only the prison in its path of destruction. God, or in this case maybe Satan, works in mysterious ways.

In this diary of my experiences, I have been extremely critical of the ADOC. However, to be fair, I must say that from the moment I stepped out of the van at Limestone, the difference in the way things were run was evident. With the exception of one egomaniac lieutenant and one doctor with a chip on his shoulder (I will get to these shortly), the entire staff at Limestone that I came into contact with acted with professionalism and treated the inmates with a certain level of human respect. I know that dealing with criminals is tough, but the difference between the administration of duties at Limestone versus Elmore was like night and day.

Unless an inmate was unruly, he was generally listened to and treated as fairly as possible. If within reason, legitimate requests were met and not just brushed off. Also, you weren't cursed every breath. Overall conditions were much better, and the food, which was supposedly sent from the same central warehouse, was far superior. I arrived at Kilby weighing 256 pounds. I arrived at Limestone weighing 179 pounds. The food and conditions in my combined six months at Elmore took 77 pounds off me.

Entrance processing at Limestone wasn't even remotely like Elmore. Everything was done professionally, orderly, and somewhat politely. We were issued everything we were to need and not left to sort through and fend for ourselves. Also, care was taken to make sure that our uniforms and State issued boots fit properly. We were also issued visitation whites to be worn only for family visitations. As much of a surprise as these improvements were, there were still reminders of Elmore. As we inventoried what I had brought from Elmore, I discovered that while my property was still in lockup there (Elmore) the previous night, much of it (coffee, snacks, etc.) had been stolen. Supposedly, only the guards at the Elmore back gate had access to it.

Upon arriving at the pre-release dorm, I was surprised and shocked to discover that we had air-conditioning. I realized that being on our last step before freedom, we were given certain privileges that other inmates didn't have, even in LCDC. Still, it was a pleasant surprise.

Inmates from all over the ADOC were in the prerelease

dorm at LCDC. Some were "short timers" like me. Some had spent most of their lives in the system. Most of these "long timers" were well-behaved and anxious for a taste of freedom. Many of the short timers were dumb punks, still looking to toot their horn as "made men."

Among the new cast of characters in my life were:

Briskee—another young black man that I would become attached to like a son. More about Briskee later.

The Great Cambino—An intelligent kid from the wrong side of the tracks, my bunkmate, not even 20 years old. Cam was already a system veteran. Although bright, he had a ghetto mentality and was always picking fights and getting into trouble. However, he was polite and protective of me as the OG (old guy) upstairs.

Bush—older inmate (70+ years old) yet a short timer who had only been in Kilby and still didn't understand the system. He sometimes let his mouth get him in trouble and only his age and the fact that we were in pre-release kept him out of serious trouble.

Jamie—a young guy from back near home who supplied me with coffee, for my first couple of weeks until my Mom could get a little money onto my books.

Lee—an avid reader/philosopher with whom I exchanged books and thoughts.

Ginn—rough cut and tough, but a genuinely good guy.

Cowboy—could have auditioned for the campfire scene in "Blazing Saddles." Could out-fart any human being I have ever known, even as a teenager. He performed a symphony every night.

The Cheshire Cat—I tagged him with this name because he reminded me of the *Alice in Wonderland* character. He was a real asshole. Always stirring up trouble. He couldn't complete a sentence without saying "know what I'm saying" or "you feel me."

Among other names that others or myself had tagged on to some of the inmates (some openly—some only in my mind) were Dagwood, Don King, Lost Boy, Eddie Munster, Cro-Magnon, Shocker, Tim Robbins, 240 Shorty, My Cousin John, Dumb Donald, Curious George, Charlie Chaplin, Peter Pan, the Boy from Brazil, Banjo Boy (from Deliverance) and Gold Mouth. You can use your imagination as to how these names were derived.

I had names for some of the correctional officers as well. Among these were Big John, Mr. Clean, Bob White (he could whistle like the bird), and Lieutenant Doofus.

Most of the guard's nicknames are self-explanatory. In the case of Lt. Doofus, maybe a little explaining is necessary. He came across as one of those ex-Boy Scout/Marine wannabes who was starving for some kind of authority. He was always tooting his own horn and trying to impress the inmates with his supposed abilities and his silly idea of wit. He really pissed me off one day when we were sent to classes early because of air-conditioning maintenance and I had laid my head on the classroom table to rest. He came in and scolded me, saying that if I wanted to sleep during class I could go to the gym where they sent the problem inmates. We were actually in class early and the teacher hadn't arrived yet and didn't arrive for another 20 minutes. Despite being aggravated, I set up and watched the educational program that was playing on the classroom TV—*Divorce Court*. Instead of supervising F—dorm (pre-release), this doofus lieutenant should have been put in charge of *F Troop*!

Despite the few officers (Lt. Doofus would scold you if you referred to them as guards) that were immature and rude, most were very professional and humane. I can only attribute this difference to a more professional approach from the administration at LCDC that trickled down to most of the COs.

As I mentioned previously, the food at Limestone, although a similar menu, was light years ahead of Elmore, mainly because of attention to preparation, temperature, seasoning, and the fact that we weren't herded like cattle with only a few moments to eat. I would put around 10 pounds of weight back on during my three months here. The added weight was due to the improved chow overall and because I received more frequent visits from the girls and Mom. During these visits, they would treat me to "Big Azz" burgers from the visitation commissary.

Basic daily healthcare, nutrition, sanitary needs, exercise, library availability, laundry, commissary, and so forth were provided and run efficiently and professionally. The one exception was advanced healthcare. Again, I will talk about my experience with one particular asshole of a doctor later on.

All in all though, my time spent at LCDC was bearable. Conditions were cramped and loud, but at least we were treated somewhat like human beings. Although I wouldn't recommend it to anyone for their summer vacation, it seemed that I had at least exited hell and could see some kind of hope on the horizon.

Someday I'll Be Saturday Night

I'm feelin' like a Monday, but someday I'll be Saturday night"
— Bon Jovi

I didn't become a huge fan of Bon Jovi until one day when I heard the song "Someday I'll be Saturday Night." If you've never heard the song, you should YouTube it and listen. The song deals with optimism in the face of adversity. Over the years, it has become my personal anthem when I am feeling down. Sometimes life is a roller coaster. One minute you are up; the next you are down. At LCDC, I finally witnessed a few good qualities in the ADOC. However, turmoil in my personal life kept this tune playing in my head during my stay here. Back to that situation shortly.

Attached to the prerelease dorm at LCDC were classrooms. Each inmate was given a schedule of classes that he was required to attend. The subjects covered included anger management, substance abuse, finances, positive thinking, the Bible, and others. Yes, I did say the Bible. Among the daily routines were readings from Rick Warren's *The Purpose Driven Life*. It surprised me that in today's politically correct climate, and with the positions being taken by the current administration in Washington, that the Feds were not raiding Limestone and shutting down the classes. I hope that this book does not give them any ideas. To me, God in the classroom was refreshing.

Although many of the classes were extremely dull and some of the lower life forms attending them were so disruptive it was almost impossible to concentrate, I made up my mind to get as much out of the classes as I could. Two of my classes however, were incredibly beneficial and I probably took away from them as much as I did from any college course that I ever attended.

One of these was the video course on Dave Ramsey's "Financial Peace University." I wish that I had been exposed to Dave Ramsey years before. Maybe I would've followed some of the principles that he teaches and not have gotten myself into this predicament to start with.

The other course that I really looked forward to was based on Stephen Covey's *The Seven Habits of Highly Effective People*. I had seen this book over the years and almost bought it several times, but for some reason never did. Again, I wonder if some of the principles laid out in Covey's book would have changed some of the directions of my life that led me here to the ADOC. My favorite quote in the entire book was "As individuals, groups, and businesses, we're often so busy cutting through the undergrowth, we don't even realize we're in the wrong jungle."

Substance abuse was a regular topic in our classes. We were constantly watching shows such as *Intervention* and *Meth Mountain*. A great number of the occupants of the pre-release dorm were methheads preparing to be sent back to their kitchens and labs. Meth is a terrible drug. Have you ever seen what it does to the enamel on a user's teeth? One blond-haired blue-eyed kid in our classes had Brad Pitt/Hollywood looks. However, when he smiled, you would have thought that he was a hillbilly from the movie *Deliverance*. His teeth were rotted out of his head as a result of Meth use.

Some of the punks in pre-release just couldn't comprehend that the classes were for their benefit and were constantly disruptive, showing their asses and their ignorance. A couple even started "gunning" (masturbating) under the classroom tables, directing it at some of the female volunteers. This resulted in our losing the tables for a period of time. How the volunteers and the classification officers could keep their cool and not kill some of them, I don't know. Speaking of the classification officers, at Limestone they were required to perform their jobs and they seemed to try hard. Shame on Elmore and Ms. Minniemee.

Many of our classes at Limestone were sponsored and taught by volunteers from Asbury United Methodist Church in Madison, Alabama. I would like to express my deepest appreciation to Jack and the other volunteers from Asbury for the sacrifice that they made. They showed love and concern for people in our situation, when so many other "godly people" only offered lip service at best. Asbury practiced what they preached, unlike so many other pseudo Christians that I know. They weren't just about singing their own praises. They were a breath of fresh air. To them we were not out of sight and out of mind.

Even in the worst of situations, you can find people to show you that you should keep your head up, regardless. In the foxholes of Elmore, I had made two such friendships in Soda and Chad. At Limestone, I met Briskee.

Briskee was an enigma. He was from the wrong side of the

tracks. A 30 something, uneducated black man with a speech impediment, Briskee had a lot of hurdles and could easily have had a chip on his shoulder, yet he stood out. He was kind, courteous, and eager to learn. He quoted the Bible well enough to intimidate a preacher. Most of the inmates in here were overgrown children, punks who rapped all night and wore their pants sagging to their knees. Not Briskee.

Briskee and I became good friends, two men from different worlds. The one thing that we had in common was that we had both spent time in Colbert County jail. I had spent only ten days there; Briskee had spent well over a year.

The story that Briskee told me about his experience with Colbert County and my old friend, Judge Snatcher's court, made me shake my head. Although, Briskee admitted that he had committed crimes as a younger man, he said that the crime that he was serving for was not his, and that he was railroaded by a combination of the judge and his appointed attorney. He said that he was basically forced to take a plea although evidence showed that he was not the perpetrator of the crime. He stated that he was told by his attorney, "Nigger, you will plea, or *WE* will throw the book at you." This statement was from *HIS ATTORNEY*! If his story is true, and with my experiences and in my opinion, he was much more credible than any evidence of credibility that the Colbert County Circuit Court had ever demonstrated to me, this situation is yet more potential evidence of Colbert County's version of perverted justice. You do your research and decide. I'll base my opinions on the actions of someone like Briskee over the actions of those "paid to conjure" any day.

As a disclaimer, many inmates professed their innocence. Briskee, however, acknowledged his wrongs and what he told me in no way would speed up his release. He was already scheduled for release. I'm sure that my repeat of his story will be viewed as hearsay, and rightfully so. I hope that someday some civil rights activist will dig into Briskee's case and substantiate the truth, whatever it turns out to be. I hope none of this evidence has conveniently been misplaced.

Many of the reality shows that make light of divorce in a court situation really upset me, because of the mockery that they make out of marriage. For many people who do take marriage and their vows seriously, divorce is like undergoing an amputation.

Despite my feelings on the sanctity of marriage, I finally realized that what was inevitable, was inevitable. After no real effort to visit me or to show any real signs of care or love, I knew that DJ had turned her attentions elsewhere. Instead of putting things off any further, I wrote to her and told her that I wanted for her to start divorce proceedings.

I was attempting to break a thirty-year spell. Writing the letter took all the courage that I could muster, but I knew that if I didn't, I was just setting myself up for rejection upon release. In reality, I think I hoped that I would get a response begging for me to reconsider. This would not be the case.

One of the things that solidified my decision to write the letter was hearing that DJ and family just happened to be on vacation, at the beach, at the same time as a certain person of interest, whose wife had just died, and whom DJ had a crush on in high school. Upon learning of this coincidence, I remember telling my mother that this situation was not good and that I would now have new competition for DJ. This prophecy wouldn't take long to materialize.

Every day, as I watched Rachel Ray on her cooking show, with her dark complexion, dark hair, and dark eyes, I was reminded of DJ. I hoped from down deep that she would throw me a lifeline and show some sincere affection and a desire to stay together. Instead, she threw me an anchor with no rope.

The day her response letter came, I was shaking as I ripped open the envelope and started reading. In it, DJ stated that she had read my letter over and over and had been distraught over it, but reluctantly she guessed that I was right and she would start proceedings. The words seemed about as fake as a pro wrestling match. I could tell that a divorce was what she had wanted all along, but she had to put on a show for everyone, especially in light of the way that she had abandoned me.

For days after receiving her letter, I lay listlessly in my bunk, the words to Dolly Parton's "I'll Always Love You" floating through my head (maybe it was the Whitney Houston version). Months later, I realized that the song in my head should have been Def Leppard's "When Love and Hate Collide." It would be a while before the fear of the unknown subsided and I realized that there were better things out there for me. But for now, I was still fantasizing that things between us would change and we would work our marriage out some way. However, deep in my heart, I think that I knew that our life together was over and it cut like a knife. DJ had done so much damage to my heart over the years that I swore I would never trust it to anyone else ever again. In retrospect, never make such promises to yourself, for you never know when that one person who will change your perspective is going to walk into your life. Such would be the case for me just a short time later.

Waiting My Turn To Get On The Plane!

"Does anyone remember laughter?"
—Robert Plant, Led Zeppelin

One of my favorite movies of all time was Steven Spielberg's production of Peter Benchley's great novel *Jaws*. In a very memorable scene from the movie, Robert Shaw's character "Quint" is recounting to Brody (Roy Scheider) and Matt (Richard Dreyfuss) about his horrifying ordeals following the sinking of the US battleship *Indianapolis* during the final days of World War II. He relived the events of the 1,196 men who went into the water, of which only 317 survived the sinking, the exposure, and the hordes of man-eating sharks. After four days in the water, the survivors were spotted by a Navy plane and rescued. In the narrative, Quint relayed that he was most afraid while "waiting on his turn to get on the plane." Obviously, he feared that he would come to the brink of rescue only to be snatched from underneath by the jaws of a predator.

In some ways, I could relate to his fear. I had watched so many inmates over the last year come up for release, only to be shot down at the last minute by some complication or "hold" discovered at the last minute. There were butterflies in my stomach, wondering if this scenario would happen to me. From my experiences with the ADOC, I had no faith that the system was run efficiently enough or kept you informed enough to head off any roadblocks. Although a failed businessman myself, from what I had seen of the Alabama corrections system as a whole, I'm not sure that the people in charge could efficiently run a lemonade stand. Fortunately, what I had witnessed so far in my short stay at Limestone, gave me some reason of hope. However, there were still snafus here as well.

One inmate in pre-release, named Robert, had been sent there after being approved for SRP. On the day of his scheduled release, he was notified that the SRP representative had decided, after the fact, that he needed to go through a SAP program (which to my observations were about as effective as trying to potty-train a two-week old Yorkie). This decision was on the whim of a social worker and not court ordered. The program added another eight weeks to his incarceration. Robert's mother was already waiting at the front lobby for him when he was informed of this change of status. My, my, my, how some people get a kick out of playing with other people's lives.

During this time, I tried to get myself in a little better shape physically by walking and working out on the exercise yard or "The Beach" as it was referred to. I exercised as best I could, while fighting the pain from my injuries. As I walked the track with my radio daily, I listened intently, hoping to hear one of my new favorite songs, "Home" by Daughtry. The words inspired me and kept me going. I also watched the progress of the tornado clean-up beyond the prison fences. The bonfires of the burning debris burned throughout my entire stay at LCDC.

As much as I tried to get myself in shape, for every step forward I took two steps back. With the conditions of incarceration and the beatings that I had taken, my back problems, my neck problems, and my vision continued to get worse, even since my escape from Elmore. I went to the nurse's station repeatedly and eventually was referred to the prison hospital to see the camp doctor. In prison your health is always in "guarded condition"—pun intended. The staff's schedule, not your pain, dictates your needs.

The doctor seemed very pleasant when I actually got to see him several days later. Prison healthcare gets in no hurry, but I was glad to get a chance finally to find out just how badly damaged my body was. After I told the doctor about my previous back surgery and about the problems incurred since my incarceration, he said that he was going to order an MRI to see exactly what was going on. I left that day thinking how much better this doctor was than the healthcare joke at Elmore. Two months later I wasn't so sure.

After checking the medical appointments for weeks, I finally put in for and got another appointment with the doctor, just days before my release. I wanted to know if there was something serious going on in my back and neck. After having been informed that DJ had dropped me from her insurance, I knew that I wouldn't be able to afford a trip to the doctor when I got out.

After nearly a three hour wait in the hospital hallway, I was finally called into the examination room. I could immediately sense that the doctor, who had previously been very pleasant, wasn't in the best of moods. I was ignored by both him and the nurse for several minutes. Finally, he asked what I needed today. I explained that I had come back in to check on the MRI that he had ordered.

After glancing at his chart, he snapped, "Administration canceled the MRI. You have only five days left to release. We can't spend $2,000 on you just to treat pain!"

Upset, I replied, "Why didn't they do the MRI two months ago when you first ordered it?"

The doctor stared at me with a look of contempt and arrogance and said, "We don't owe you anything! Of course, with your attitude, I'm sure you'll be back soon anyway!"

Puzzled and irritated, I asked in the calmest tone that I could manage, "What did you say?"

"OUT!" the doctor screamed at me.

After a short pause, I quietly got up and walked out of his office. It took every bit of strength and self-control in me not to knock the arrogant prick's head off. I was too close to going home to mess up now.

I don't know what the reason for the doctor's mood was that day and why he acted to me the way he did. I showed no kind of attitude to warrant his behavior. Later, as I reflected on his behavior, I came to the conclusion that it was nothing that I had done, but just the quality of the physicians employed by the ADOC. Really, why would someone who invested in all those years of medical school, stoop themselves to working in a prison where the work was terrible and the fees probably not so good. Maybe this guy was the medical professions version of a plea jockey. Obviously, he was one of the castoffs of the medical profession who couldn't make it in the real world of professional medicine.

"Hey, Doc! Now that's attitude!"

PART IV: TREADING WATER

Going Home

"If it weren't for my lawyer, I'd still be in prison. It went a lot faster with two people digging."

—Joe Martin

August 14, 2011, 5:30 A.M.—you can imagine the nervousness and the anticipation running through my body as I, along with Cheshire Cat was led to the camp gymnasium to await our release. Although release was supposed to happen at 8:30 A.M., because it was Sunday visitation it would be close to 11 o'clock before the call came. For over five hours I paced, until I was sent for and told to report to exit processing. There I was given the clothes that my family had brought for me to change into and my exit paperwork. While doing the paperwork, I learned from the processing guard that there was some kind of a hold on Cheshire Cat, because of a demerit, and he would not be leaving. Although I wasn't overly fond of Cheshire Cat, I felt sorry for him. I also didn't understand why the ADOC was just now coming to this conclusion. Why wait till he was in the gymnasium waiting to be picked up?

As I reached the Plexiglas exit door, I could see Jessi's beaming smile. My heart leapt out of my chest. We hugged and then quickly made our way to the parking lot where Jenni and my mom waited. After quick hugs and kisses, we hastily made our exit drive from the prison property. Immediately after going through the gate, I broke down and cried. The "Prodigal Son" was going home! "Won't you fly high, Free Bird, yeah!"

Although I had been telling the kids that I wanted a salad bar for my first meal as a free man (it's crazy some of the things that you miss the most and fantasize about while behind bars), I selected Red Lobster for our reunion meal. I love Red Lobster's slaw as much as I do salad bars. You can imagine what it was like to relax and enjoy a meal with my girls and my mom, as we laughed and caught up.

Besides the joy of being reunited with my family, I couldn't wait to get to Mom's house to see my dog, Big Boy. Would he remember me? When I walked into the backyard, he paused for only a second before he leaped on me and almost licked me to death. Whoever coined the phrase "Man's Best Friend" had a canine like Big Boy.

The day after I arrived home, my good friend Rob came to see me. Rob had been great to write, send money to my commissary account, and to check on the girls while I was gone. He informed me that he would put me to work doing odd jobs for his company, and that he had an old car that he would let me use to get around in until I got on my feet. It was great to know that I still had friends like Rob.

The next few weeks would be an emotional roller coaster. Reacclimating myself to the free world, while still being uncertain about the direction of my future, was filled with anxiety. It was so wonderful to experience so many things that I had missed over the previous year: salad bars, real milk, napkins, private showers, personal possession of a remote control, *Jeopardy*, and plain ole' Free Will. It was nice to be able to concentrate and have a say so on even little things like which way the toilet paper roll should go on. I wasn't constantly being told what to do or how to think.

I also had plenty of time to reflect on things associated with my incarceration that I would never miss: 3:30 A.M. chow, the drone and beat of rapping at any hour of the day or night, mystery meat (a.k.a. Chernobyl Meatloaf), the constant smell of body odor, sleeping with spiders, state whites and orange jumpsuits, stainless steel toilets with no seat, having my head shaved, cuffs and leg chains, being ruled by sociopaths, and the knowledge that you were forgotten and written off by so many.

It was a few days before I saw DJ for the first time. She was bringing something by my mom's house and I had to run out and catch her before she drove away. My emotions were running wild. Unless you have lost everything that you have in life you probably don't understand. Could I salvage our family? Did she still love me down deep? Was she willing to start again with me for the sake of the girls? The answer to all these questions was NO. I thought that maybe with time she would reconsider.

Although I still didn't have a grip on what I was going to do for permanent work or the direction my life was taking personally, I wanted to address my conviction and my failures publicly. I drafted a statement to my former customers and a couple of the small local newspapers were kind enough to print it. The letter went as follows:

I have now served the sentence imposed on me by the Colbert County Circuit Court. As I prepare to reenter the workforce, I am eager to start restitution payments to the customers caught up in my collapse.

This list includes the customers who have court ordered restitution, those whom I was found to be innocent of wrongdoing, and those who have shown kindness and patience. I thank the District Attorneys in the surrounding counties who either dismissed or deferred my charges in order to try and allow me to work toward restitution. I am not sure yet as to the speed of payments. I have healed somewhat from my pretrial accident and am capable of taking on more types of job opportunities than before. Keep in mind that with a felony on your record, good employment is hard to find. I will do my best to make this as speedy as possible. However, in order to remain free to do this, my court ordered restitution has to take priority.

If you are a former customer that I failed to fulfill a contract to, please mail your contact information and any documentation to the following address. If you know of someone who was caught up in my company's collapse, please relay this information to them.

Mike Harrison/regarding ArcStone
Russellville, AL

I appreciate your help with this. I apologize for the hardships that my failures have caused. However long it takes, I plan to get this taken care of so that someday I can regain my reputation.

Mike Harrison

I had a moderate response to my letter. Most of my records had been lost for some reason during my incarceration. Nevertheless, I immediately started sending monthly payments, although small, to each who responded to my letter.

During this time, I also wrote letters to the ACLU and to the Equal Justice Initiative about my case and my pending appeal, asking for legal assistance. Unlike the governor's office, I received responses from both agencies. In very polite letters, I was told that although they would love to take my case, they could not take on every single case and that there were more serious and pressing situations that were more demanding of their limited time and resources. However, they did offer me suggestions as to other avenues to pursue. I understood their position. There were other people in more serious situations than mine that really needed their help. I did, however, appreciate their response as well as their consideration and suggestions.

Upon considering the response to my letter to my customers, I decided to make a public plea in an effort to save my marriage of 30 years and the life that I had known. The Franklin County Times was kind enough to print the following statement for me in their paper:

> *Don't Take Your Marriage for Granted—over the last year I have had time to reflect on a lot of the shortcomings in my life. Among those are the mistakes that I've made in my marriage.*
>
> *I discovered some advice given by Stephen R Covey in his book The Seven Habits of Highly Effective People. "A man was complaining that the feeling of love wasn't in his marriage anymore and asked what to do. Covey answered:*

"Then love her. If the feeling isn't there, that's a good reason to love her. My friend, love is a verb. Love—the feeling is a fruit of love, the verb. So love her. Serve her. Sacrifice. Listen to her. Empathize. Appreciate. Affirm her. Are you willing to do that?"

Guys, take my advice. Appreciate what you have. Don't take chances and try to be something that you aren't.

Don't lose your focus and fail, thus embarrassing and disrupting both your families. Give her security and a future to look forward to.

Don't make her a golf widow. Don't throw past mistakes in her face. Don't neglect her, because that is the worst form of abuse.

Don't say things in anger that you don't mean. Realize that she hurts and suffers, too.

Learn from your mistakes. Hold her hand. Make her feel loved. Realize that she is your best friend before you lose the best thing that you ever had.

Mike Harrison
Russellville

I wrote these words because I was facing the great unknown. Whether I had lived a 30-year marriage of love or a 30-year marriage of infatuation and complacency, I don't know. What I do know is that I wasted my time while pouring out my heart publicly. DJ was gone. During the next few days and despite a lot of outpouring from my heart, it was evident that she was too resentful of the position I had put her in. For the next few weeks, I was an emotional wreck, both from self-pity and from watching my girls suffer. And I wasn't even officially divorced yet!

Later, while exchanging emails with a potential employer, I noticed a quote on his letterhead that stated: "Laugh when you can, apologize when you should, and let go of what you can't change. Letting go doesn't mean giving up, it means you're moving on."

Reading those words really hit home with me and slowly started to change my way of looking at things. Although I had initially put brakes on the divorce, because it was so hard to let go of 30 years, I finally decided it was time to move on. DJ and I would never make it.

After the initial feelings of betrayal, I decided to cut ties before my feelings got me into trouble and sent back to prison. I made a final divorce offer to DJ, which she was anxious to accept. She was eager to move on. Our divorce was final on November 1, 2011, less than three months after my release.

Both of my girls urged me to get on with my life. They told me that I should start dating and offered to set me up a profile on some online dating sites. I told them that I didn't need a dating service, that I was still very capable of knowing how to approach a woman. Besides, I was concerned about how I would approach my background on an online site's profile. Also, I used to make fun of some of my friends who had used these services.

Several of my friends offered help and advice to get me back in the world of dating. Some even offered advice on advanced dating. I think that they figured (and rightfully so) that I was suffering from sex depravation. One of my buddies handed me a package one day containing Viagra. "This stuff works great," he said. "It's like a whole new world. You should try it."

"No thanks," I said. "I've never needed it in the past to get there, and I sure as hell don't want to take four hours to get back!"

My time "barhopping" and trying to meet women in that way was short-lived. First of all, I was way out of practice. Secondly, most of the action seemed to happen late, and I was usually toast by 9:30 to 10 o'clock. And finally, my girls seemed to object to the ages of some of my potential conquests.

After a while I relented and let the girls sign me up for an online dating service. Although I'm sure that there are plenty of security measures involved, you can still meet people semi-anonymously that way without having to bear your entire soul from the get-go. At the urging of my daughters, we selected Christian Mingle as the dating service that I would apply to. They seemed to think that I would potentially meet a better class of women there. I think that they were right. The "Christian" label scared many less-than-righteous types away.

To my surprise, I enjoyed the process of online dating. After a while, I proceeded on to the next stage and started going on dates with some of the ladies that I had met on Christian Mingle. A couple of these progressed into multiple dates and I even disclosed the events of my past few years to them. These ladies seemed to be very understanding and sympathetic. Most all the people on these sites have some kind of baggage, whether it is just bitterness from a bad divorce or financial problems. It is, however, a good medium to ease into dating. I really enjoyed the dating and the companionship. However, you do have to be careful, even as a man and even on Christian Mingle. There are dating service "Cyber Stalkers" out there. I had a dose of one myself.

A word of advice to all who do start dating through an online site, women and men alike: Go slow, be thorough, and never put yourself in a dangerous or compromising position. I was eager to disclose the skeletons in my closet as my dating progressed past the initial introductions. However, I can see how easy it could be for someone hiding a malicious intent to prey on eager participants.

Moving on, one day in October I saw a newspaper article stating that an Alabama Correctional Lieutenant had been charged in the beating death of an inmate at one of the State Correctional facilities. The current State Attorney General had made the statement, "Neither the ADOC or this office tolerates the use of excessive force in controlling inmates, and when officers cross the line, they will face the serious consequences of their acts." BULLSHIT! The only reason that this statement was made was because they couldn't hide the fact. Excessive and unnecessary force goes on every day in the ADOC. Real accountability would be pure hell not only for the ADOC but also on the State Attorney General's office. A watchdog organization had to send letters to Federal, State, and local officials before any charges were brought. This is the way Alabama's legal and penal system works.

Every Silver Lining Has It's Cloud

"One tequila, two tequila, three tequila, floor."
—George Carlin

Appeal and Probation: During our pre-release instructions at Limestone, we were instructed to contact our probation officer immediately after arriving home. After several unsuccessful phone attempts to find out who my probation officer was, so that I could comply, I drove to the Colbert County Probation office.

No one there seemed to know who I was assigned to, but ultimately it was decided that I was on unsupervised probation and did not have to report monthly. Wow! The ADOC must have really done the job that Judge Snatcher had intended. The dangerous criminal, who warranted a level 4 prison camp, must now be reformed! All the criminal element must have evaporated out of me. I no longer needed supervision. Of course, I guess that I had no more marketing value left in me. Was this vendetta over?

In 1960, the Chevrolet Corvair was Motor Trend Magazine's "Car of the Year." A few years later, it was dubbed "unsafe at any speed" by consumer protectionist Ralph Nader. In today's safety minded society, I doubt that same Corvair would be a popular choice on the car lot.

At one time, smoking was debonair, trading stamps were the rage, and phone booths were on almost every corner. Also, 8-track tapes were the coolest thing available in the 70s; however, most kids today don't even know what you are talking about when you mention them.

Things come and things go, sometimes because something better comes along or sometimes because the flaws and weaknesses of it are discovered.

As many have said before, on paper the American Justice System appears to be the best thing out there. However, being invented and controlled by humans, it is inherently flawed. When you throw in the county level biases of narcissistic and agenda driven politicians, the system stinks to high heaven. By the time that you follow the system down from the limelight of big-time media and public scrutiny present at the upper levels, to the level of state districts and counties, you sometimes find a system based solely on promoting and protecting itself. Its own rules and interpretations are made based on their value in the next election or the contributions made to the pocketbooks of the politicians or their supporters. Then, as a result, the appeals process is set up to promote failure and to protect the local courts decisions and verdicts.

This self-protection became even more evident as I was exposed to the rules and the process of appeal. The most glaring thing to me that I had never been aware of as a "non-criminal," is that when appealing from a Circuit Court, you were not appealing what you consider an unfair rendering of sentence, but rather the appeal has to show a lack of proper procedure by the court. Basically, if I understand this correctly as it was explained to me, unless this procedural blunder was made, the court is automatically correct in whatever decision was made and in whatever sentence was passed. If no recorded procedural errors are made by the attorneys or the Judge, you are basically screwed.

Later on, I ran across comments made by a popular political blogger stating that lower court decisions are almost always affirmed, whether with merit or not, because of the cost of appeal. I take this fact to mean that, in the eyes of the system, with an investment already made in a conviction, an appeal could affect the net profit. After all, the Corrections System is big business in Alabama.

John Odem recommended to me that I should hire a different attorney for the appellate process so that I could use "ineffective counsel" as a part of the appeal. At first I thought John was just scared that he couldn't get paid. Later, however, I realized that what he said made sense and was in my best interest. Also, over time I saw John go out of his way for me so many times, that I knew his position was not about the money.

As mentioned before, after some discussion, my mom and I had decided to hire Jim Lawless, the attorney who had represented me in Morgan County. He seemed eager and quoted a fair price. I met with Jim a couple of times when I was still at Limestone, in preparation of a possible appeal. As we went over portions of the trial transcript, which I had to purchase from Colbert County, our discussions made me aware of another confusing fact that I had previously been unaware of. The appeals first had to go back through the same court that I was tried and sentenced in—Judge Snatchers Court. Holy Shit, Batman! WTF? This was crazy. Jim acknowledged that there was no way that Judge Snatcher was going to overturn her own court's verdict and take a black eye on her rulings and sentencing procedures. However, it was a formality that we had to go through to get to the next level. Once we got to the intermediate court, he said that he felt like we had a fair chance to get something done. In his research, as well as my own, we had found several precedents that should help get my convictions overturned.

As expected and anticipated, the appeal hearing in Judge Snatcher's court was just a predetermined formality, designed to hinder, frustrate, and postpone matters. If any doubt was ever in play, just like in the trial, the DA had the last chance to impress. Not that it mattered.

My hearing followed some other procedures in which Judge Snatcher seemed very pleasant, smiling, and cutting up with the attorneys. When my case came up, her demeanor instantly changed. She became cold and crude. I remember afterward that my youngest daughter Jessi, who had attended with my mom and some friends, asked me, "Why does the judge dislike you so much? She totally changed her attitude when your name was called. She didn't show that for the other people present for hearings."

I didn't know how to answer her. I didn't know why. I had probably said less than a couple of dozen words to the judge throughout the entire ordeal. With the attitude and demeanor she expressed toward me, you would've thought that I was Charlie Manson or Adolf Hitler. Was this attitude because she considered me a criminal? Hell, she dealt with criminals every day. Was it because some of the "victims" were her friends or supporters? Very possibly. If nothing else, these were voters.

Basically, I think that it comes down to the fact that Judge Snatcher does not like for her kingdom to be challenged. She made a sneering remark that she was aware of the deals that had been worked out in the other courts. I came to the conclusion that when I would not take a plea and bucked her system, I was a marked man. Although this Queen Bee would be a wannabe in a real civilized court or in a board room, she was Lord, God, and Master on her private turf.

After going through the motions routine, I left Jim to proceed with the appeal to the next court. He assured me that he would do his best and would keep me informed of his progress. Do the names Judas Iscariot and Benedict Arnold mean anything to you? I wonder if 40 pieces of silver were laid in front of Jim. Well more on this situation later.

For now, it was time to find a job. Being self-employed for so long, I knew that I would be a little rusty as I started looking for decent employment. I was determined, however, that despite being a convicted felon, I would get past this. If I were diligent, I could do it.

Maybe it would never have come to this if I had originally entered an insanity plea, meaning if the DA really thinks that I am guilty of intentionally doing this, then HE must have been insane! Oh, I forgot, here, intent is whatever the court defines it to be, never mind history, Webster, or even the truth; they don't apply in small town Alabama justice.

Because the court had tagged me as a criminal, no potential employer was likely to take my word that I was mislabeled. Most companies would understand debt; however, a convicted debtor was unacceptable.

The job situation looked bleak. With my back and neck pain becoming even more chronic and the vision in my right eye being a concern, I still could not be too selective in my search. With no insurance, I saw no hope of my physical problems being solved any time soon. I cursed the court and the ADOC every time I gritted my teeth with pain. Despite the huge challenge I had in front of me, I had to persevere! Screw the Court! Screw the ADOC! This country boy will survive!

The Song Remains the Same
The Great Job Hunt

"As a face is reflected in water, so the heart reflects the person"
— Proverbs 27:19 (NCT)

As a Southern middle-class Caucasian hitting adulthood in the 70s, I never imagined what it must have been like for a young black man to have sought an advanced job during that era. Whether by prejudice or perception, many companies were hesitant to place minority candidates in positions of authority or in positions where they made public representation.

Those who criticize the work of Dr. Martin Luther King and his followers should put themselves in the shoes of those who were born without the social advantages that many of us have been blessed with. Those disadvantaged citizens, who have strived to overcome, have hurdled great obstacles to advance in American society. Although the Civil Rights movement has had its share of people who took advantage of it, for personal gain from both without and from within, Dr. King's dream has slowly started coming to fruition.

Although human nature will never allow a perfect world, whether you live in Georgia, Manhattan, Kenya, or South Africa, attention to human rights issues has come a long way. This statement is in no way saying that discrimination doesn't still exist, for many states still lag behind, Alabama included. Here voting districts are still often laid out along racial lines and are designed to influence voting results. Racial prejudice is still prevalent. As a result, the voices and opinions of many citizens are kept in check.

Having grown up on the right side of the tracks, my perceptions of life in my home state have taken a drastic dose of reality since being incarcerated. This change came about because I have been exposed to the injustices that have for so long been dished out on those from the wrong side of the tracks.

Fast forward: Living now in Dunwoody, Georgia, a suburb of Atlanta, is almost like living in a different world. Dunwoody is a wonderful place. Here you see all races living equally, both in the corporate world and in after-hours suburbia. Sure, there are areas of Atlanta that are still divided along racial lines, but the opportunity to succeed is here. Although this view may not be shared by many in "the movement" who like to keep their positions and power by continuing to magnify themselves, all you need to do is to look around.

As it pertains to employment in Atlanta, a minority applicant sometimes has advantages over a white male. Affirmative action has almost gone too far in some cases, and now discriminates against the majority applicant. Major obstacles still abound, but where a man is willing to work hard to elevate himself, he can, regardless of his race. There are scores of minority Americans who have risen from the ashes to become great and prominent citizens. Hey! Our last President is black! Maybe we have overcome!

The same cannot be said for a convicted felon, especially in Alabama. There is no Dr. King battling for our opportunities. There is no real movement to speak of to help us find real employment. Sure, upon release you are issued a couple of meaningless certificates that are supposed to aid you. Also, there are state programs to help find menial work for re-entry. But my experience is that these programs are just government-funded scams to pad pockets of those not in need.

Checking the felon box on an employment application is an almost guarantee not to get an advanced position. Sure, most applications say that is not automatic rejection, but if you believe that then you probably also believe in tooth fairies and the Easter Bunny. I'm not saying that a conviction should be hidden, but in my case, I have to check the same felon box as a paroled rapist or child molester. Basically, it is just one more weapon of the court to ensure that you won't get into a position to come back at them. The state had, in my opinion, been guilty of identity theft; it took my identity and replaced it with one that hindered any chance of being a threat to them.

I had a mountain of debt and restitution in front of me. As I looked high and far for an opportunity for an income, so I could begin repaying my debts, I ran into hurdle after hurdle. With my experience and my gift of gab, I give a pretty good interview. On countless occasions I was told that I was overqualified. Other times, employers were eager to hire me until they found out that I had a felony. On three different occasions, I was told that I *had the job* after my first interviews, despite the felony, if they could get approval from their superiors. On two of these occasions I was rejected by Human Resources, and on the third I was informed that being a felon, I could not be issued a state license to sell insurance. Would I be regulated for the rest of my life to careers that required memorizing phrases like, "Would you like to supersize that?" or "Good morning, welcome to Wal-Mart!" By the way, do McDonalds and Wal-Mart hire felons for management or clerk positions?

Having no luck around home and having weathered a lot of bad, one-sided gossip, I came to the conclusion that I needed to get away. I needed to leave Alabama to try to give myself a shot at recovery. It would be tough leaving my home, but everything was just stacked against me there. I expanded my job search. To my surprise, I was soon contacted, interviewed, and offered a job in Atlanta. I have to mention that there was no felon box on the application. I was moving to the Peach State. The devil was going down to Georgia!

Ramblings

"There is no greater agony than bearing an untold story inside you."

—Maya Angelou

Hometown U.S.A.: Wanting to build a better life for his family, an aspiring farmer decided to pursue his career in a raw and newly populated territory. He purchased property from the local land company and started working the soil. He was successful from the start. As the years passed, his success continued and there was more and more demand for his crops from the local towns. Being the primary local source, he decided that he had to expand his production or other farmers would move in and take away some of his customers. He mortgaged his land to buy more property and seed. At the same time, others seeing his success did move in to compete with him, causing him to have to lower his prices. Having more expenses now and fighting to maintain enough business to offset them, he looked for other ways to supplement his business. Many people in the local towns urged him to raise cattle and sell beef to them since they had no property to do so. He agreed, but with the property mortgaged, he couldn't borrow any more money from the bank to buy the cattle, so he took deposits from his customers to purchase the young cows so that he could fatten them for beef. He bought enough cattle to fill his initial orders and for additional seed needed for feed. As these cattle were ready for slaughter, he would turn over the balances due into cattle and seed for the next orders due. This process worked well for years. He called this "cash flow."

Then one day, out of the blue, a famine hit his territory. Much of his crop withered away. Potential customers for his new beef venture were scared by the famine and moved away. As the cattle on the next wave of his existing orders were processed, he had no new money coming in from either new cattle sales or from his famine ravaged crops, to buy new stock. When he couldn't fill all his existing beef orders, the townspeople who had invested deposits and not yet received their beef were furious with him. Some of them contacted the local magistrate, accusing the farmer of running a scam. Instead of giving the farmer the necessary time to formulate and exercise a plan to reimburse the customers, and despite the famine, the magistrate saw an opportunity to please some of his influential constituents and arrested the farmer.

All the accusations against the farmer were put in the territorial newspaper and his reputation was ruined. He was stereotyped as a criminal because he owed a lot of money and the creditors wanted to place blame. This attitude persisted despite the fact that, due to the drought, farmers and other business people were failing all over the land.

As a result of the publicity, the farmer couldn't get anyone to give him a fair liquidation price for his tools or equipment, all of them look-

ing for a bargain-basement price from a desperate man. Even with some equity in his land, he was unable to sell it.

Because he couldn't immediately pay his debts, he was convicted and sent to Debtor's Prison. The bank repossessed his land and his wife left him looking for a more stable life with someone that would have a regular paycheck and who wouldn't embarrass her like he had, by ruining his name.

Debtor's prison was abolished in England in 1869. In the US, debtor's prisons were eliminated federally in 1833, leaving the practice up to the states. I lived in a debtor's prison from August 2010 till August 2011. They can call it what they want to, theft of property, theft by deception, whatever. Theft constitutes intent. I had no intentions of failure or from depriving anyone of anything. I was trying to survive a famine!

Before I go further, let me make some more disclaimers. I am a bitter man. As I have stated, in prison I have learned many emotions that I had never experienced before: bitterness, hate, self-pity, etc. In our pre-release classes at Limestone, we were urged to fight these emotions. I fight them every day. Nevertheless, every day that I was incarcerated, I got a little more bitter. I pray that I will eventually overcome this.

Let me also say, I'm responsible for setting the wheels in motion. My failures as a businessman, staring into the face of a storm, caused my eventual downfall. My oversights and my failure to practice safe and sure business decisions, plus my level of stress during the economic collapse, sealed my doom. I let down my customers, my employees, my family, and myself. Once my ship had sunk, the sharks smelled blood in the water and attacked. I was wounded and helpless during the feeding frenzy that followed. However, let me also say, despite the facetious statement that I made earlier in this book: I AM NOT A CRIMINAL!

Imagine you are traveling to a ballgame. A friend asks if you can give his child a ride to the game because he has a conflict, and you agree. You are driving down the road on the way to the game, casually glancing around, when a big rig truck meeting you swerves into your lane. You immediately yank the steering wheel to avoid a collision. But say you overcompensate your maneuver, your tires are worn and do not grip well, and you lose control of the car, hitting a tree on the side of the road. Your friend's child is killed. You are frantic and don't know what to do. You are in shock but you must call your friend to make him aware of what has happened. What can you do? Your life has changed in an instant.

Although this is a horrible scenario to use as an example, answer this:

1. Even though the truck presented itself as a potential obstacle for you, did your poor maneuvers and worn tires ultimately contribute to the injury to the child—YES!
2. Does this fact make you a murderer?—NO!

First Blood

"If the system turns away from the abuses inflicted on the guilty, then who can be next but the innocents?"
— Michael Connelly, *The Concrete Blonde*

Growing up, I loved detective movies and TV cop shows. As a kid, I played at being Steve McGarrett, Frank Bullitt, Hutch, Dirty Harry, or a member of the *Mod Squad*. On other occasions, I was Lewis Erskine of *The FBI* (Efrem Zimbalist Jr.'s character) or Steve Keller from *The Streets of San Francisco* (played by Michael Douglas). I also sometimes imagined that I was a real-life cop like Frank Serpico or Buford Pusser.

Over the years, I followed such screen characters as Colombo, Cagney and Lacey, Virgil Tibbs, Sonny Crockett, Clarice Starling, and Raylan Givens (Timothy Olyphant's role on *Justified*). My love of books made me a regular follower of Alex Cross, Harry Bosch, Jack Reacher, Lindsay Boxer, and my all-time favorite, Dave Robicheaux.

I no longer have dreams or aspirations of being a cop. Today, my favorite movie is *The Fugitive*. If you had lived through my experiences, you would understand why!

I had never imagined being on the opposite side of the fence and what it would be like. Sure, I had seen *Cool Hand Luke*, *Brubaker*, *Escape from Alcatraz*, and *The Shawshank Redemption*, but those were just movies. That was Hollywood! It wasn't real to me. I would never have to go through anything like what those characters endured!

Now that I have gone through jail and prison time, I don't like what I see—on either side of the fence. I hate the criminal element in our country, as well as the criminal presence in my home state. But you know what? I've discovered that sometimes criminals hide behind gavels, robes, ties, and badges. Some of these people mock the very civil liberties that they are sworn to defend.

I grew up a big believer in the importance of the justice system and the punishment of criminals. I still am. I have seen first-hand how bad our criminal element is. However, our legal system, at least in Alabama, has been prostituted by self-serving, callous bureaucrats who think that they are above the very constitution that they are supposedly defending. The laws are structured and perverted to allow those with wealth or power, and their lawyers, to dictate what is right and what is wrong. The very people who send citizens to prison do not always follow constitutional procedure or provide humane discipline to those in their charge. However, they, as justice providers and implementers of punishment, claim immunity to the same levels of accountability.

Although I'm now living in the free world, I have been instilled with a sense of uneasiness and a total lack of respect for cops. I know that I'm guilty of stereotyping, just like I was stereotyped as a Bernie Madoff type, however it's difficult not to view the law enforcement community in this manner after what I have witnessed.

My best friend growing up went into law enforcement. I still consider him a great friend. I know numerous others in the profession whom I consider fine people. I know that there are also a lot of good people working in the corrections systems. Many brave men and women have sacrificed their lives to promote goodness in law and order enforcement. However, the police and the corrections systems today, particularly in Alabama, have been so infiltrated with bad elements and as a result have become so rotten that they now seem to attract mostly the gung-ho types. A grand and honorable profession has now been prostituted by egos and ignorance.

Every time that I watch TV and see one of these I.C.E. (Inflated Cop Ego) programs, as I refer to them, I become incensed. Guns and egos do not mix! Hey, maybe that would make a good name for a band at the police ball — Guns & Egos. Who knows, maybe there is already one called that.

I am more scared of cops with egos than I am of criminals. Instead of being humble and professional, they want everyone to see how important and tough they are. These gung-ho, bad-ass cops are, in many cases, sociopathic and narcissistic.

For those honest and upstanding peacekeepers out there, I apologize for my stance. However, if you condone many of the things that I have witnessed that exist within the realm of your profession, then you are just as guilty for looking the other way as those are that perpetrated the atrocities or contributed in the negligence.

This is not to say that any of the actual guilty parties are going to own up to their crimes or shortcomings. Even if they know that they have been a party to inappropriate behavior, they will probably see the guilty parties as being someone else. That is what sociopaths and narcissist do. With due respect to all the good policemen and policewomen out there, this attitude of authoritative entitlement and immunity is what has made me a crusader against the current corrupt state of the justice system.

Many people were appalled at the ineptness of the Aruban police during the Natalee Holloway case. Trust me, you don't have to look to the Caribbean to see ignorance and corruption in law enforcement. Just look at the state that Natalie and I both called home.

Maybe if these jobs paid more than just a chance to be in authority and required more real education than a multiple-choice psyche test, we would have a better overall class of law enforcement. It's bad when the picked-on, attention starved kids in high school and the dumb hot-headed jocks who can't get a real job wind up as police officers. Those of you who fit this definition know who I'm talking about. Of course, I am sure it is not you. Narcissism never admits guilt. Once again, to those of you who do not fit this description, I apologize if I am offending you.

After my ordeal, I could have chosen to have become an isolationist and a radicalized conscientious objector to our government. I could have moved to a remote part of Montana and yelled my objections at the moon. Instead, I choose to express my feelings and observations in words and in print.

I hope that my words and my willingness to defend them will enhance my credibility and shed light on the judicial travesties going on within our borders. I also hope that these words will hit the guilty parties below the belt and force them into accountability.

If you were to witness many of the police that I have seen in my travels, you would think that you were watching a right-wing militia group. Hell, I think that many of them have aspirations of being some kind of gun-toting vigilantes. I witnessed and experienced, first hand, enough unprovoked verbal and physical abuses of power to destroy my once held respect for the profession. When did law officers become para-military enforcers, instead of peacekeepers, anyway?

The words "Sworn to Serve" emblazoned on many patrol cruisers should instead read "I'm da man" because of the character and disposition of its occupants. News Flash—just talking trash and strutting around beating your chest does not make you tough. Most guys who have to proclaim their toughness will usually shit in their pants when confronted with a real and non-restrained opponent. What happened to the polite and professional TV cops of my youth?

I've watched the TV SWAT competitions with the participants walking around with their elbows stuck out like gunslingers and I've seen them brag about how tough they are. They make me want to throw up. A lot of these guys couldn't fight their way out of a wet paper bag—if it fought back. However, you let them spot a pedestrian texting and driving, and they become Supercop! They love to demonstrate their authority, while they enforce the law.

Sure, there are some tough, sincere and professional policemen out there, but for every one of these, there are probably several "Billy-bad-ass" types. Many of these are guys hired straight out of high school because they liked guns and becoming a cop seemed cool to them. I'll bet that some of them would fit the following criteria: Age > I.Q. But put a badge on them and they automatically qualify to be granted authority. Intelligence, mental competence, and character take a backseat to the badge. That is not to mention that they provide cheap enforcement labor for the court system.

Would it not make sense to require the hiring of our policemen to come from our military? I'm not referring to just Weekend Warriors, but rather to combat tested troops or at least full-time service veterans with substantial experience in keeping order and carrying firearms. At least in this situation we would have better trained and seasoned individuals who have been exposed to the real world of right and wrong. Also, it would provide another screening of the mental and physical makeup of the applicant, as well as provide employment for soldiers after their service. Sure, there are examples of soldiers who go off the deep end, but they are at least usually held accountable for their actions, unlike many small-town cops and corrections officers. The cops and COs with military experience that I experienced during my incarceration generally had a more grounded and professional approach to their jobs.

I will also bet you that if in Alabama "Piss Tests" were given (to detect the presence of drugs) as a measure of accountability, BY A THIRD PARTY, a large percentage of the policeman would fail. I remember one time, years ago, that a friend invited me to go on a deep-sea fishing trip with a group of local policeman. They picked me up at my home and I was surprised to find that they were all drinking beer in the van. Also, as soon as we got to the vacation condo, out came a bag of pot.

My travels within the legal system have left me with a bad taste in my mouth. I feel like I am always "on the lam." When the local police park across the street from my office, watching for speeders, I am on pins and needles. Are they watching me? Will they be walking through my office door? I have developed such a distrust for cops that I quickly hang up on phone callers soliciting funds for the Fraternal Order of Police, something that I used to contribute to regularly.

Just like surgeons are schooled to save lives, gung-ho, ego-driven investigators (as well as many of the image conscious prosecutors pulling their strings) are schooled in the art of destroying lives. Then when their theories are proven wrong, they fight tooth and toenail denying it. You don't believe me? Just watch random episodes of 20/20, Nightline, or American Justice and form your own opinion.

Correctional officers are just another brand of police. A while back I heard a radio ad advertising the glamorous position of CO. Bullshit! They need to put another ad to hire criminals to protect people from many of these guys. Growing up, I watched videos of the Holocaust. I couldn't imagine how the Nazis could be so cruel and inhumane. I don't understand how any human could become inhumane. Once I experienced some of the COs in the Alabama Department of Corrections, I still couldn't explain this question. However, I did come to understand that cruelty was a trait present in many humans, even today. Although they try to hide their atrocities, the ADOC is guilty of crimes against humanity. Even if they're not guilty of gassing millions of people to death, they are guilty of treating thousands of inmates inhumanely. How long will it be before the state decides that gas is a good option?

If the ADOC were governed by the NCAA, they would be cited for lack of institutional control. Maybe the State of Alabama should defer control of the ADOC to the NCAA. Maybe then, someone would do something about it.

Television is a false impression of what much of law enforcement has become today. Sure, there are real professionals out there who carry their job with dignity like the folks on Bluebloods, NYPD Blue, CSI, and Criminal Minds. However, there is a large percentage of the law-enforcement profession who exhibit none of the traits of dignity.

One of my favorite authors is James Lee Burke. In his book *Creole Belle*, he stated, *"People wonder how injustice is so often denied to those who need and deserve it most. It's not a mystery. The reason we watch contrived television dramas about law enforcement is that often the real story is so depressing, nobody would believe it."*

I apologize, yet again, to those good law enforcement officers whom I offend. I do not, however, apologize to those parasites who have invaded a once proud and honorable profession. It was not me who created this disrespect, but rather those who have prostituted what the badge once stood for. A callous and arrogant small town cop is no better than a big-town cop who is on the mob's payroll. I once had a great respect for the law enforcement profession overall, but no more! As Rambo would say, *"You drew first blood!"*

Law School Fodder

"They like to get you in a compromising position,
They like to get you there and smile in your face,
They think they're so cute when they got you in that condition,
Well I think it's a total disgrace."
—John Mellencamp, "Authority Song"

Criminals can wear many different disguises. Many times, they wear a suit and tie. Many times, a criminal is strictly a liar that disrupts others' lives for his/her own benefit. Think about it hard. This is the definition of lawyers and politicians. Granted, all lawyers and politicians are not liars and crooks. I have several friends and acquaintances in these professions, and some of them are fine people. You notice that I said some.

The requirements of the legal trade make it hard for a lawyer to be ethical. They are given lots of slack in their approach to morals, and the temptations of money and power are great. The term "lawyering up" should be considered a synonym for "contracting leprosy."

If a defendant or a witness in a criminal case were to try to mislead the court and the jury, he would be in grave peril of recourse. With lawyers, it is common practice, without consequences. In the movie *A Civil Action*, the lawyer portrayed by Robert Duval states, "If you fall asleep in court, the first words you speak when you wake-up should be 'Objection, Your Honor.'" Ditto to that one.

Lawyers and politicians are generally professional liars. They are the masters of smokescreens and manipulations. It is nothing for a lawyer to spin a far-fetched theory and present it as fact to a jury. It seems that law schools must concentrate more on theater and less on pragmatic legal courses. They seem to consider these theatrics an integral part of their profession. They use quick-bite media sensationalism. Their job is to work you between a rock and a hard place.

Prosecutors perform these dramatized hypothesis and lies with no recourse. With their immunity, they have nothing to fear. Lies, speculations, and character assassinations are the tools of their trade. If lawyers' noses grew every time they lied, like Pinocchio, it would be very difficult to maneuver around a courtroom. In another line by Robert Duval's character in *A Civil Action*, he says, "The truth—I thought we were talking about a court of law—come on, you've been around long enough to know that a court is no place to look for the truth. You'll be lucky to find anything here that in any way resembles the truth."

The public seems to accept this fact. Lawyers lie, politicians lie, and we grin and bear it. They never seem to have severe ramifications brought against them, other than some bad publicity and an occasional election lost. For example, Richard Nixon, Anthony Weiner, John Edwards, the list goes on and on. And let's not forget, "I did not have sexual relations with that woman."

It's almost easier to believe headlines in the National Enquirer than most lawyers when they have an agenda. If lying were considered a crime for lawyers, to the extent that it is for perjurers on the witness stand, the legal system could really clean up crime by locking them up. Instead of a Hippocratic Oath like doctors take, I believe attorneys and politicians must take a Hypocritical Oath. Marines utter the phrase "Semper Fi" or "always faithful." If most lawyers or politicians uttered this phrase, even if they were formerly a Marine, they should have their tongues cut out for lying.

A good ole boy district attorney should never lose a case. They have all the cards. They are like crooked dealers in a casino with the house (the judge) covering their back. They get the first and the last punch. The DA, when backed up by a corrupt or system loyal judge, can interpret the law as they see fit. Many times, a person's stature and position in society decides whether something that they are accused of is a crime or not. Constitutionality doesn't mean anything. Reasonable doubt is abused. Their theories and speculations are presented as facts. Many of the things that they prosecute pale in comparison to their own vices. However, they look at their own vices just as they would "smoking in the boy's room."

If you don't think that most small-town prosecutors and judges don't take care of each other, could I interest you in a buy one, get two free deal on some men's suits? The smoke and mirrors of good old boy justice is very similar to a lot of the ridiculous lies in modern marketing practices.

Of course, money talks. The right dollar figure can buy you anything in a courtroom. I wish that I could've afforded F. Lee

Bailey, Robert Shapiro, Johnny Cochran, or even My Cousin Vinnie!

Have you ever wondered how much sense it makes to publicly elect a judge or a district attorney? What qualifications does the general public have to determine who is capable and who is not for these positions? It's kind of like the way high school cheerleaders were elected in the old days. It's strictly a popularity contest or who can outspend and out publicize the other. High school cheerleader elections have advanced into a more modern and intelligent world. They are selected by competition and upon their merits. Not so for Alabama's county judges and district attorneys.

The former Alabama Supreme Court Justice, Sue Bell Cobb, had problems with the way Alabama's judges were elected. She voiced this prior to her resignation, however, her views didn't seem to be very popular in political circles in Montgomery.

In John Grisham's novel *Gray Mountain*, popular election of judges is referred to as an abomination, implying that elected judges are highly susceptible to influence by big money campaign contributions from corrupt organizations and lobbyist. I realize that this novel, as well as some of the other books and movies that I have referred to, are fiction. However, many of the events described in these works parallel actual happenings. Also, many non-fiction works describing the fallacies of small town courtrooms are referred to and are available, as well.

In the world of nature, science, and politics there is good, and there is bad. There are good rats and bad rats, good snakes and bad snakes, and there are also good lawyers and bad lawyers. However, what determines whether a lawyer is good? Is it character, truthfulness, dedication, or honesty? There are some lawyers, prosecutors included, whom I have met in my trials who exhibit some, if not all, of these traits. However, in many corrupt, southern county courts, if you are looking for an honest and ethical prosecutor or judge for that matter, you just might have a better chance of finding Bigfoot.

In a rural community, its uncanny how dirty lawyers and politicians think that they don't sometimes have common acquaintances with those that they prosecute. Do they not think that sometimes, mutual acquaintances have one drink too many and get very chatty and loose lipped? Based on things I've heard, I've wondered sometimes what the curriculum was like at the Good Old Boy School of Corrupt Law. Maybe these were some of the courses offered:

- Jury Manipulation 101
- Misdirection of Facts 220
- Procedural Methods of Character Assassination
- How to Present Hypothesis as a Fact
- Turning Political Correctness into Social Popularity
- Dismissing DUIs for Family and Friends
- Hiding Personal Vices from Your Public
- Acceptable Racism in the Courtroom
- She Don't Lie, She Don't Lie, She Don't Lie! (Cocaine as a Courtroom Tool)

Many trials in small-town America are no different than the Salem witch trials. Innocence or guilt is not a real factor. The big issues are, win at all cost and protect the system. There were times when I felt like I was being thrown into a pond to determine my guilt or innocence, just like in the witch trials. If I had floated, I was guilty. If I sank and drowned, then just maybe I was innocent. But so what, the Judge and the DA were immune. They didn't have to answer for anything if they are wrong. Who came up with this idea of immunity for judges and prosecutors anyway?

In a very famous Alabama murder case, a set of twin sisters were tried for the death of one sister's husband, who was a doctor. One twin was found guilty and the other innocent, although basically the same evidence was presented against both. Ironically, the sister found guilty had notoriety as being promiscuous, while the sister found innocent regularly attended church. A former state assistant attorney general following this case referred to the jury process as an imperfect science. He compared it to a baseball umpire calling balls and strikes, sometimes, the strike zone moves around.

In many trials, there are questions as to why the burden is even put on the juries. If there is no evidence of guilt, is it not the judge's responsibility to dismiss the charges? I asked the same question about my trial. Believe it or not, there are judges out there, even in Alabama, who take this question of evidence seriously.

In a nationally publicized trial about an Alabama man accused of killing his newlywed wife on their honeymoon while diving on the Great Barrier Reef, the judge dismissed the case before the defense even called a single witness. He stated that the prosecution had shown no proof of guilt and had based its entire case strictly on speculation by another diver. The funny thing was that the Alabama Attorney General, the boss of all the county DAs, had taken the case personally for the publicity. He was furious when the case was thrown out and ridiculed the judge in the media. Was this court not the same system that had put him in his position? It wasn't fun to him when the cards didn't go his way. He was used to having a stacked deck. He didn't like the fact that the judge played by the rules. Kudos to the judge.

If you want to get an idea of how the Alabama judicial system generally works, Google and watch an episode of *48 Hours* entitled *Lies and Whispers*. This show documents the decade-long case of Daniel Wade Moore, a young man convicted of murdering a doctor's wife and subsequently sentenced to death. He was later released because it was discovered that the state assistant attorney general had withheld evidence that could have potentially exonerated him. The judge refused to allow him to be retried, citing double jeopardy. The state, however somehow, overruled the judge and tried him again. This time the jury became hung and a mistrial was declared. Just prior to Moore's third trial, more withheld evidence became public. The third jury found Moore innocent.

The assistant state attorney general ridiculed the jury publicly. The jury's response was, "They selected us!" They also stated that there was no evidence to show that Mr. Moore had committed the crime and that lack of evidence had cast their suspicions elsewhere.

Judge Thompson, the judge in the Daniel Wade Moore case who had thrown out the first conviction, was also the judge in one of the county cases where my charges were dismissed. He stated on the 48 Hours television program, concerning the Moore case, that it wasn't justice to the victim to put an innocent man in jail.

He took that stand with the knowledge that he himself might be facing political suicide by doing the right thing.

If every judge in Alabama did his or her job the way Judge Thompson did in the diving case, true justice would be more likely to occur. If all judges took their responsibility to the law seriously, Alabama would have a better system. Instead, and in too many cases, they give credence to the good old boy stereotype, by which other parts of the country view us. However, where there is light, there is hope. Maybe if scrutinized, more of these court jesters would view their jobs in a more professional and ethical manner. Maybe right and wrong would have more meaning instead of scores, publicity, and favors. Maybe it is our job as citizens, churches, and potential victims to make sure that this accountability takes place.

Speaking of lawyers and accountability, after my initial mock-appeal hearing, when I tried to contact my appeals attorney, Jim Lawless, I found that he had changed firms. After an exhaustive few weeks of trying to track him down and countless unanswered messages to see where my second level appeal stood, I finally reached him by phone. He stuttered around and apologized for being difficult to get in touch with, told me that he would pull my file, and call me right back to give me an update. I know lawyers are generally slow to return calls (they are the anointed and their time is so much more important than that of the rest of us), but I am still waiting on that phone call from Jim.

Obviously, Jim failed to file for the next level or had some reason for skipping out on me. Maybe it was because the other cases which he was suddenly working in Colbert County didn't give him time to work on my appeal. It's not like my mom hadn't been paying him. Was this an ethical way of doing things, abandoning my case without even notifying me, or was it grounds for disbarment? Maybe it's just the way the system works in Alabama county justice. In the military, it would be called treason.

Needless to say, I have had a bad taste left in my mouth from some of the courtroom jesters that I have had to deal with. Maybe James Oglethorpe had the right idea when he founded the Colony of Georgia as an alternative to the overcrowded debtor's prisons of 1700s England. Lawyers were prohibited. According to Oglethorpe, Georgia was to be "free from that pest and scourge of mankind called lawyers." Oglethorpe and the trustees detested them, believing each colonist was capable of pleading his own case. Maybe it's no coincidence that a certain debtor and Criminal (me) ended up in Georgia.

PART V:
BACK FROM THE DEAD

A Commentary from Monte Cristo

"Yes; and remember that two legged tigers and crocodiles are more dangerous than the others."
—Alexandre Dumas, *The Count of Monte Cristo*

The legal and judicial dogma recites a list of slogans that include sworn to serve, reasonable doubt, circumstantial evidence, tried in a court of law, and convicted by a jury of your peers. I'm sure that each of these platitudes was initially uttered with conviction and with sincere intent. However, in many courtrooms today, small town and big town alike, the meanings have been twisted and reinterpreted to benefit investigators and prosecutors. With their own interpretations and if the judge does not hold the Constitution in high regards, the prosecuting officials can have their way. In many cases, there is no justification to the direction that judges can take a courtroom. They can throw favor in whatever direction they fancy. I don't think that this liberty was the idea that our forefathers intended, but when you have a state that elects judges in a popularity vote, sometimes this is what you get.

As mentioned, former Alabama Chief Justice Sue Bell Cobb,

prior to her resignation, stated her displeasure with the way Alabama judges were elected. She also unsuccessfully pushed for reform within the Alabama Department of Corrections in order to reduce overcrowding. Although in her resignation statement she cited "family reasons," for why she was leaving office, I wonder how much was due to the State's resistance to reform.

Speaking of the ADOC, which is a very rotten element in Alabama's assortment of alphabet soups, it seems to be run with no rhyme or reason. Sure, you can say it is a correctional system or even a punishment system, and you would be correct in theory, but this is not the point I'm making. I'm talking about the inept way in which this department is run. From a business standpoint, it is mismanaged to a point of disbelief. Take this from an expert in mismanagement and business failure. Who is running this show? Are they not accountable? Maybe they should be prosecuted for squandering Alabama's citizen's tax deposits!

In addition to the state tax money allocated for the ADOC, according to an article in AL.com dated December 19, 2010, Alabama prisons were the single biggest recipient of Alabama's educational stimulus dollars from the US government. Yes, I said "education stimulus dollars." According to the article, the ADOC received $118 million of $1.1 billion in stimulus funding given to the state by the US Department of Education since 2009. The money supposedly covered health care cost for the 26,000 inmates and salaries and benefits for the 4,200 employees for a 3 ½ month period, according to officials. That's $4,500 in education stimulus per prisoner, roughly 4 times the amount per student in kindergarten through 12th grade. Take it from someone who has been inside, nowhere near this kind of money is spent for the education or medical treatment for Alabama's prisoners. This claim is a farce! Whose pockets are these funds going in? Besides, 4,200 employees for 26,000 inmates, that's one employee for every 6.2 inmates. What are all the fences and bars for?

Altogether, according to the article, Alabama has received more than $3 billion in federal stimulus funds for education, public works, and other purposes, yet every time you talk to local public officials, including my hometown tax assessor, they talk about how the state is broke. Why is this? Our state has plenty of resources. Could it be because too many Good Ole Boys have their hands out? I might be opening a can of worms or even Pandora's Box with this assertion, but so be it. Heaven forbid that someone question them or threaten their Federal Cash Cow.

Yours Truly,

"The Count"

I Know You're Out There Somewhere

"The mist is lifting slowly, I can see the way ahead, and I've left behind the empty streets that once inspired my life."
—The Moody Blues, *"I Know You're Out There Somewhere"*

This world is full of givers and takers. This fact is true, not only in politics and business, but also in personal relationships. The sad fact is that the percentage of takers far exceeds the percentage of givers. These expectations are reflected by the high number of marriages and relationships that end in divorce and separation.

Whichever of these titles that I would label myself, from a material standpoint I had nothing left to offer a companion. All I had left was my mind, my heart, and my soul. Any woman that would become seriously interested in me would be inheriting a ton of baggage. Although my incarceration was behind me, the hurdles set in front of me by the system were formidable. The judicial system wants to keep you down to ensure that you are no future risk to them.

As I have said repeatedly, I started the train rolling on my situation by not handling my affairs correctly. I will live with this burden for the rest of my life. By theorizing my intent and incarcerating me, the State of Alabama effectively eliminated any reasonable chance of recovery on my part. Granted, because of uncontrolled growth and later economic upheaval, I was in debt, delinquent on taxes, and searching for answers at the time of my business closing. However, incarceration, being labeled a felon, and placing garnishments and levies on any menial wages that I could earn, did not hasten any restitution and basically insured a prolonged punishment, of which there was no end in sight.

The system doesn't regard any obstacle they put in front of you. Never mind that you were locked away. Never mind the difficulties that they put on you in finding respectable work. You can't even have a checking account to buy a modest amount of groceries, without fear that it will be taken away without notice. Was a year of my life not worth some kind of credit?

Although I was dating, my budget really didn't allow for it. At the time, I viewed this as a sort of rebellion against the system. The system wanted to make sure that I couldn't enjoy life or try to better my situation. Those who incarcerated me wanted me to be like many ex-cons and start drinking or drugging and contribute more to the business that is their system. They certainly don't envision you returning to normal society.

Nevertheless, even after my move to Georgia, I conversed and occasionally went on dates with a handful of women. Many of these were one-and-outs, but a few evolved into more than one date. I made a point, if I went out with a woman more than two or three times, to tell her about my background. This honesty had mixed results. Although I maintained cordial friendships with all these ladies, the thought of dating a convicted felon seemed to dampen what usually started out as excitement in their approach to me. I had anticipated this reaction and accepted it as the way my social life was going to be. It was what it was. I resigned myself to the fact that it might be a very long time before I ever had another really serious relationship with a woman. Boy, was I wrong!

On January 1, 2012, only months after my release and my divorce, I met a lady at a restaurant for our first actual date. Although we had been talking for a short while on the phone, New Year's Day was the first time that I laid eyes on Diane. Wow, the moment that I saw her get out of her van and walk toward me, I was smitten. Something in the way she walked and carried herself just expressed confidence. On top of that, she was beautiful!

The date was a hit. Our conversations went so smoothly. We were so alike, yet at the same time, so different in many ways. We were both instantly at ease with each other. Here was a woman who could talk current affairs, politics, religion, and even football. Turns out, she was originally from Tennessee and grew up following the Volunteers, one of Alabama's most bitter football rivals.

We kind of let time get away with us that day at Pappadeaux's. After I left to go back to my room, which was an extended stay hotel room, that I referred to as "the Closet" (I had to be careful with that one), I was on cloud nine. I really liked this woman. Then, as always, the cloud came over me and I wondered, "Would she understand when I told her all about me?"

I enjoyed my date with Diane so much that I called her the next day and asked her if she would go to Smith's Old Bar with me later that week to watch the Alabama Crimson Tide play for the National Championship. She accepted quickly. What a blast we had as Alabama rolled to another championship.

Diane and I went on several more dates and I met her kids over the next couple of weeks. I had not anticipated being this crazy about a woman so soon. Di seemed to be as interested in me as I was in her. She knew that I was recently divorced (she had been divorced for almost two years at the time) and that I was living out of a room near where I worked. I dreaded telling her about my time in prison. How would she react? Although Di was the sweetest and seemingly the most understanding person that I had ever met, this revelation would be a big pill to take.

Finally, one night I just did it. I told her that I had something very important to tell her and over dinner I spilled my guts. Although my story seemed to shock her, she didn't get up and run away. Instead, she seemed sympathetic and consoling. I told her to research my case, that I didn't want her to base her opinions strictly on my words. She told me that she would, but to not worry, that she understood that bad things sometimes happen to good people.

Di did her research. It really surprised me how much was available on the Internet about my case. She read many of the forums, even in the Birmingham media, with people who didn't even know me expressing outrage for what I was convicted of. Diane told me that if anything, what she had read just solidified her feelings for me. We continued to date regularly and started growing closer and closer. Several weeks later, she told me that she had something that she wanted me to read. It was a letter that she had written to me. At first I was a little worried, then as I read the letter, my worries evaporated. This is the letter that Diane wrote me:

April 14, 2012

Mike,

You are so adorable and have so many wonderful qualities. I have been so impressed with you! I'm impressed with your intellect, your humor and attitude about life and the way you adore and care for your family. And I am impressed with how you have endured the hardships of your life and how you somehow came through it all.

You have endured the weight of the world for so long now. You have proven your strength. You survived the most horrific emotional journey of slowly losing your business, admitting failure to your employees, who I'm sure adored you and respected you immensely. In reading that chapter (of my journal), I could feel the emotional toll of having the last glimmer of hope destroyed when the phone call came from your friend who changed his mind about buying ArcStone. I felt the desperation of a man who would have done anything to save his family and employees from any hardship or financial loss.

Then, looking for some way to make sense of your plight and to survive amongst prisoners who were a mixed bag of misfits, you found those who were deserving of compassion and friendship. Some you encountered were evil and wicked, some damaged and strange, some trapped and disadvantaged from the first day they entered the world. Across the board, most of them never felt the love and support of family or friends; or the love and humility that a God and Savior can bring to your heart and life. They only knew survival at any cost.

Then the realization that your "keepers," the prison guards, *may be even more hostile and dangerous than the criminals you are housed with. They had the power to withhold basic necessities and even beat you with no cause. You learned about wardens who abused their power, and callously created an environment where basic human needs were not acknowledged.*

Mike, you have proven yourself. You have mentally and physically survived more than most people could endure without being broken. I can tell that you have had the will to stay strong for the sake of Jessi, Jenni, and your mom. And only God could give you the strength and love and wisdom to make it through the events you have endured.

Love is what makes our lives worth living and that is a valuable lesson that some people never learn. You have learned the lesson and I hope that you are drawn to me because of my heart's desire to love and put relationships above all else. To brighten someone's day is what I live for, and of course to be a loving example to my kids.

All this is to say...you don't have to be strong anymore, or "James Dean-like." I adore a man who is in touch with his feelings and especially one who has feelings for me! You have allowed yourself to "feel," and I'm glad you picked me to love. I think I am in shock right now, but I will grow to embrace and feel that our love is "real"!

I do love and adore you more than I can express. Hopefully someday the words will become more descriptive and you will feel and see the love that I have for you. As love grows, I believe it should become deeper and more precious. That's the kind of love I dream about and desire for us. Now I struggle

with believing this is not a dream, but very soon I will be "all in" and getting mushier by the day.
   Love you,
   Diane

Diane is a giver! She is the most loving and compassionate woman that I have ever met. In all things, she puts others above herself. Maybe God was showing me that life wasn't over. He had sent me an Angel.

When Justin Hayward of The Moody Blues wrote the song "I Know You're Out There Somewhere," it was generally accepted that he was talking about a first love. In my own personal interpretation, the song means searching for that one true love that you always hoped to find, that someone who would love you back without qualifications. For Diane to accept me as I was and despite where I've been, shows love without fear. I had never experienced this level of affection from someone before, but whatever path brought me here was worth it.

The secret of your beauty,
and the mystery of your soul,
I've been searching for in everyone I meet.

Maybe God was really looking out for me. I had never experienced anyone like Diane. He had sent me a woman who was loving beyond all my expectations. As Di and I continued to get to know each other, my mind flashed back to an adage that I had seen while still incarcerated at Limestone. It stated:

Love----believes all things. As love grows, so does our willingness to trust and to grant another chance. Love refuses to make another's failures terminal and is willing to accept the risk of being hurt again. There is, after all, no such thing as risk free love.

—Proverb on a Prison Wall

BRAVO!

Losing My Religion

"It is not the healthy who need a doctor, but the sick. I have not come to call the righteous, but sinners to repentance."
—Jesus Christ, Mark 2:17

The Bible talks about the broad way and the narrow way. It is generally believed that this is talking about believers versus nonbelievers. The question is what constitutes a believer? Do pseudo Christians who claim to believe in Christ and claim to follow his example, while doing otherwise, qualify as true believers? Will they walk the narrow way, or will they follow the broad way to their final destination? There are a lot of "Smoke and Mirror Christians" who need to ask themselves this question. Then again, we all need to ask ourselves this question.

This observation is not to say that any Christian is without fault. Perfection is not possible, we are humans. But to use our imperfections as an excuse to interpret Christ's examples and instructions, in any way that we want, is a very dangerous thing. Christ taught love and compassion. He taught against hypocrisy.

"If you love those who love you, what credit is that to you? For even sinners love those who love them. And if you do good to those who do good to you, what credit is that to you? For even sinners do the same."

—Jesus Christ (Luke 6:32)

Although I consider myself a Christian, because of my belief in God, I do not consider myself a strongly religious person. I think that religion has diluted the very foundation of Christianity.

Before you go to blasting me for my views, I admit, I'm a long way from perfect and don't have all the answers, but I do try my best to not go around acting holier than thou from a church pew while setting my own rules on the street. Admittedly, I am fighting a lot of new emotions and tendencies that I didn't know before the Alabama Justice System instilled them in me. Well, there I go making my own excuses. That's probably very un-Christian like, but it is what it is, and I'm not going to lie about it.

Perhaps a lot of the problem today is the fact that so many people practice "faith by proxy." The church business has grown to be enormous. It also seems to be very lucrative. There is nothing wrong with attending a large congregation of Christians; I attend one myself. However, in my opinion, we need to be very careful about certain things.

"Religion is what keeps the poor from murdering the rich."

—Napoleon Bonaparte

Money and faith are like oil and water. They don't mix very well. When they do come together, temptation comes into play.

This temptation may be for power or for financial gain; however, the apostles taught heavily against this mindset. Faith is not a business. You cannot buy your way into heaven. Using the works of a congregation as faith by proxy will get you nowhere if you do not truly participate. However, many Christians today view their faith as a type of cooperative, where they get brownie points for regularly or routinely occupying a pew. If you don't take your faith home with you, it gets you nowhere. If you don't make your faith personal, it means nothing.

"Preach the Gospel at all times and when necessary use words."
—Francis of Assisi

A truly incredible book entitled *Letters from a Skeptic* by Dr. Gregory K. Boyd and his father Edward K. Boyd chronicles the letters of a son wrestling with his father's questions about Christianity. One of my favorite statements from the book reads, "Christianity isn't a religion or an institution of any sort: it's a relationship. Within the religion of Christianity there are, and have always been, genuine Christians—people who have a saving and transforming relationship with Jesus Christ. This fact accounts for the tremendous good Christianity has brought to the world (in spite of the evils). But the 'religion' of Christianity, the 'institution' of the church, is not itself Christian. Only people, not institutions, can be Christian."

In no way do I believe the author is saying that it is wrong to worship in a congregation or group. I feel that he is simply cautioning against the faith by proxy concept. Our church families cannot answer to God for us. We are accountable for ourselves.

Churches are ways to elevate our faith and our good works. They are not places to hide in and disguise our outside hypocrisies. This thought pattern goes beyond just the Christian faith.

> *"However many holy words you read, however many you speak, what good will they do you if you do not act upon them?"*
> —Buddha

I'm saying all of this to reach a couple of points. The first point is that until you have fallen, and looked at things from the ground, you don't realize how many people don't practice what they preach. They make up their own set of Christian rules. If the Bible doesn't fit their day to day agenda, they rewrite it, however, every Sunday they are putting on their best faces. I guess their attendance and their claims of righteousness serve as the penance they need to get to the next level. Maybe they don't understand the meaning of "pay me now or pay me later."

The other point that I'm trying to make is that so many modern Christians are complacent in their service and in their faith which are dictated by their group's perception of the "Thou Shalts" and of the "Thou Shalt Nots." By getting lost in their congregation or by choosing their battles (meaning the direction of their service) they sometimes overlook the very things that Christ gave us directions for. Christ didn't tell His apostles to minister always to the good or to the visible, but rather sometimes he instructed them to go to the Samaritans.

Prisons and jails house a lot of Samaritans. Sure, there are churches that minister to the incarcerated. I applaud them and their efforts. Some of these do truly wonderful work in the face of adversity. Others are there simply to provide lip service and to make a show. As I mentioned in an earlier chapter, some of the members of Asbury Methodist Church in Madison, Alabama, take Christ's directive about ministering in prisons to heart. Every church and its members should follow their example.

Every prison camp that I was in had some kind of a Christian ministry. Some were very fulfilling and some I really don't know how to explain. However, Islam has a strong foothold in Alabama's prisons. Some camps have far more Muslim services then Christian services. Although most Muslims are very polite and upstanding people, many of the radical factions use prison systems as their recruiting grounds — Ground Zero. If Christians want to fight a Holy War, prisons are the front lines.

Andy Rooney once said, "Christians talk as though goodness was their idea, but good behavior doesn't have any religious origin. Our prisons are filled with the devout."

Although I don't share the atheistic views that Mr. Rooney professed, his statement was an accurate observation. The bad news is that while many Sunday School Christians downplay Jail House Christians, they practice much of the same two-faced philosophy that they condemn. Wrath, greed, sloth, pride, lust, envy, and gluttony are considered the Seven Deadly Sins. How many "Billboard Christians," ones who love to toot their own horn and to point fingers at others, are guilty of multiple of these sins? Throw in gossip, backstabbing, lying, hypocrisy, callousness, and unfaithfulness, and the narrow way might become outright desolate. Also, "pew-fixtures" with these traits have to live an internally miserable existence. Maybe all these conflicts add credibility to the words of Billy Joel's hit song, "Only the Good Die Young," when he sings, "I'd rather laugh with the sinners, than cry with the saints."

George Bernard Shaw stated, "No man ever believes that the Bible means what it says; He is always convinced that it says what he means." Do you ever wonder why a multitude of preachers can read the Bible, interpret different things, and yet all be right?

I consider myself a Christian, yet I have been guilty of many of these traits and still fight a lot of them, as do most of you. The thing that we have to be careful of is not to look down our noses at others in their plights and think that because we haven't been exposed on our own shortcomings that we are any better than them or don't owe them some compassion. I know that after living with a different culture from the other side of the tracks, it gave me a new perspective. Many of these people have never known the kind of life that some of us grew up in, yet we judge them even beyond their criminal record.

Sure, these people are sinners, but so are we all. Some of us are just in denial or think that there are degrees of sin. Christ and the apostles in their ministry targeted the sinners. Does this example not solidify the fact that we should really try to minister in the jails and prisons instead of just offering lip service? Sure it does. Maybe a stronger presence from churches would negate some of the corruption in the correctional system. From my viewpoint, it seemed to have had a big influence even when you look at the differences between Limestone and Elmore.

If we are really ministering to sinners, focusing on the Sunday morning pews would be a good start. There are plenty of sinners present there to minister to. Then we need to follow Christ's instructions and go forth into the world, including the jails and prisons. It is easy to be labeled a Christian, but to have a Christian aura, you have to really want it. Just wearing the title is worthless. Over the centuries, many horrible acts have been performed in the name of Christianity—atrocities during the crusades, persecution of the Native Americans, the Spanish Inquisition, and looking the other way during the Holocaust.

In *Letters from a Skeptic*, Dr. Boyd says, "Thus, I want to sharply distinguish between the Christianity I'm defending and the Christian church; the two need not have anything more than a name in common. I wouldn't dream of trying to defend all that's been done under the label 'Christianity.' Like you, I am enraged by a great deal of it."

However, can atrocities of the Church not be just callousness and self-righteousness? Christ did not teach these traits as being acceptable. Maybe many of these callous churches should practice under the name "The Southern Hypocrisy Church" or "The First Feel-Good Church." I know that after my downfall, I didn't receive a single call or word of encouragement from the congregation that I had been attending at the time. Also, not a single soul from there called or came by to welcome me home. Is the story of the Prodigal Son in Luke 15 not in their Bibles? I guess they didn't have time for sinners. However, the congregation would soon be making regional and national headlines for very non-Christian like actions going on within their walls. As it turned out, they had bigger demons to exorcise than me.

Tim Keller wrote a book, which I read just prior to my incarceration, called *The Prodigal God*. It takes the story from Luke 15 and examines it from the eyes of the older "good" brother. It basically showed the failures of the older son by assuming his entitlement. Keller's synopsis meant a whole lot more to me after my return.

By casting these stones, I know that maybe I am not being very Christ-like. I hope that God will forgive me for the emotions and the anger that runs through my veins these days. This anger is my cross to bear. Maybe we all need to do a lot of soul searching.

So, while these nations feared the LORD, they also served their idols; their children likewise and their grandchildren, as their fathers did, so they do to this day.
—2 Kings 17:41

Hair of the Dog

"How fortunate for governments that the people they administer don't think."

—Adolf Hitler

Have you ever been kicked when you were down? Have you ever been picked on by bullies? Have you ever been laughed at because you were down on your luck? Many of us can answer yes to at least one of these questions. Those who can't answer yes to any of them just don't have a clue.

The next question is, how do you respond? Do you take it and grin or do you arch your back and fight back? Oprah Winfrey once said, "Where there is no struggle, there is no strength." I believe that this statement has been proven repeatedly throughout history.

When the Colbert County DA and his pal, the judge, jumped on me I was down. I was hurting, both mentally and physically, not to mention the hurt over the financial problems I faced. They were beating on a whipped and cowering puppy. Through the time of my arraignment and my trial, I didn't know if I was coming or going. Some of my depression was due to medication because of my surgeries, but most was simply because of the shock and the stress from the collapse of my business and the subsequent ordeal.

This state of shock is no longer the case. So, "Here's Johnny! I'm back"! And I'm no longer a wounded and cowering puppy. This dog bites! If biting's not an option, this dog will just piss on your leg. Maybe it's your turn to find out what it is like when shit happens.

During my ordeal, as Austin Powers would say, "I had lost my mojo." The fight had gone out of me and I had no mulligans in the bag. I was caught with my pants down. I was embarrassed and groping in the dark. If nothing else, the ridiculous, hillbilly legal system of Colbert County, Alabama brought me to my senses. I'm now ready for fight. After all, Bear Bryant once said, "Don't give up at halftime. Concentrate on winning the second half."

There will be no ambush this time. To quote a great line from the movie *Full Metal Jacket*, "I'm so happy that I'm alive, in one piece and in short, I'm in a world of shit, yes, but I am alive and I'm not afraid."

I'm sure that others have endured much more than I was exposed to. Nevertheless, I was exposed to much more than I should have been. No, I was not killed, but I could have been. No, I was not raped, but I could have been that as well.

To all those small businessmen who read this journal, or for that matter, to anyone who has lost their direction or had bad circumstances befall them, you could have been in my shoes. I was not some career criminal that the court sent to my fate. I was an

Everyday Joe, just like you. Please, take mind to keep your focus, limit your risks, and be wary of all the bureaucratic wolves that will tear at your flesh if you stumble and show vulnerability.

I'm sure you can say that my words are "contempt of court." You're damn right! I am full of contempt for this Mickey Mouse Court. Because of being on probation, I have been cautioned against these words, but I've simmered long enough. If Colbert County wants to come after me for contempt, bring it on. All I've got to say is that the queen and her merry court better be ready for a much better prepared legal team this go around. I consider lawyers to be a necessary evil in most cases, but I'm sure that I can put together a team with enough ethical awareness and Constitutional capabilities to take you on. I'm looking forward to it. Maybe we can drag the skeletons out of all our closets and let them have a good legal debate! And on top of that, ah-ain't-skairt-neether! (Translation for all of you Yankees: I'm not scared either!)

Einstein's theory of relativity states that for every action there is an opposite and equal reaction ($E=MC2$). I'm ready to be the MC2 behind the E! As Michael Buffer would say, "Let's get ready to rumble!" You stole a year of my life because of my personal failures, just to escalate your own egos. You've tried to starve me and have allowed damage and neglect to my physical wellbeing. You've contributed to the disruption of my family and hindered my recovery, as well as becoming a roadblock to the restitution of my customers. All this persecution because of your own interpretations of intent in what should have been a civil matter. You need to go back to law school and study the Constitution.

It's time for "good old boy" courts to come into the 20th century. Maybe as protectors of the public, judges and prosecutors should be required to spend a few nights in the very place that they are so quick to condemn people to. Maybe they will enjoy the mystery meat better than I did. (Only after my release and by chance did I inadvertently learn from a meat salesman, that his company sold their out-of-date products to the ADOC). If the public, as a whole, could see what kind of a cesspool this is and what you are, maybe they would not just fire you, but rather tar and feather you and send you for a vacation there.

Sweet Home Alabama

*"People generally see what they look for,
and hear what they listen for."*
— Harper Lee, *To Kill a Mockingbird*

I am an Alabamian and I love my home state. I'm proud of my Southern heritage, and the Bible Belt upbringing that I was raised in. I say y'all, yunder, and fixin' to. Family to me is kinfolk. I know that fireflies are really lightnin' bugs. I have dined on poke salad and know that a barbeque sandwich should be served with the slaw on it. I know that the tastiest part of a fried catfish is the tail and that the only acceptable way to fry okra is in a skillet. I know what the term "fair to middlin" means. Also, the words "Roll Tide" jump off my tongue with regularity.

However, Alabama has a dark side, a Jekyll and Hyde persona that I had never experienced growing up. Although I had grown up during the time of the Civil Rights movement, I really didn't comprehend what people of color and those who aided them were going up against. The good old boy system does as it pleases and without a conscience. It makes its own rules. Once you get caught in its maelstrom, you are sucked under to drown.

The brightest fruit can rot from within. The most graceful and sleek athlete can be stricken with disease from within. So can states and political government systems.

Alabama has a cancer growing within it. It is the callous and indignant presence of the self-serving politicians and administrators within its governments. That is not to say that these types of people are not present in other states; however, the level of corruption in Alabama makes us a joke to the rest of the country. Our county and state systems are packed full of power mongers. Together with their puppets, they use their positions in a self-serving fashion. Just because the good ole boy's families, friends, and close allies cannot see or won't admit to their shortcomings, doesn't make these injustices any less factual. Maybe it's time for our citizens to open their eyes and really take an interest in those that we elect, rather than just taking part in a high school level popularity contest. Politicians, judges, and public officials should be held accountable for their actions in both legislative and monetary decisions.

Many of these good old boy powerbrokers spread their smiles and favors around enough to stay in power for upwards of a decade or roughly the average job length of an Alabama Highway Department paving project (How many men in reflective vests does it take to watch a piece of road construction equipment to make it work, anyway?). Many of the same elected officials run companies or are connected to firms that are recipients of state contracts. In my home area, many of the same persons responsible for social and economic decisions have sat behind the same desks for years and years, drawing a healthy salary, while scores of jobs have left the area. This lack of progress is called mismanagement (take the word of a man convicted of mismanaging)!

I'm sure I will be criticized heavily for the words that I have written. After all, I would not plea to the "crimes" that I was accused of, and obviously I'm spouting off because of the bitterness in my heart. What right does a convicted felon have to criticize the system, anyway? Go ahead, throw stones at me. I can still see the way things work in my home state, and I have a constitutional right to express my observations. I am not Neil Young! I am a Southern man and I am gonna be around, anyhow!

Once again repeating myself, I was guilty of a lot of things, including having a failed business. However, I was not willing to lie and take a plea to what the state of Alabama demanded of me, stating that I had intentionally defrauded anyone.

In the book *To Kill a Mockingbird*, author Harper Lee wrote the following:

"They're certainly entitled to think that, and they're entitled to full respect for their opinions... but before I can live with other folks I've got to live with myself. The one thing that doesn't abide by majority rule is a person's conscience."

The good ole boy subculture in Alabama lives in a fantasyland of entitlement and self-fulfillment, which may be close to the mindset present during the pre-Confederacy South. Those who cross them are cast into a no-man's-land, maybe only slightly more modern and humane than the 19th century. As a result, as a state we lag behind much of the remainder of the country in many social and educational scores while the fat-cats keep their pockets full with the funds that should be devoted for such improvements. Whereas a state infrastructure project can be dragged out and milked for astronomical lengths of time, when issuing levies on a failed businessman, the billing department for the Alabama Department of

Revenue works at warp speed. Maybe Mercedes Benz should make a special edition 'Alabama Revenuer' model. It would probably be advertised 0 to 60 in 0.1 seconds. Hyundai could then counter with a slalom model, designed to navigate the miles of permanent orange barrels obstructing many Alabama roads.

PolicyMic reported in a study compiled jointly by Indiana University and City University of Hong Kong concerning the corruption in our state governments. In this study, Alabama ranked as the sixth most corrupt state in America. My heart and sympathies go out to those in the top five.

The study considered multiple factors, including violations of federal anti-corruption laws between 1976 and 2008, and generated a corruption index tied to the number of government employees. The report states that *"States with higher levels of corruption are likely to favor construction, salaries, borrowing, correction, and police protection at the expense of social sectors such as education, health, and hospitals."* This revelation seems to tie directly to the education money diverted to the Alabama Department of Corrections, mentioned in an earlier chapter, does it not?

Although ranking as the 6th most corrupt state by the Indiana/City U. study, in a 2014 study in *Kids Count Data Book*, which is funded by the Annie E. Casey Foundation, Alabama ranked 44th for the second consecutive year in child well-being. This study used data from indicators in the areas of economic well-being, education, health, family, and community. We ranked dead last in math proficiency among eighth graders. Maybe if those in charge would use the Federal stimulus money as it was intended, our state could pull itself out of the cellar. Instead, they let the wrong people have access to it with questionable intentions and results.

The Indiana/City U. Report also says, *"Not only do these states, including Alabama, have excessive state spending, but they also spend more in areas of the government that are susceptible to corruption, like construction jobs, governmental employee wages, and law enforcement."* It goes on to say, *"Many of the corrupt states exhaust a lot of money on big infrastructure projects for which the money trail is not fully transparent to the public. Extortion, bribes, and kickbacks may cause a rise in expenditures. These states also pay police and correction officer's higher wages. And areas which are not so easily corruptible—like public welfare, education, and health—see much less state funding. On average, the 10 most corrupt states spend $1,308 more per capita than the remainder of the country."*

Where is this money going? In a Wall Street.com special report, Alabama ranks as the fourth poorest state in the country with the seventh highest percentage of residents below the poverty line, this despite many states having higher levels of immigrant workers coming into the borders. We spend more and yet our citizens live poorer. Once again, whose pockets are these funds going in? Eventually, due to the constant scavenging from our corrupt politicians, the country will again have to come beggin' to town. How much more of this will Washington stand for?

According to Wikipedia, Alabama also ranks fourth nationally in the number of state prisoners per capita. This number is more than twice that of New York, Washington, Minnesota, and New Jersey. Alabama's prisons are not an industry, Huh! Tell me then, is this because our citizens are inherently more prone to commit crimes? Do we rank anywhere near that high in any other industry? Well, besides maybe football.

I use the term industry literally. Do you really want to fall for the farce that the ADOC is costing the state money, instead of being an instrument to funnel Federal dollars into our crooked politicians' pockets? If you fall for their creative accounting, maybe you're a candidate to help transfer some email solicitor's free millions from Nigeria. I'm sure that you won't mind giving them your personal banking account info.

The bottom line, however, is that as long as we keep these parasites in office, we have no one to blame but ourselves. If we allow ourselves to be party to corruption and callousness, then shame on us. Will we continue to see what we want to see and hear what we want to hear? Perhaps time will tell.

There is an old joke that goes: "How many Alabama football fans does it take to change a light bulb?"

The answer: "Two. One to change the bulb, and another one to talk about how good the old bulb was!"

The Alabama Judicial System is not football, but the old bulb is broken and has been for a long time. We need to install a new and improved bulb and pump it full of new juice. Alabamians do not stand for complacency and inferiority in football. We should not stand for it in our government or the education of our children. There is not always, "next year."

Maybe we should elect Nick Saban as governor or even anoint him Emperor. His track record for building a clean and prosperous program far exceeds anything that anyone in Montgomery has done. Maybe he could return the state to prominence, like he has our Crimson Tide football team. In all seriousness though, I doubt Coach Saban would want to tarnish his image by becoming a politician.

Note: If we did hire Nick Saban to rebuild our state and get it to the top, maybe we could also hire Paul Finebaum to expose all the Harvey Updikes hidden within our state and local governments.

As you enter Alabama on Interstates 20, 65, 59 or 10, you will see a sign proclaiming, "Alabama the Beautiful." Physically our state is beautiful. Now maybe it's time for us to become "Alabama the Healthy." We cannot accomplish this feat as an Orwellian or Good Ole Boy State.

At the rest stop entering Alabama from Georgia, there is a stone monument with the engraved phrase, "We dare defend our rights." This term should not apply just to using arms against outside forces. It should also be used as a battle cry against the tyranny and corruption within our borders. As Alabamians, we have to get past good intentions and proceed to take the ethical foundation and reputation of our state to heart.

Maybe one day Alabamians will take a stand against the power brokers that have controlled and hindered the growth of our state for so long. Perhaps, when they do, we will take our place among the elite in our country in something other than football. But first we must open our eyes, throw complacency aside, and decide that common sense is not unconstitutional. When we come to this realization, we will tell the good ole boys to take a hike, and we will start thinking for ourselves. Maybe it is time to reinvent the ice cube.

I'm sure that the good ole boys will put up a big fight. A lot of mudslinging will occur, aimed at those who challenge them. Change won't be easy and these people will get very nasty, but just remember, "When you pray for rain, be prepared to deal with the mud."

In Alabama today, organized crime is alive and well. Here it is often called state and local government. What do we do with all these good ole boys, you ask? In the infamous words of the Outlaw Josie Wales: "To hell with them fellers. Buzzards gotta eat, same as worms."

Harsh, huh? "Yeah, I reckon so."

Baggage
Diary of a Madman

"So go ahead. Fall Down.
The world looks different from the ground."
— Oprah Winfrey

Sometimes I feel like I have lived through a dark and dreary Spaghetti Western. The theme music to "The Good, The Bad and The Ugly" rings through my brain. As the reel turns, playing the last few years of my life, everything seems so dim and in despair. I feel that I have hit rock bottom and my life is hopeless. Then, just as everything starts to really weigh on me, the picture jumps forward in time.

Through the gloom, as I focus my attention on the new scene, I hear ole Josie Wales criticizing me for wanting to mope in my pity. "Dying ain't much of a livin', Boy," he says. The words strike a chord. If I just lay down and die, Colbert's court jesters have won! I can't have that! I'm not dead! I'm not a madman. BUT, I AM MAD! Maybe I can't beat you in your one-sided kangaroo court, but I can certainly take you on in the public eye. Perhaps these memoirs can serve notice of my contempt and as a vocal revenge for the abuse to which you have subjected me. Who knows, maybe this is just a start. I hold no respect for your piss-ant court and its renderings. Your morals and character do not warrant respect, so *"Don't piss down my back and tell me it's raining."*

Many people think that prison is like a country club. I have heard this statement many times through the years. I probably at one time thought the same thing. Perhaps some federal facilities are—I don't know. The one thing that I do know, is that some of the prisons in the Alabama Department of Corrections are a hell on earth. My own physical and mental baggage is a testament to that.

Besides the obvious scars and damage (neck, back, eye) I have, courtesy of the vacation that the State sent me on, there are other scars I carry with me. The correctional system tries to steal your speech and your manners, as well as trying to make you question your faith and your very reason for existing. As a result, you learn automatically to see the bad side of everything and everyone, instead of the good. You become the devil's advocate in most aspects of your life. They attempt to turn you into an animal that they can keep penned up, so that you can be of no future legal threat to them. If you are financially broke, they insure your right to "improper" council by appointing a handler for you, not to protect your rights, but rather to insure their position.

Then the State, regardless of your charges or your situation, strips you of your right to vote, your right to bear arms, and whether they admit it or not, the right to find advanced employment. The pursuit of happiness takes on a whole new concept with a felony conviction pinned on you from these kangaroo courts. I can't vote, by design, against those who have railroaded me. Also, being the violent criminal that I am, I cannot even carry a shotgun and go dove hunting with my step-son or my sons-in-law, not to mention the fact that, as a heinous villain, I have forfeited my Constitutional right to protect myself.

If you really wonder why cops and uniforms make me nervous, check this story out. In a 2013 article in the Montgomery Advisor, it reported stories of beatings and sexual assaults by correctional officers in three ADOC facilities, including Bibb Correctional Facility, Donaldson Correctional Facility, and Elmore Correctional Facility (where I was incarcerated). The article was based on the investigative work of the Equal Justice Initiative (EJI), an organization founded to be an advocate for civil rights and humane treatment.

According to the report, in just a six-month period, there had been nearly a dozen reports of prisoners at Elmore being handcuffed, stripped naked, and then beaten by several guards. The report also stated that the Warden and other high-ranking officials were involved in some of the beatings and other misconduct. There were also reports from the other facilities that correctional officers forced young male inmates to perform sex acts and then threatened disciplinary action if they were reported. Some of the inmates collected physical evidence and turned it over to the ADOC. The evidence corroborated the reports but little was done to punish the perpetrators.

The Equal Justice Initiative issued the following findings:

At Elmore Correctional Facility, there is a dangerous group of officers. One man was beaten by multiple guards while handcuffed and legs shackled. He was beaten till he was unconscious.

After being transferred to the prison infirmary, it was determined that his injuries were too severe to treat, so he was transferred to a free world hospital, where he was treated for numerous facial fractures and severe damage. Another inmate who was beaten by a group of officers was afterward paraded around the facility by the Warden as an example to others.

At Donaldson and Bibb, male officers in multiple instances had forced young male prisoners to perform sex acts. They coerced them by threatening disciplinary action if they refused. Afterward they were threatened with discipline if they reported the incidents. The EJI found that on instances where the violations were reported, there was no response from the Alabama Department of Corrections internal investigations unit.

Where are the U.S. Marshalls and the Federal Grand Juries? If Rodney King's civil rights were violated, then so were these individuals' civil rights. Sure, maybe there wasn't a passerby recording it with a video camera (the ADOC makes sure of that, except in Sergeant Cole's case), but it is hard to believe that with all the national media reports on Alabama's prisons that the Feds are not all over them.

A June 2014 report on www.vice.com entitled "The Horrific State of Alabama's Prisons" goes into depth about the corruption and the incredibly high rate of inmate murders in Alabama prisons, in comparison to the remainder of the country. In particular, the report focused on The St. Clair Correctional Facility. Journalist Ray Downs used information from the Equal Justice initiative as well.

His article states that when Jodey Waldrop, a 36-year-old inmate at St. Clair was murdered on his bunk on June 3, it was the third time a prisoner had been murdered inside St. Clair's walls during the past 10 months, and the fifth time in the last 30 months. He put that fact in perspective by reporting that the average nationwide homicide rate for all state prisons for the last 10 years is 52. That number is in relation to 1.35 million inmates. St. Clair has fewer than 1500 inmates.

The EJI's director, Bryan Stevenson, says that St. Clair's problems are because of overcrowding, a warden who doesn't care what prisoners do to one another, and drug dealing guards who sometimes order hits on inmates. He stated, "There is a lot of illegal activity by correctional staff—they are smuggling in drugs, cell phones, and other contraband. These officers bring the stuff in and have inmates collect the money. When people refuse to pay, oftentimes violence is ordered by the officers to make sure that they recover what they're supposed to get."

Louisiana's Angola prison is notorious as having once been one of the worst detention centers in the country. Efforts have been made to change Angola. Now you have much less violence in a prison that is four times the size of St. Clair. According to many, the ADOC has far surpassed the past reputation of Angola. Trust me, the ADOC's lack of institutional control starts at the top and then filters throughout the system. They simply have no initiative to do their job in a humane manner. They simply don't care. Their job is to manage the state's Cash Cow and collect their lucrative salaries. Have inmates surpassed marijuana as Alabama's number one cash crop?

One of the friends I made when I was confined at Elmore was Chad. After my release, I found out through letters that Chad had been transferred to St. Clair. He was there during the time of most of these murders. It could very easily have been him. Although Chad was incarcerated on the three-strike plan, due to crimes of his youth that he confessed to me, he is probably the closest thing that I have seen to an ADOC success story. He keeps to himself, minds his own business, offers assistance when needed, and is a problem to no one. Every day he continues to spend incarcerated in the ADOC can only corrupt, not correct him, but after 14 years he is still incarcerated for the crimes of a drug dependent young man. He lost everything he had due to his youthful ignorance and dependencies. Chad has completed every program available to prove that he is rehabilitated. Yet with no family to fight for him, he still languishes away in Alabama's torture camps.

Author Harlan Coben seems to have an informed view of prison systems. In his book *The Innocent* he writes,

> *Society wants to peddle that rehabilitation crap on the public. But I know better. You may have gone into that place an okay guy, but you want to tell me you're the same man now? The prison system has its share of critics. Most problems are obvious and to some extent organic, what with the fact that you are, for the most part, caging bad people with other bad people. But the one thing that was definitely true was that prison taught you all the wrong skills. You survive by being aloof, by isolating yourself, by fearing any alliance. You are not shown how to assimilate or become productive—just the opposite. You learn that no one can be trusted, that the only person you can truly count on is yourself, that you must be ready to protect yourself at all times.*

In trying to help Chad since my release, I have discovered another fallacy within the Alabama Department of Corrections. Parole board members are not always and generally seldom qualified for their positions. These are strictly political appointments. One prominent Alabama parole attorney I spoke to about Chad's situation stated that inmates were strictly subject to the whims of the board members. The attorney also laughed and stated that over the years many of the board members had been legislator's family members, friends, ministers, and on at least one occasion, their hairdresser. Maybe, upon parole, in addition to the ten bucks and a bus ticket that a parolee receives, they could get a new doo and a tint.

In trying to get Chad a cut to move his parole hearing date up, I spoke to a high-ranking official within the parole board. I vouched for Chad's character and expressed my fears for him. She seemed like a very nice lady, but she told me that he had already received a small cut and would not be eligible for another review for a year. I mentioned that in the wake of the bad publicity at St. Clair that other, more violent, inmates had received much larger cuts. She told me that she was sorry but that because of policy he could not be considered for another year. She then said that if they did not stick to their rules that they would be bombarded with phone call requests every day.

Heaven forbid that the parole board has to increase their workload to do the right thing. After all, the real duties of these people are to protect the system and to collect a paycheck in the process. Right and wrong take a backseat when they come in contact with Alabama's red tape and bureaucracy.

This perverted ideology is the mindset of the political system in Alabama; take care of your own and make sure you have someone to cover your ass. Would it not make more sense to put some of the unpaid ex-cons that the Innocence Project had exonerated on the parole board, along with a group made up of clergymen, civil rights advocates, and individuals elected specifically for that purpose? Why of course not! That might jeopardize the state's judicial Cash Cow and expose them to recourse.

But again, there is no recourse. At least for the people providing the business for the prisons there is none. Prosecutors and judges carry immunity. They are not held accountable for what they do. They can lie and manipulate all they want. They can send all the innocent people to jail that they want to. They are immune. All that matters here are conviction rates and what promotes their careers and the bankroll in their pocket. This system is crazy!

What other business is there where the managers are not held accountable? In big manufacturing companies, can the managers conduct business like this state does and not be held accountable? Hell no, they would be fired.

What about in churches? If it was discovered that priests or ministers acted like many of our state officials, the congregation would demand that they be excommunicated or undergo an exorcism!

We should start holding state judicial officials accountable for their actions. Maybe for every inmate proven to be innocent, the prosecutor should have to serve an equal number of days. After all, with report after report from neutral parties about the state of Alabama's prisons, these prosecutors are, in my mind, criminals themselves. If I am a criminal because of the backwash of my failed business, then they are certainly criminals for sending innocent individuals into a living hell. Do parents discipline or correct their misled child by penning them up with snakes and other wild animals?

Rouge prosecutors don't take fairness, circumstances, ethics, or even the Constitution into consideration if they have a Court bench to back them up. They don't mind sending a sacrificial lamb to slaughter, nor do they consider any collateral damage that occurs from their actions. It's all about the score and promoting themselves. We don't need prosecutors that are on a crusade, but rather we need prosecutors who have the Constitution and the citizens' interest in mind, rather than their own.

In court, those crusading prosecutors often use a "birdshot" approach by throwing as many charges at you as they can come up with, in order to confuse and influence the jury. Chances are some pellets are going to hit. With a judge in their corner, you may as well be running through a mine field. When you have a failed businessman with no resources left to fight with, it is easy for a court to label him as a Bernie Madoff and use him as a patsy to make themselves look good to their public.

If that businessman had been such an accomplished thief, why didn't he have the resources to fight the prosecution in a formidable manner? I guarantee you that in that case, things would have been approached differently. If the accused thief had been a popular NCAA quarterback would he have ever even been charged with theft or even something more serious if violent offenses were involved? I guess money and public opinion would dictate that case.

In third world countries, when public officials get out of

control, a coup de grace many times follows. I view the Colbert court system and the ADOC as well below the civilization level of many third world countries. Maybe a coup is in order. These people need to be held accountable not only for the atrocities in their prisons, but also for their hypocrisy and poor leadership in general. Alabama is lagging behind in too many areas while the Fat Cats keep filling their pockets. Rise up, Alabama! And then, "Let's get on our knees and pray, so we don't get fooled again!"

In the movie *The American President*, Michael J Fox's character, Lewis Rothschild, has the following conversation with the president, played by Michael Douglas, concerning people and whom they follow:

Lewis Rothschild: "People want leadership, Mr. President, and in the absence of genuine leadership they'll listen to anyone who steps up to the microphone. They want leadership. They're so thirsty for it they'll crawl through the desert toward a mirage. When they discover there's no water there, they'll drink the sand."

The President: "People don't drink the sand because they're thirsty. They drink the sand because they don't know the difference."

As citizens of Alabama, we need to learn the difference. We need to come out of the Dark Ages. We need to step up to the plate and show our pride in being born an Alabamian. Once again, it's time for our leaders to be held accountable and for us to elect moral, honest, and non-self-indulging people into our leadership roles. It's time for us to take as much pride in our leaders and our image as we do in our football. If we continue to fall victim to shallowness, we will eventually drown when exposed to the deep end.

Reflections and Resolve
Food for Thought

*"I see you've got your fist out, say your piece and get out.
Guess I get the gist of it, but it's alright."*
—Jerry Garcia, "A Touch of Gray"

Maybe I screwed up. Maybe I should have taken the easy road, the cheap way out. Maybe my stubbornness and convictions made me too dumb to stay out of jail. Maybe I should have done what the court expected of me by lying and taking a plea. Maybe that compromise would have made things a lot better. NAAA! I couldn't have lived with myself. Sometimes resolve and willpower just hurt. Regardless of the names they call me or the labels that they attach to me, I know that I am a far better and more ethical person than the hypocrites that went after me and hung a conviction around my neck.

Don't Quit!

*When things go wrong, as they sometimes will,
When the road you're trudging seems all uphill,*

When the funds are low and the debts are high,
And you want to smile, but you have to sigh,
When care is pressing you down a bit,
Rest, if you must, but don't you quit.

Life is queer with its twists and turns,
As every one of us sometimes learns,
And many a failure turns about,
When he might have won had he stuck it out;
Don't give up though the pace seems slow—
You may succeed with another blow.

Often the goal is nearer than,
It seems to a faint and faltering man,
Often the struggler has given up,
When he might have captured the victor's cup,
And he learned too late when the night slipped down,
How close he was to the golden crown.

Success is failure turned inside out—
The silver tint of the clouds of doubt,
And you never can tell how close you are,
It may be near when it seems so far,
So stick to the fight when you're hardest hit—
It's when things seem worst that you must not quit.

-Anonymous

A lot of men far greater than I have faced trials and adversity and succeeded. To succeed, you are constantly facing risks.

Sometimes, no matter how hard you try, things just blow up in your face. Sometimes it happens because of bad decisions and sometimes simply because of circumstance. Character is shown by how you react to your failures. Do you simply allow yourself to continue to be beaten down or do you give it your all in an attempt to persevere?

"We must never despair; our situation has been compromising before, and it has changed for the better; so I trust it will again. If difficulties arise, we must put forth new exertion and proportion our efforts to the exigencies of the times."
— George Washington

Time takes its toll on you physically; it's inevitable. As long as you keep your sanity and character, you are still a winner.

Age wrinkles the body. Quitting wrinkles the soul."
— Douglas MacArthur

Resolve can overcome everything that tyrants can throw at you. However, for resolve to be successful, you have to stay the course.

"Prison itself is a tremendous education in the need for patience and perseverance. It is above all a test—of one's commitment."
— Nelson Mandela

Hypocrisy claims character and virtue. Resolve lives it.

"God knows our situation; He will not judge us as if we had no difficulties to overcome. What matters is the sincerity and perseverance of our will to overcome them."

— C.S. Lewis

Sometimes we have to focus on the future in order to atone for the past. Example: The Apostle Paul persecuted Christians till his conversion. He then became a staunch advocate for Christ and evolved into the saint that we know him as.

"Forgiveness is about empowering yourself, rather than empowering your past."

—T. D. Jakes

In order to rise above our trials, we must remember that we are leaders and not allow ourselves to become followers.

"Battles are fought in our minds every day. When we begin to feel the battle is just too difficult and want to give up, we must choose to resist negative thoughts and be determined to rise above our problems. We must decide that we're not going to quit. When we're bombarded with doubts and fears, we must take a stand and say: "I'll never give up! God's on my side. He loves me, and He's helping me! I'm going to make it!"

—Joyce Meyer

Sometimes even great men are made out to be the enemy. It is our job to put the images of our youth aside, mature and see greatness for what it is. Growing up in 60s Alabama, I watched as Dr. Martin Luther King was made out by our state leaders to be a heretic. Thank God, I was raised by a father who didn't judge a man by the color of his skin.

> *"If you can't fly then run, if you can't run then walk, if you can't walk then crawl, but whatever you do you have to keep moving forward."*
> —Martin Luther King Jr.

As moral people, we should take up the fight of those who are oppressed and not follow a path simply because our handlers have instructed us to. This statement is especially true for those of us who profess to be Christians.

> *"Well we are not afraid, we are not afraid*
> *We shall overcome someday*
> *Yeah here in my heart, I do believe*
> *We shall overcome someday"*
> —As sung by Pete Seeger and Peter, Paul and Mary

We Shall Overcome should not only be considered an anthem for racial equality, but for all who are oppressed. Whether you like Pete Seeger's version, Joan Baez's, or that of Peter Paul & Mary, this song and the speech by Dr. King should mean something to anyone who has ever been in a crisis.

> *"Count it all joy, my brothers, when you meet trials of various kinds, for you know that the testing of your faith produces*

steadfastness."

—James 1:2-4

It took facing the wrath of the establishment for me to really open my eyes to the truth about the injustices sometimes dealt out by those in power. Interpretations of right and wrong take on a whole new perspective when dictated by narcissist.

> *"More than that, we rejoice in our sufferings, knowing that suffering produces endurance, and endurance produces character, and character produces hope."*
>
> —Romans 5:3-4

The establishment will attempt to strip you of your dignity and of any ability to be a threat to them. They will attempt to prohibit you of any course of financial recovery.

> *"Naked I came from my mother's womb, and naked I will depart. The LORD gave and the LORD has taken away; may the name of the LORD be praised."*
>
> —Job 1:21 NIV

The name Job always arises when persecution and perseverance are discussed. Reading his story and observing everything that he endured, who then am I to lie down and roll over?

> *"One who gains strength by overcoming obstacles possesses the only strength which can overcome adversity."*
>
> —Albert Schweitzer

Tyrants hate exposure. If you are vocal and question the shortcomings and brutality of those who abuse you, they will attempt to assassinate your character.

"All the world is full of suffering. It is also full of overcoming."
—Helen Keller

Helen Keller was probably the most famous native of Tuscumbia, Alabama, which is the county seat of Colbert County. Although blind, Helen Keller could see things that those with physical vision could not. If she were alive today and walked the few blocks from her home at Ivy Green to the courthouse or into the jail a block away, what would she say? Would she have kind words to say to those placed in charge of peace and justice, or would she call them barbarians?

"The test of success is not what you do when you are on top. Success is how high you bounce when you hit bottom."
—George S. Patton

The world can be unfair. Televangelists can use their "inspiration" and a tax-exempt status to make millions from an uneducated flock, with little or no repercussion. Politicians can do the same with their influence-for-pay and a campaign contribution fund. Speaking of politicians and televangelists, a certain DA that I know does a very good impersonation of Televangelist Robert Tilton. They are both very proficient at clouding the issue by babbling in meaningless tongues.

Despite the tolerance for these phony preachers and politicians, if a small businessman with limited connections and a depleted bank account were to adhere to similar practices, he would be accused of theft by deception. Is what is good for the goose not good for the gander? Maybe these legally protected thieves should find out the meaning of, "What goes around, comes around." Sometimes you're the windshield, and then sometimes you're the bug.

> *"Defeat is a state of mind; no one is ever defeated until defeat has been accepted as a reality."*
>
> —Bruce Lee

The system not only performs a character assassination on those it prosecutes, but it also participates in recovery assassination. How can a man recover to pay his debts when he cannot even open a bank account for fear of it being seized without notice? Never mind that you have to buy groceries and try to pay bills to survive.

Even if you try to enter a deal with the state on tax issues, you are at their mercy as to whether they honor it. Is locking you up and hindering your recovery not worth something?

> *"In life, you'll have your back up against the wall many times. You might as well get used to it."*
>
> —Paul "Bear" Bryant

I've resigned myself to the fact that with my baggage, and the burden that the State of Alabama has put on me, that I will never become the CEO Emeritus of anything. Rather, I have to settle for being the CEO anonymous of nothing. The state offers no actual rehab courses designed to aid in financial recovery. Yet, I have to keep my head up and move forward on my own. In doing so, I must remember the words uttered by a number of great or well-known individuals that inspire me.

"It is hard to fail, but it is worse never to have tried to succeed."
— Teddy Roosevelt

*"I've missed more than 9000 shots in my career.
I've lost almost 300 games.
26 times, I've been trusted to take the game winning shot and missed.
I've failed over and over again in my life.
And that is why I succeed."*
— Michael Jordan

"Losing doesn't make me want to quit. It makes me want to fight that much harder."
— Paul "Bear" Bryant

"Sometimes life hits you in the head with a brick. Don't lose faith."
— Steve Jobs

"If you could kick the person in the pants responsible for most of your trouble, you wouldn't sit for a month."
— Theodore Roosevelt

"Do not be anxious about tomorrow, for tomorrow will be anxious for itself. Let the day's own trouble be sufficient for the day."

—Jesus Christ

"There's no present. There's only the immediate future and the recent past."

—George Carlin

*"If you wake up and don't want to smile
If it takes just a little while
Open your eyes and look at the day
You'll see things in a different way"*

—Fleetwood Mac

*"You may say I'm a dreamer
But I'm not the only one
I hope someday you will join us
And the world will be as one"*

—John Lennon, "Imagine"

"I believe that if life gives you lemons, you should make lemonade… And try to find somebody whose life has given them vodka, and have a party."

—Ron White

If everyone who had ever failed gave up, life as we know it would not exist. The Good Ole Boy court system however, is afraid of the Phoenix that rises from the ashes. A comeback kid presents them real problems. They don't want their victims to persevere, for then, they can be called to answer for their true colors.

I strive to be the Phoenix, the Comeback Kid. I will fight to the bitter end. I will overcome. I will not go down as just another casualty of a corrupt system.

Lauren Hillenband is the bestselling author of *Unbroken: A World War II Story of Survival, Resilience, and Redemption* and also of *Seabiscuit: An American Legend*.

In *Unbroken*, she chronicles the story of Louis Zamperini, an Olympic runner in the 1936 Olympics, who was later shot down over the Pacific in 1943. Zamperini and the other survivor of the crash, were adrift for 47 days (a third crash survivor died on the 33rd day) before being captured by the Japanese. They were then imprisoned and tortured as POWs until their liberation in 1945.

In her book, Hillenbrand makes the following observation: *"Dignity is as essential to human life as water, food, and oxygen. The stubborn retention of it, even in the face of extreme physical hardship, can hold a man's soul in his body long past the point at which the body should have surrendered it. The loss of it can carry a man off as surely as thirst, hunger, exposure, and asphyxiation, and with greater cruelty."*

My hardships with the ADOC pale in comparison to what Louie Zamperini and other wartime POWs went through. My sufferings were not even close to theirs. However, in comparison, there is one thing that stands out about mine. The POWs were in the hands of cruel wartime enemies. The injustices and the inhumane treatment that I received and witnessed was at the hands of Americans, employees of the State of Alabama to be exact. I wonder how many teachers in the state's education system realize that they are co-employees of people who conduct themselves in this manner.

Winding Down

"Direction, not intention, determines your destination."
—Andy Stanley

Most fairy tales have a happy ending. After enduring danger and hardships, the hero or heroine overcome the wicked step mother or the evil queen. The big bad wolf and the evil witch are slain. Then the subjects in the fairy tales go on to live happily ever after.

Let me take stock in my current situation. I am a fifty + year old convicted felon with the financial consequences associated with a failed business. Also, I carry the restrictions associated with being an ex-con and have a number of physical limitations brought on by my travels through incarceration. I am still fighting my way through the briar patch. A retirement involving a daily round of golf is not in my future, so I needn't have aspirations of becoming the Lord of the Pings. I have serious back and neck issues, chronic fatigue, and rapidly diminishing eyesight. Since my incarceration, I've had two major spinal surgeries (5 fused vertebrae), in part due to neglect from the ADOC, and I've had 2 eye surgeries to try to correct the damage inflicted during the attack at Elmore. Gravity is no longer my friend. I'm running on empty. Can I possibly live happily ever after with all these burdens? Can I find Shangri La, Valhalla, or even Margaritaville?

The answer to the above question is sure, why not. You play the hand that is dealt to you. Job, of Old Testament fame, did. Although you can be angry and continue to fight the injustices that were cast upon you, you still have to go on with your life. You can't just lie down and roll over. After all, as they say, life is all about how you handle Plan B. In my case, my experiences may not have made me any smarter, but I am certainly more seasoned.

Prison ages you at an accelerated rate and damages you emotionally. Nevertheless, it has made me even more determined to find a silver lining. My determination and gumption have gotten me this far, so I can't stop now.

What exactly did the pursuit, conviction, and persecution inflicted on me accomplish? I'm sure the results are not what the jury was conned into believing they were voting for.

The D.A. succeeded in:

1. Hindering the payback of my customers. Many have been paid back privately, outside the court's supervision, and others are in the process. If I had been left alone to liquidate and get to work, without the harassment and the negative publicity, I could have been much further along with recovery and restitution. Being branded a thief and thrown in jail, on the pretense of intent, does not aid in bouncing back from economic fallout.
2. Sucking a lot of much needed re-payment money into court and legal fees.

3. Performing a character assassination on me, while I was trying to dig out and find a way to do the right thing.
4. Exposing me to danger and teaching me the mindset of criminal minds.
5. Teaching me that many criminals hide behind the law.
6. Practicing hypocrisy.
7. Opening my eyes to the true nature of many of our state and local officials.
8. Grabbing himself some political headlines.
9. Exposing me to mistreatment and thus contributing to my current physical problems.
10. Teaching me the emotion of hate!

Writing my memoirs did not come with instructions. Much of what you have read was written, sitting Indian style on a bunk, as I lived it. Now I have to start writing the next stage of my life and my recovery. This narrative is a labor of love and has been necessary to ease the pain in my soul. This pain is the unwanted introduction to the emotion of hate that was created by my enlightenment to the true nature of some "revered" human beings.

As I expound on my travails and put them into perspective, a philosopher I am not. I'm no Socrates, Confucius, or Machiavelli. Heck, I'm not even a W.C. Fields, Yogi Berra, or even an Al Bundy! Nevertheless, I've been where I've been, seen what I've seen, and experienced what I have experienced. I am simply writing down those events. They can ridicule me and call me a tainted individual and a liar, if they choose. It is what it is and I have spoken the truth.

If you think that I should just forget what these people have done to me and let bygones be bygones, read the words of intellectual Thomas Szasz when he states, "The stupid neither forgive nor forget: the naïve forgive and forget: the wise forgive but do not forget." I'm still fighting through the stupid stage.

To once again quote Bear Bryant, he said, "When you make a mistake, there are only three things you should ever do about it: 1. Admit it, 2. Learn from it, and 3. Don't repeat it."

I made a lot of serious blunders in the final years of my business. I lost focus on how to safely and efficiently plan for the future. If I had carried my business prowess onto Shark Tank, the panel would have chewed me up and spit me out. Mr. Wonderful would have called me Mr. Blunderful.

I had lived through so many good times that I didn't prepare for the bad ones. As a result, a lot of people got swept up in the aftermath. My customers and my family suffered from my not taking care of matters properly. I certainly hope that I have learned some lessons from my shortcomings.

The debts to many of my former customers have been taken care of or are ongoing by a slow but steady repayment plan that I have implemented. However, there are others who have not responded to my newspaper or written requests for information. I am easy to locate through family, friends, or my attorney. If you have not responded or if I have yet to contact you, please get in touch with me so that I can get the process going. I have been unable to locate many of my business records since my release. I do not want to leave this world without making things right with my customers. Throughout this whole ordeal, my biggest regret has been the loss of my reputation.

My life certainly changed for the better the day that I met

Diane. Di is a silver lining to the cloud that has been the last few years of my life. Not only did I meet a woman who accepted me for what I am and where I had been, but also one who cared for me enough to take me under her wing and to want to fight my battles with me. With the love that Di has shown me and the love that I have for her, I would go through all my trials and tribulations again if that is what was necessary for me to find her.

On a beautiful day in October, just ten months after we had met, Diane and I were married in a private ceremony at the beach on Jekyll Island, Georgia. In attendance besides us were the preacher, a photographer (who also served as the witness), and a few party-crashing sand fleas. Despite my legal and physical problems, with Di to go home to, I can say that I have not had a bad day in my life since the day we married. She has been worth everything that I have been through. Along with her came two great step kids, Rachel and Eric (city kids who consider Starbucks the essential nectar of life), a football crazy father-in-law, whom we call Big Daddy, who is a rabid Tennessee Volunteer fan (orange causes me to break out into a rash), and a jet-black cat named Stormy, whom I renamed Speed-Bump because he loves to lay across every path of travel that I take in the house.

Although I have found happiness, it has not deterred my resolve to expose the cesspool that is Alabama politics and the judicial system that they use to keep themselves in power. In a quote from another of my favorite authors, Randy Wayne White, he states, "A society whose moral ideas inhibit their own defense will always suffer defeat by the very predators they deem immoral." Before, I was easy pickings. I was naïve to the system. No longer!

I hope that those who fabricated my "intent" and incarcerated me, remember that no good deed goes unpunished. I have made it my life's ambition to expose you for what you are.

I'm sure that those that I have exposed will rally all their friends, family, supporters, and underlings to try and discredit me, but so be it. Let the character assassination begin again. I've already taken my lumps and stand ready for your backlash. I'm ready for you and have a bag full of dirt to sling as ammo.

If you ask me if I think that most of Alabama politics is corrupt, my answer would be to just open your eyes. My eyes were opened when I was exposed to the Nazi tactics that the state allows to go on, under their noses, in order to keep the status-quo that they so desperately want to preserve. If they are working for us as Alabama citizens, how can they allow these travesties to go on as they pretend to be decent and God-fearing public servants? How many public officials have you heard decrying the State for their failures in these matters? Few! It takes outside sources to call attention to the abuses and then they, our elected officials, resist any change to their precious system because it may further expose them.

These officials can't admit making wrong decisions or taking part in wrongful convictions. This would open a whole new can of worms called Liability and Accountability. Heaven forbid that doing the right thing might cause some court official to have egg on their face and to have to answer for it.

You may think that I have lost my respect for authority. That statement is not necessarily true. Authority is like respect; it should be earned. Someone should not be considered an authority figure simply because they were appointed to a position or because they won a public popularity contest. You say, "How can this be accomplished? If we don't give elected officials authority, who is Authority? Elected officials are granted authority everywhere."

This statement has merit, but the preceding question is not my point. My point is that we should collectively use our intelligence in electing these people and then rigorously hold them accountable. At least in my home state, the same cronies are elected year in and year out and they make a mockery out of us. They disregard ethics and the Constitution and make Alabama their personal gold mine.

If individuals want to enter public service, then it should be just that and not a springboard to wealth and power. They should not be allowed to promote themselves by simply putting badges on a hired group of enforcers. Those put in positions of authority should be scrutinized as our employees. Someone along the way forgot who works for whom. Could this situation be because they handle things that we do not want to see or be exposed to? If so, then we have allowed a new element into our society—the "legal criminal." I think that this was the very thing that our forefathers revolted against when our country declared its independence.

Elected and appointed officials should be thoroughly trained and tested before they are allowed to be in office. A high bar should be set and enforced in order to be able to become a public servant. Creating this bar is up to us. We should not allow conniving and greedy power brokers to manipulate us by ignoring our principles and by hiring ignorant underlings to enforce their wishes. Maybe, as informed and aware citizens, we can elect officials who can create an Altered State of Alabama, one that respects human rights and the real interests of society, not just certain individual's financial gains.

Have you ever not wondered why many politicians spend so much money on political campaigns? Is it for the salary that is a fraction of what they spend to get elected or maybe just because they really want to be in a position to do good? REALLY?

I always scoffed at people who watched professional wrestling and insisted that it was non-choreographed and real. I always told them that if it were real, all the participants would be arrested for criminal violations. I also insisted that if politicians were truly guilty of the pre-election claims by their opponents, then they should be in jail as well. It's funny how these claims surface just before elections. Just prior to this writing, the speaker of the Alabama House of Representatives was arrested on 23 counts of ethics violations. He had been in office since 1998. If true, did it take that many years and a lack of confidence in winning, by his opponent, to bring these violations to light? If the opponent wins, will he be up on charges in a few years?

The political in-breeding in Alabama has become ridiculous. The old cronies suck the state dry and the "new blood" is quickly taught the rules and the tricks of the trade. The lies and corruption in Montgomery are staggering. Don't take my word for it, do your own research or insist on a National TV watchdog to do so. If I am wrong, then maybe Pro Wrestling is legit.

I know that as I have written in this journal, I have been all over the place. And I realize that as I have rambled through this text, I have repeatedly criticized those that I feel have served me injustice. However, I probably have failed to recognize enough of those who have stood behind me through adversity, every step of the way. My mom, my girls, my family, and a few very loyal friends have never wavered in their support for me. To all of you, I send you my eternal gratitude and love.

Through the suffering, my mom, JoAnne, and my two daughters, Jenni and Jessi, took every punch thrown their way and stood their ground for me. They did this in light of the fact that I had lost the legacy that I had built for them and replaced it with public scrutiny and scorn. Nevertheless, they stood strong and kept their faith in me.

Both girls have now married and I have two great sons-in-law, Brian and Tyler. Jenni and Brian have given me two incredible gifts in my grandson Harry and my granddaughter Addie. Harry is a handful, like his Pops, and Addie is a doll. I'm looking forward to Jess and Tyler adding to the fold.

I'm sure that if this book is successful in drawing the attention that it is intended to do, a lot of fair-weather friends will claim some of these praises as being directed towards them. Those of you who talked about and criticized me behind my back or gossiped to others about me know who you are and so do others. Word travels fast in a small town. However, I forgive you just like I forgive the jury that followed the state's wishes and sent me to Elmore. I'm sure that there were plenty of former friends and upstanding citizens present in the arena of ancient Rome, cheering the lions on. It's tough going from popular to pariah overnight.

As for the members of the jury, you saw the awful picture that the court's theatrics and theories painted of me with no real knowledge of what goes on behind the scenes. How could you know the difference between fact and fiction, when the DA presented to you a Broadway production? You were not accustomed to the win-at-all-costs shenanigans, stereotypes, rumors, and innuendos that the legal profession uses to influence you. You also were not aware of what really goes on behind the scenes of a state incarceration, just as I was naïve to the fact prior to my failures and my vacation courtesy of the State of Alabama. If you were, you would have needed shock absorbers to cushion the truth.

In the motion picture "The Judge," the attorney played by Robert Downey Jr. defends his father, who happens to be a judge, in a murder trial. His father is played by Robert Duvall. As the two are debating tactics for jury selection, Duvall's character talks about selecting jurors of good character. Downey's character replied that what they needed instead, were jurors that they could convince to swallow their own tongues and who had seen Sasquatch.

In retrospect, and from my experience, they really wanted both. Good people are probably more prone to be impressionable. I have no doubt that you, the jury who convicted me, are all good people. The DA wants good people on the jury. He wants people whose goodness he can manipulate with his theories, resulting in a sense of responsibility to follow his wishes. Nevertheless, you did what you felt was right at the time. All you knew was that I owed money and the context that the DA put it in. I wonder if the result would have been the same if you had been able to do your own research, not only into my case, but also into the Colbert judicial machine as well. Sometimes, just because something is politically correct, doesn't mean that it is the right thing to do.

We need fewer "psychic" prosecutors and more who deal in fact. Then maybe we could avoid "theory-fed juries" and "reasonably doubtful convictions."

The Colbert court system basically passes off convicted subjects, and for that matter accused subjects as well, to their jailers to treat as they wish. There is no real attempt to follow humane protocols during their incarceration. As citizens and wards to those that we incarcerate in our state, we should not simply view them as animals. Sure, some need to be kept away from our children and the public. Still, there are those who, with the appropriate care and attention, could become positive members of our society. They just need to be identified and given a real chance. We should view these individuals with the same compassion that we feel for a puppy or a kitten on an ASPCA commercial. However, we need to appoint or elect educated and ethical people to implement this.

On to other subjects.

To the mother of my children: we spent thirty, sometimes happy and oftentimes tumultuous years together. I guess sometimes love just hurts. As I stated before, spouses are victims as well. You were a victim not only of the system, but also of my neglect and loss of focus as well. I understand that you did what you had to do to protect your own sanity. In reality, our marriage was over years before this all went down. I hope that you find happiness in life, as I have, and I pray that we can all live in peace and enjoy our kids and grandkids.

To all those who once considered me family, before my downfall; I apologize for the embarrassment and hardships that I put you through. If roles had been reversed, who knows, maybe I would have reacted the same way. I wish you all a wonderful life.

As Don Henley put it in his hit song:

I've been tryin' to get down to the Heart of the Matter
But my will gets weak
And my thoughts seem to scatter
But I think it's about forgiveness
Forgiveness
Even if, even if you don't love me anymore

As I struggle to put things in the past truly behind me, I am constantly searching for guidance and answers. One day I read the following adage posted on Facebook:

Someday, we'll forget the hurt, the reason we cried and who caused the pain. We will finally realize that the secret of being free is not revenge, but letting things unfold in their own way and own time. After all, what matters is not the first, but the last chapter of our life which shows how well we ran the race. So smile, laugh, forgive, believe, and love all over again.

—Unknown

I hope and pray that, with time, I can learn to accept this stance and purge the anger that resides in me.

Turn the Page

"What does it profit a man if he gains the whole world and 3 putts the last green?"
—Fred Corcoran

I hope and pray that each of you will read my story with an open mind and take to heart the things that I have relayed to you. No matter what you think of or believe about my personal situation or guilt, please be aware that our state has some serious problems and needs our help. Even if you have made up your mind that I am guilty of everything that I was charged with, that opinion still doesn't change the crimes that are condoned by those running our courts and branches of our state. Those who are callous and look the other way are just as guilty! Pilot washed his hands of the conviction and crucifixion of Christ, but that made him no less responsible.

*"Yes, there are two paths you can go by, but in the long run
There's still time to change the road you're on.
And it makes me wonder."*
—Led Zeppelin, "Stairway to Heaven"

We need people of good, moral fiber in our leadership positions. You don't assign fat people to guard a buffet! If we as citizens of Alabama don't open our eyes, we will continue to be left behind as other states push ahead both economically and morally. If that fact doesn't mean anything then just ask yourself, "What would Jesus think about us not becoming aware and involved in fighting the injustices going on within our state lines?" We can have justice without funding a police state.

I once dreamed of being a cowboy or a policeman, but I have now been enlightened. I now have a new set of heroes in my life. Among these new heroes are all those who fight social, economic, and judicial injustice. I've even learned to appreciate those who are referred to, by their critics, as tree-huggers.

I am especially impressed with those that campaign against unfairness and injustice dished out by our court systems. These include Barry Scheck and Peter Nuefeld of The Innocence Project. Take the time to research the work that these people undertake. Go on their blog and read the story of Michael Morton, who was also featured on the CNN special "An Unreal Dream." Maybe you will be as impressed with the Innocence Project as I am and will follow and contribute to its cause.

Another organization that I look up to is The Equal Justice Initiative. The founder, Bryan Stevenson, has taken on the challenge of fighting for those that no one else is willing to fight for. In an interview with Terry Gross of "Fresh Air," he states, "We have a criminal justice system that treats you better if you're rich and guilty than if you're poor and innocent." His memoir, *Just Mercy* chronicles his journey to becoming an advocate for those whom society has abandoned. In his book, he makes a statement that parallels a point that I have tried to make in this script. He states, "We are all implicated when we allow other people to be mistreated. An absence of compassion can corrupt the decency of a community, a state, a nation. Fear and anger can make us vindictive and abusive, unjust and unfair, until we all suffer from the absence of mercy and we condemn ourselves as much as we victimize others." Please read this statement again slowly and give deep thought to it.

Bryan Stevenson is a Harvard educated civil rights attorney. His book is scathing of the court system in Alabama. The stories he relays will make your blood boil and if you are a resident of Alabama, it will make you question many of the things that you grew up thinking. I am white, not black; however, I have seen the side of our state system that has oppressed minorities for over a century and continues today. Mr. Stevenson's book should sit on every Alabamian's bookshelf right alongside *To Kill a Mockingbird*. It should be required reading for every schoolchild in Alabama.

There are many other organizations who promote human rights. Among them are "Amnesty International," "Human Rights Watch," and "Not on Our Watch." Among the celebrities who support these and other great organizations are Bono, Brad Pitt, Angelina Jolie, John Cleese, Danny Glover, Madonna, Bruce Springsteen, George Clooney, Jackson Browne, Elton John, Michael Stipe, Joan Baez, Adele, and former President Bill Clinton.

The work that these stars and organizations provide around the world is admirable. I ask only that they join The Innocence Project or the Equal Justice Initiative in bringing attention to the atrocities going on within our own borders and particularly within our prisons. Not all inmates are guilty. Even if they were, human rights should apply regardless. In today's media driven, socially aware world, more attention is given to the humane treatment in kennels and animal shelters, than for those locked away in prisons. Correctional facilities should be a place for reform, not for mistreatment or abuse of power.

Hey, Rolling Stone Magazine, how about you guys doing an investigative report on my home state's judicial and correctional systems. You seem to call it as you see it. Chris Cuomo of CNN, how about you doing the same? You seem very fair and balanced in your approach to investigative reporting as well. Maybe if you all got involved you could make a difference and in the process, open the eyes of our state's youth, as they will eventually become our leaders. Hopefully, you can also help to keep the hounds at bay while you substantiate my claims. Maybe your scrutiny will ease the backlash and keep their teeth away from my throat.

Alabama routinely (again in 2015) sets up some kind of lip-service prison reform bill in an attempt to pacify the feds and the socially conscience public. YET, very little ever seems to get done, other than to invent new avenues of ADOC revenue. Many of our "public servants" have become self-servants.

In Clint Eastwood's movie (based on David Baldacci's bestseller) *Absolute Power*, an aged and wise businessman made the statement, "Selling sin is easy." Maybe it is time for the ADOC to quit selling sin and to start selling reform.

If Alabama was serious about protecting human rights, why not put an independent office in each prison facility, manned and paid for by members of these watchdog groups (for obvious reasons), to ensure proper and humane treatment of its prisoners and due diligence on appeals and rehabilitation. These watchdogs could keep an eye on the criminals that are watching the criminals. All of these police misconduct cases that the public sees on the news are an every-hour occurrence in a prison dorm.

REMEMBER, MY STORY COULD BE YOUR STORY! I was attacked by the diatribes of a vindictive county court. Although I came from a comfortable middle class background, attacking me was politically correct. Imagine if I had come from a poor minority background.

Every small business man is confronted with potentially life changing decisions on a daily basis. A loss of focus, a few bad decisions, some bad breaks, and you could be in my shoes. In realizing this possibility, please keep a proper perspective of human rights and our obligations to ensuring them. Let's not be callous and indifferent to the shortcomings of our system simply because we are shielded from them and because these failures are not a pleasant subject.

In making your life and business choices, concentrate on focus, character, and direction. If you don't, failure could bring out the scavengers that prey on the weak and they will devour you. Learn from me: cross your "T's", dot your "I's." Run your business with respect and treat it like a lady.

In addition to The Innocence Project, and the other organizations that I have previously mentioned, I urge all of you to subscribe to the podcast *Wrongful Conviction with Jason Flom*.

You will find the stories mind boggling. It will make your blood boil.

In closing my ramblings, I hope that each of us can strive to become less complacent with what goes on around us. I wish that each of us will open our eyes and become more involved in the accountability of those whom we select to be in positions of authority. Lastly, I pray that we will set a goal that despite the grind of our daily lives, we will think about and strive to care for those that are *Out of Sight and Out of Mind*.

Postscript
August 2017

"The only thing there is to say
Every silver linings got a touch of gray
I will get by, I will survive"
— The Grateful Dead, "A Touch of Gray"

This world is a never ending cycle of change. As I look back on the past events in my life, the recent and current happenings, and the unknown of the future, sometimes my head spins wondering what God has in store for me.

In September of 2016 we lost "Big Daddy", Diane's dad, who died at the age of 95. This man was a hoot. He made everyone laugh. He was also a shrewd businessman and a great source of wisdom. We all miss him very much.

Then on Valentine's Day of 2017, I suffered one of the worse days of my life. I lost my Mom. On her return trip from a Thanksgiving visit to my girls in Alabama, she suffered a stroke. Over the next two and a half months she endured extended stays in three hospitals in Chattanooga and Atlanta. After discovery of the reason for the stroke she also underwent open-heart surgery and came through like a champion. However, after an unexplained early-morning fall at a rehab center, she succumbed to a brain hemorrhage a week later. I had lost my Rock and my greatest source of strength.

Although losing Mom was heart wrenching, the long hours that we spent together in the hospitals illuminated the love between mother and son even more, if that was possible. Mom will always be in my heart and my faith gives me no doubt that she is in good hands. Every day since my Dad's death in 1999, she has mourned him. I'm sure that they are having the glorious honeymoon that they never had before, but so richly deserved, this one in eternity.

In addition to the losses of Mom and Big Daddy, I also lost Big Boy due to a tumor. Big Boy was the best dog any man could ever ask to have as his companion. If dogs do go to heaven, I'm sure he is there with Mom and Dad.

On the positive side I've also been rewarded with some recent joy in my life. In July of this year Harry and Addie got a cousin. Jessi and Tyler gave us a beautiful baby girl, Etta Margaret. God could not have given me three more beautiful and perfect grandchildren.

Etta was named for two of her great grandmothers. One of them was Maggie, my Mom's mom. Maggie was a real piece of work. The family stubbornness and resilience was passed down from Mama Maggie. Etta was born with a full head of hair which she obviously inherited from her Pops. I wish Mom could have met her.

Diane and I are creating an incredible life together. We are so alike in some ways and so different in others that we are a perfect match and face life together in all things, good or bad. Our future looks to be wonderful as we weld our families together.

In late 2015, I went before the Alabama parole board and gained parole for my friend Chad who had helped me cope with the struggles of incarceration. In early 2016 Soda was released. With the help of a state senator in Georgia, The diligence of my co-workers Susan and Casey, the willingness of the Georgia Interstate Compact Division, and with a lot of determination we were able to get Chad and Soda transferred away from Alabama and into Georgia. Here they are off the street, back into the workforce and contributing to society as they build a new life for themselves.

Di and have basically adopted Soda as our Godson. He lives in our basement apartment and has become part of the family. Ours has become a real *Modern Family*. We are trying to offer him guidance as well as an introduction into middle class life. We also serve as a buffer to decisions and critique his girlfriends.

In Alabama it is business as usual. In the state house the usual insults and indictments are flung right and left between many of the same old cronies, Governor Bentley has resigned over an alleged affair with an aide, and riots and murders continue within the walls of the Alabama Department of Corrections. The new governor, Kay Ivey, takes over as Alabama's second female governor. Maybe a lady can take control of this mess when the men preceding her couldn't.

On the national scene we have a new President in Donald Trump. I pray to God that our new president can rise above the political in-fighting and get a grip on Washington. Like him or not, he is our new leader and we need to ask God to give him direction.

Also in Washington, president Trump has appointed Senator Jeff Sessions of Alabama as our new Attorney General. I have mutual acquaintances with AG Sessions and they all refer to him as a good man. Good man or not, I also pray that Mr. Sessions has a better grip on his underlings in Washington than he did as Attorney General in Alabama.

Our country and my home state of Alabama both need prayer and a lot of due diligence. We all have a lot to overcome as we strive to come together. We must rise above law and disorder.

In closing I will recite the words of Kid Rock:

"And I will vow to the shining seas and celebrate God's grace on me, I was born free!"

Acknowledgments

Thank you to my script editor, Adele Brinkley at A Pen in Hand, for such a wonderful job.

Thank you to my daughters, Jennifer Denton and Jessica Killen, for keeping the faith and for all the content contributions and editing help.

Thank you to my step-daughter, Rachel Haviland, for many hours laboring over my manuscript and for correcting my poor grammar.

Thank you to Susan Viviano for teaching this old dinosaur how to use Word.

Thank you to Casey Wasinger for all your contributions and ideas.

Thank you to Bob and Jan Babcock at Deeds Publishing, for helping me to navigate this difficult process.

And especially, thank you to my wife, Diane Harrison, for believing in me and making this all possible.

About the Author

Alabama born. Alabama raised. Mike, a baby boomer was born into the deep South during the civil rights era. A longtime businessman in Alabama, Mike now resides in Atlanta, Georgia, with his wife Diane.

CPSIA information can be obtained
at www.ICGtesting.com
Printed in the USA
BVHW03*1733300818
525861BV00001B/4/P